HARVARD POLITICAL STUDIES

PUBLISHED UNDER THE DIRECTION OF THE

DEPARTMENT OF GOVERNMENT

IN HARVARD UNIVERSITY

INTERNATIONAL SOCIALISM AND THE WORLD WAR

INTERNATIONAL SOCIALISM
AND THE WORLD WAR

BY

MERLE FAINSOD

OCTAGON BOOKS

A DIVISION OF FARRAR, STRAUS AND GIROUX

New York   1973

Reprinted 1966
by special arrangement with Harvard University Press

Second Octagon printing 1973

OCTAGON BOOKS
A DIVISION OF FARRAR, STRAUS & GIROUX, INC.
19 Union Square West
New York, N. Y. 10003

LIBRARY OF CONGRESS CATALOG CARD NUMBER: 66-17499
ISBN 0-374-92679-4

Printed in U.S.A. by
NOBLE OFFSET PRINTERS, INC.
New York, N.Y. 10003

TO MY MOTHER

PREFACE

The concept of an international labor community has loomed large in the speculations of Socialist theorists who have sought a counter symbol to parry the attractions of the nation-state. From the First International organized in Marx's day to the latest effort by Trotsky to create a Fourth International, a series of attempts have been made to give it institutional expression.

This volume on International Socialism and the World War embraces only a small part of the history of the international labor movement. It is intended as a case study in the disintegration of the international Socialist community under the impact of national passions aroused by war. In tracing the process of dissolution, particular emphasis has been placed on the sequence of events leading up to the organization of the Third International. If the narrative appears to come to an abrupt stop with the birth of that organization, the reader is due the explanation that the present work is intended as the first part of a larger study which will be concerned with the post-war rôle of the Third International.

*   *   *

Not the least of the joys of a preface is the opportunity it affords to acknowledge, however inadequately, the author's gratitude to those whose advice has been of inestimable value in the preparation of his book. To Professors C. J. Friedrich and A. N. Holcombe, of Harvard University, whose recommendations made possible the publication of this volume, with the aid of the Louis Adams Frothingham Fund, thanks are due. To Professors B. C. Hopper and R. Emerson, also of Harvard University, I am deeply indebted for helpful criticism and counsel. For stenographic and editorial assistance, I am profoundly obligated to my wife. None of the above, however, bears any responsibility for errors of fact or interpretation.

Leverett House,   M. F.
Harvard University,
Cambridge, Massachusetts
March, 1935.

CONTENTS

CHAPTER I

THE BACKGROUND OF SOCIALIST INTERNATIONALISM

Labor internationalism is a relatively recent development in the field of international organization. In the minds of many observers, its origins are irrevocably associated with the work of Karl Marx. But the idea of an international association of labor to make common cause against oppression and exploitation antedates Marx. It appears in inchoate form in the writings of the Utopian Socialists of the early nineteenth century, and in the aspirations of a section of the Chartist movement.[1] It remained for Karl Marx to bring the concept to the fore with an arresting force.

Marx's analysis of the operation of capitalism led him to formulate "laws" of the disintegration of capitalist society. He envisaged all history as a history of class struggles, and capitalist society as a battleground where the rising proletariat encounters declining capitalism and overthrows it. The Marxian view transforms the proletariat into an irreconcilable group which refuses to share the consensus upon which the state is founded. The national state is considered not as a collectivity embracing the welfare of all those who live within its boundaries, but as a power mechanism—as an instrument of the ruling class to enforce dominance over the ruled. The state under capitalism, according to the Marxist, is controlled by a dictatorship of capitalists, regardless of the garb in which they cloak their domination. As Marx and Engels proclaimed in the *Communist Manifesto:*

> Modern industrial labour, modern subjection to capital, the same in England as in France, in America as in Germany, has stripped him [the worker] of every trace of national character. . . . The workingmen have no country. We cannot take from them what they have not got. . . .[2]

The net result of this kind of theorizing is to deny altogether the compulsion of the national loyalty. Marx's battle-cry, "Proletarians of the world, unite!" was designed to make the workers vacate the vertical compartments called nations and align themselves in a new horizontal stratum based on class. Thus the Marxian theory looked forward to an

---

[1] See L. Lorwin, *Labor and Internationalism,* New York, 1929.
[2] Karl Marx and Friedrich Engels, *The Communist Manifesto,* Marx-Engels-Lenin Institute edition, Moscow, 1933. 26, 35.

1

international association of workingmen which would seek to overthrow the rule of the bourgeoisie and supplant it with a society dominated by the proletariat.

It was Marx who recognized more clearly than most of his contemporaries the close connection between capitalist internationalism and labor internationalism. In a very real sense, he argued, labor internationalism may be regarded as a by-product of capitalist internationalism. For one of the results of the growth of capitalism was to develop the world market and to promote trade between nations on a much larger scale than ever before. The era of invention which heralded the progress of modern industrial capitalism worked to break down the barriers between nations and to multiply the possibilities of communication between them. The mobility of capitalism and the spread of capitalist methods of production served to standardize industrial processes and to make the position of workers in one country dependent upon their condition elsewhere.

In the *Communist Manifesto,* Marx and Engels drew attention to this development:

> The bourgeoisie has through its exploitation of the world market given a cosmopolitan character to production and consumption in every country. To the great chagrin of reactionaries, it has drawn from under the feet of industry the national ground on which it stood. . . . In place of the old local and national seclusion and self-sufficiency, we have intercourse in every direction, universal inter-dependence of nations. . . .
>
> The bourgeoisie, by the rapid improvement of all instruments of production, by the immensely facilitated means of communication, draws all, even the most barbarian, nations into civilisation. . . .
>
> National differences and antagonisms between peoples are daily more and more vanishing, owing to the development of the bourgeoisie, to freedom of commerce, to the world market, to uniformity in the mode of production and in the conditions of life corresponding thereto.
>
> The supremacy of the proletariat will cause them to vanish still faster. United action of the leading civilised countries at least, is one of the first conditions for the emancipation of the proletariat.[3]

Thus the struggle for proletarian internationalism is viewed as a natural outgrowth of the condition created by the spread of capitalism. It was this struggle which Marx proposed to organize and wage through the First International (1864-1876).

In the latter-day studies of the First International, particularly those

[3] *Ibid.,* 19, 35.

written under the aegis of the Communist International, there is a tendency to identify the revolutionary preachings of Marx with the program of the First International, and unduly to exaggerate the Marxian color of the association.[4] The tendency is readily understandable. The desire to incorporate the International in the revolutionary tradition and to provide the Communist International with an aura of historic respectability produces the incentive. The fact that Marx delivered the inaugural address and drafted the provisional rules lends an element of plausibility to this interpretation. The theorists of the Communist International have been particularly active in fostering this view. It needs correction.

The First International came into being chiefly through a union of French Proudhonists[5] and British trade-unionists.[6] The effort of Marx to weld the combination into a revolutionary amalgam was resisted from both sides. Marx formed a temporary alliance with the British group to combat the anti-political views of the Proudhonists. In this effort he was successful, but at no time was he able to gain universal acceptance for his theories. The British trade-unionists abandoned him as their own policies veered toward class collaboration, and as they became frightened at the revolutionary implications of the Paris Commune with which Marx identified himself.[7] No sooner had the Proudhonist danger subsided than a new threat presented itself from the anarchist supporters of Bakunin.[8] The anarchist virus spread widely and dominated the Latin countries. Marx succeeded in preventing the followers of Bakunin from capturing

[4] A striking example is G. M. Steklov's *History of the First International*, New York, 1929.

[5] Proudhon (1809-1865), an influential figure among Parisian workers, sought to transform all producers into small owners, by organizing producers' cooperatives which would exchange their products in proportion to the labor incorporated in them. Relying on economic rather than political organization, Proudhon believed that these cooperatives would render the state and the capitalist class superfluous, and would preclude exploitation of labor.

[6] The outlook of British trade-unionists was primarily insular, and their demands for shorter hours, higher wages and better working conditions contemplated no basic reorganization of society. The tendency of employers, however, to import foreign workers as strike-breakers, forced a small element of international consciousness upon the leaders.

[7] For Marx's evaluation of the Paris Commune see Karl Marx, *The Civil War in France*, London, 1921.

[8] Bakunin (1814-1876), a revolutionary romanticist, emerged from a Czarist prison and Siberian exile to spread the gospel of universal anarchy. In 1868 he founded the Alliance of Social Revolutionaries which declared itself anti-God, anti-state and anti-political action. Bakunin attempted to indoctrinate the First International with the program of this Alliance.

the apparatus of the International; he could not prevent their influence from pervading a considerable section of the potential membership, particularly in the Latin countries. By allying with the French Blanquists (whose conspiratorial and insurrectionary tactics he could not accept) he contrived the ejection of the Bakuninists. The result was to leave the International a whited sepulchre. The anarchists broke away on the one hand; the moderates on the other.

Thus the history of the First International reflects the whirling eddies and the changing tides in which the labor movement rocked in the 'sixties and 'seventies of the nineteenth century. The International Working-men's Association (The First International) was intended as a central agency for cooperation among workingmen's societies to advance the interests of the laboring classes; in its development it became increasingly an arena of conflict in which competing social philosophies bid for the loyalties of the working class. So bitter was the struggle that before ten years had passed what was intended as a perpetual bond of fraternity dissolved in bickering and disintegration.

The First International was constructed out of the materials at hand— trade unions, declassed intellectuals, educational societies of workers, mutual credit associations, producers' cooperatives, and a host of other miscellaneous groups—and out of this assorted array an effort was made to piece together an International Workingmen's Association. The effort failed. The elements were still irreconcilable.

Meanwhile labor parties began to take root in various countries. The period of the 'eighties especially was an era of building, marked by the growth of national parties and by tendencies toward organizational unity. In the more advanced capitalist countries it saw the triumph of the faith in political action. The anarchist influence subsided, except to make a brief but ineffective reappearance in the form of revolutionary syndi-calism. The two wings of the socialist movement which respectively strove for dominance were the moderate class collaborationist groups and the revolutionary Socialists who followed in the Marxian tradition. As these tendencies crystallized, another effort was made to fuse them into a united international of labor, though a decade had to pass before the effort was undertaken.

The Second International was organized in 1889, thirteen years after the dissolution of the First. It apeared on the scene when the tide of socialist sentiment was rising, but like its predecessor, it lacked from the first that consensus on program and tactics which alone makes real organizational unity possible. If one may paraphrase Marx, the Second International contained within itself the seeds of its own destruction. It was born in discord, and it was destined to bear the marks of that birth throughout its chequered career. Even the effort to achieve formal unity failed in 1889. Two rival congresses met side by side in Paris through the hot exposition days of that year, one predominantly Marxist in sentiment, which had been organized by the German Socialists and the French Guesdists,[9] the other, reformist in outlook, which had been arranged by the French Possibilists[10] and the British trade-unionists. All efforts to unite the two factions were unavailing, and it was not until two years later that, at the Brussels congress, they were brought together through a hollow compromise. Engels had no illusions about the nature of the union:

> Of course real amalgamation, if it comes, will not by any means prevent the continuation of violent rows in England and France; on the contrary. It will merely be an imposing demonstration for the great bourgeois public, a workers' congress of more than nine hundred men, from the tamest trade unionists to the most revolutionary communists.[11]

Engels foresaw the bitter conflicts between Marxists and reformists which were to develop within each national party and which could not be obscured by the sham solidarity of the International.

One mistake the experience of the First International taught the organizers of the Second to avoid. The new organization would have no truck with the anarchists. At the Paris congress the anarchist representatives who refused to subscribe to the program of political action were treated as enemies in the camp and were ejected from the hall. Although the anarchist delegates reappeared at subsequent congresses, the Second International was adamant in its attitude of firm opposition, and they were never permitted to play the disruptive rôle in its ranks which had resulted in the destruction of the First International.

Yet even among the believers in political action as a way to the emancipation of the working class there were plenty of discordant tendencies. Fundamentally incompatible philosophies were glossed over by a superficial organizational unity. The compromise was tolerable because the Second International never attempted to settle fundamental

[9] Jules Guesde was the leader of the orthodox Marxist group in France.
[10] The Possibilists owe their name to their more moderate evolutionary program.
[11] *Briefe und Auszüge aus Briefen von Becker, Dietzen, Engels, Marx an Sorge,* Stuttgart, 1921. Engels' letter to Sorge, July 17, 1889, 317-318.

questions of principle. Even when it seemed to commit itself to a definitive statement of party doctrine, it allowed departures in tactics which vitiated the principles to which the International proclaimed loyalty. It never established a real central authority with plenary power to enforce decisions and punish breaches of discipline. The permanent bureau which was formed at the Paris congress in 1900 possessed powers only of an administrative nature; it confined itself to handling correspondence, issuing appeals and circulars, making arrangements for future congresses, and similar clerical duties. The Second International was at best a loose organization of autonomous national units. Consequently its possibilities of unified action were limited by all the weaknesses inherent in a system where there is no central authority, no commonly accepted program of theory and tactics, no possibility of whipping recalcitrants into line except persuasion and pleading.

The root causes of the weakness of the Second International lie hidden in the disagreements on theory and method among its discordant factions. In the early history of the International these disagreements centered around the dispute between Reformism and revolutionary Marxism. The rival congresses which met in Paris in 1889 represented this division. In the German movement, in the early years at least, the party was overwhelmingly Marxist. The wing which came over from Lassalle showed a predisposition toward reformist tactics, but it was engulfed in the larger organization. In the 'eighties the revisionist tide ran small; in the 'nineties it began to swell. It expressed itself in the "Eldorado speeches" of Vollmar with his declaration in favor of "the tactics of reformist operations which will achieve the object desired by the only possible means of practical partial successes."[12] It found its outstanding theoretician and philosopher in Eduard Bernstein whose work, *Evolutionary Socialism* (1898), precipitated a three days' discussion of its conclusions at the Hanover congress of the German Social-Democratic Party in 1899, a discussion which ended in a formal resolution of dissent from Bernstein but formed the prelude to an actual undermining of the orthodox faith.[13] But while orthodox Marxism rejected the Revisionism of Bernstein, in practice it accommodated itself to the reformist tactics and demonstrated a greater concern for the day-to-day struggles than for the ultimate goal. Though the bulk of the party followed the orthodox

---

[12] J. Lenz, *Rise and Fall of the Second International,* New York, 1932, 18-19.

[13] Eduard Bernstein, *Evolutionary Socialism,* London, 1909. See preface to English edition, xxi.

leadership of Bebel and Kautsky, there arose on the left wing of the German Social Democracy a small but intransigent revolutionary group which gathered around such redoubtable leaders as Rosa Luxemburg, Clara Zetkin, Franz Mehring and Karl Liebknecht. This group expressed its impatience with the cautious tactics of the official party leadership which it labelled "Centrist," and clamored for revolutionary action.

The divisions in the German Social Democracy mirrored the conflict on the broader stage of the International. With the Revisionists allied themselves the French Possibilists, the followers of Jaurès, the Fabian Socialists and others of the same political tendency. The Bebel-Kautsky group found its supporters among the French Guesdists, the Menshevik supporters of Plekhanoff, the Hyndman group in Great Britain, the followers of Adler in Austria-Hungary, and of Hillquit in the United States, and among all those who considered themselves "orthodox Marxists." They formed the largest group in the International. On the extreme Left there allied themselves with the German dissenters the Bolshevik supporters of Lenin, the "narrow" faction among the Bulgarian Socialists, and a few other scattered groups.

Within the Second International there existed in embryo the division between Right, Center and Left Socialists which played such a important rôle in the disintegration of the International during the World War. During the war these differences became more sharply defined and the chasm between the various schools widened until the split in the Second International became inevitable. But the intellectual motive power of the split was furnished by the divergent theoretical trends within the Second International.

In the pre-war International, Eduard Bernstein was perhaps the most famous theoretical exponent of the point of view of the Right, Karl Kautsky of the Center, and Lenin of the extreme Left. In studying the ideological germs of the later split these three theorists may be taken as typical of the three general tendencies, though of course any exhaustive treatment of the subject would have to take account of many refinements and departures among those who in a rough classification are labelled Right, Center and Left. On the Left, for example, it would be a rash over-simplification to identify the theories of Lenin and Rosa Luxemburg, though in practice they often made common front.

Bernstein, as the exponent of the Right, gave expression to a set of doctrines which have since become known as Revisionism. His examination of the fundamental tenets of Marxism led him to observe that these tenets must be considerably modified in the light of later developments. Arguing that the collapse of the capitalist system was not imminent he insisted that it was a mistake to adopt tactics which assumed the immediate outbreak of a great social revolution. His study of social classes led him to remark that "the enormous increase of social wealth is not accompanied by a decreasing number of large capitalists, but by an increasing number of capitalists of all degrees. The middle classes change their character but they do not disappear from the social scale.[14] He saw, moreover, counter-tendencies at work which blunted the edge of the class struggle.

Factory legislation, the democratization of local government, and the extension of its area of work, the freeing of trade unions and systems of co-operative trading from legal restrictions, the consideration of standard conditions of labour in the work undertaken by public authorities—all these characterize this phase of the evolution. But the more the political organization of modern nations is democratized the more the needs and opportunities of great political catastrophes are diminished.[15]

Holding that the movement meant everything, the final aim of Socialism nothing, Bernstein laid special stress on

the *next* tasks in social democracy, on the struggle for the political rights of the working man, on the political activity of the working men in town and country for the interests of their class, as well as on the work of the industrial organization of the workers . . . unable to believe in finalities at all, I cannot believe in a final aim of socialism. But I strongly believe in the socialist movement, in the march forward of the working classes, who *step by step* must work out their emancipation by changing society from the domain of a commercial manholding oligarchy to a real democracy which in all its departments is guided by the interests of those who work and create.[16] (Italics mine)

Taking his stand unreservedly on the theory of democracy, he preached loyalty to the national democratic state. He argued that:

the right to vote in a democracy makes its members virtually partners in the community and their virtual partnership must in the end lead to real partnership. With a working class undeveloped in numbers and culture, the general right to vote may long appear as the right to choose the "butcher." With the growing number and knowledge of the workers, it is changed, however, to the implement by which to transform the representatives of the people from masters into real servants of the people.[17]

[14] Bernstein, *op. cit.*, xl.
[15] *Ibid.*, xii.
[16] *Ibid.*, xxii-xxiii.
[17] *Ibid.*, 144.

Bernstein, therefore, regarded the democratic state not as an organ of oppression to be overthrown, but as an instrument to be mastered and utilized for the realization of Socialism. In a highly developed democratic state, consequently, the interests of the Socialists tend to become identical with those of the state. From this proposition it is easy to make the deduction that it is the duty of the proletariat to defend the state when it is attacked or when its interests are endangered. This was essentially the position of the Right Socialists who thus justified their support of the Fatherland during the World War.

The attitude of Kautsky differed from that of Bernstein in certain essential respects. As an orthodox Marxist he took issue with Bernstein's evolutionary Socialism and believed that Socialism would be realized as a result of revolution. But to Kautsky revolution did not necessarily signify violence; it meant any kind of change which placed a hitherto oppressed class in control of the government. While lacking Bernstein's unquestioning devotion to democratic institutions, Kautsky argued that "the political situation of the proletariat is such that it can well afford to try as long as possible to progress through strictly legal methods alone."[18] Though Kautsky accepted the Marxian laws of the decay of capitalist society, he tended to interpret these laws in terms of peaceful development, rather than violence and struggle. In discussing the dictum of Marx, that force is the midwife of the old order pregnant with the new, Kautsky emphasized the fact that the midwife cannot be called upon to practice her art successfully until a natural process of development has run its course. Kautsky placed much stress on the inevitable arrival of Socialism as the climax of a long process of development in which the contradictions of capitalism become increasingly apparent. Irresponsible violence and useless bloodshed are in any case superfluous since immutable laws operate to make inevitable the final triumph of the proletariat. Since such a theory relies on the operation of impersonal economic forces rather than on the conscious, purposeful efforts of man to transform the capitalist state into a socialist state, it is easy to see how it might in practice paralyze the revolutionary driving force of the masses and inspire considerable dissatisfaction among the revolutionaries who press for immediate action and seizure of power.

The philosophy of Kautsky is permeated with a horror of useless bloodshed. Revolutionary phraseology cannot conceal a reluctance to use revolutionary tactics. In practice, the activity which Kautsky advocates

[18] Karl Kautsky, *The Road to Power*, Chicago, 1909, 54.

does not differ markedly from the policies of the revisionists. The verbiage breathes fire; the tactics are tame. Within the framework of the capitalist state, argues Kautsky, the proletariat may gain the political experience which will enable it to assume and retain control of the machinery of the socialist state. Utilizing the tools of democracy in a capitalist state, the working class can consolidate and define its power, and by making clear the strength of the respective classes within the state, can obtain the concessions which are indispensable to avoid violence. It is, therefore, readily comprehensible, that such a philosophy, compounded of a horror of violence and of a belief in the victory of Socialism as the result of the automatic operation of economic laws could lend itself to pacificism during the war and to a repudiation of the tactics of revolutionary hotheads who sought to utilize the disorganization and the unrest of wartime to drive the masses on to revolutionary battles.

There is a danger in treating the philosophy of Kautsky and the orthodox Marxists as an inflexible and integrated system, uniformly valid for the whole history of the Second International. In a study of the orthodox wing of the German Social Democracy, theory and practice must be considered together. It is a mistake to adopt a static view, to treat Kautsky, for example, as an unvarying quantity through the whole course of his development. As the German Social Democracy grew in numbers, it began to lose its revolutionary fervor; even when it was staunchly defending the ramparts of purest orthodoxy against the revisionist barbarians, within the fort important phalanxes of the working class and their leaders were beginning to suffer from a paralysis of revolutionary initiative. Beneath the brave show of revolutionary phraseology the germ of reformism was already at work. Even Lenin made the mistake of accepting the professions of orthodoxy at their face value. For him Kautsky's book, *The Road to Power*, was a revolutionary document, and his furious hatred of Kautsky after 1914 can only be explained as the hatred of one who has loved dearly and feels himself betrayed.[19]

For an adequate study of the causes of this decline in revolutionary fervor a separate volume would be needed. Pre-war capitalism was a period of expansion. The progress of industrialization guaranteed advantages both to capitalist and worker alike. It was a period of hope, of

---

[19] N. K. Kruyskaya, *Vospominaniya o Lenine* (*Memories of Lenin*), 2 vols., Moscow, 1931, II, 131. See also Arthur Rosenberg, *History of Bolshevism,* London, 1934, 68, for a similar expression of judgment.

considerable concessions to the working class which opened up vistas and expanding horizons. In a sense the destiny of particular labor movements became intertwined with the industrial structure which supported them. This was even more true of the leaders. After years of revolutionary struggle, socialist parties and trade unions began to be respectable. They achieved legal status; they became incorporated in the texture of the society about them. They developed their own bureaucracy—the business agents of unions, the party officials, the editors of the party journals, the managers of cooperatives, the representatives in legislative and governmental bodies—leaders who developed a stake in society and were reluctant to embark on dangerous adventures which might entail the loss of all their perquisites. As the labor movements grew in strength and became institutionalized, they attracted lawyers, journalists and other intelligentsia who saw the labor movement in terms of careers and who utilized labor to express their own aspirations. Thus the fiery spirit of revolt was tempered, the clarion call to revolution muted until it became a politely modulated voice. This does not pretend to be a complete picture; it does, it is hoped, give some clue to the social climate in which the revolutionary lion was tamed.

The small but intransigent group of uncompromising revolutionaries found their most effective spokesman in Lenin, leader of the Russian Bolsheviks. The theoretical position of the Left grows out of an emphasis on the revolutionary aspects of Marx's thought. Regarding the state as an organ of class domination used by the bourgeoisie to oppress the proletariat, Lenin called upon the proletariat to wage an irreconcilable war to shatter the machinery of the bourgeois state and to substitute for it a new state in which the proletariat would be organized as the ruling class. This substitution, he argued, cannot take place without violent revolution since the bourgeoisie would not relinquish power without a struggle. Democracy, upon which the revisionists placed all their hopes, is expressly repudiated:

Democracy, so-called, that is bourgeois democracy, is nothing more nor less than veiled dictatorship by the bourgeoisie . . . Marx splendidly grasped the essence of capitalist democracy when in his analysis of the experience of the Commune, he said that the oppressed are allowed, once every few years, to decide which particular representatives of the oppressing class are to represent and repress them in politics.[20]

[20] Nikolai Lenin, *The State and Revolution*, New York, 1929, 89.

The bourgeoisie through its possession of economic power is able to control all the channels for the expression of political life and thought. It is, therefore, impossible for the worker even when he is in a numerical majority, to gain power by relying on the institution of "bourgeois" democracy.

The spirit of the Leninist approach is activist. Instead of waiting patiently for the historic process to unroll, he rushes forward to meet it. Every capitalist crisis is welcomed and eagerly exploited. War is regarded as an evidence of capitalist disintegration. When nations are arrayed in battle against each other mass disillusionment grows; the resistance of the state is weakened and the time is peculiarly ripe for the workers to rise up in armed revolt and seize control. Lenin believed the task of Socialism to consist not in being afraid of civil war, but in getting ready for such a civil war and for a proletarian revolution, in directing its energies toward the transformation of the war between nations into a war between classes.

In the pre-war period, Lenin was already beginning to develop some of the theories which later were to form the basis for the program and tactics of the Communist International. In his article on "The International Socialist Congress at Stuttgart" (1908) he stated "that part of the working class had already succumbed to a species of imperialism"[21] (the theory of bribes from the surplus profits of imperialism), and he noted with concern the tendency of the "labor aristocracy" to forget the demands of international class solidarity. The split in the International was foreshadowed in his warning against betrayal by opportunist leadership. In a number of articles before the war, Lenin insisted on the revolutionary meaning of the national colonial uprisings. In 1908 he declared that "the Russian revolution has a great international ally in Asia,"[22] and from this emerged the theory of fighting a rear guard action against capitalist imperialism by stirring up revolt in the colonies.

The small circle of revolutionary Socialists were not at one in their ideology. They shared the activist attitude, the belief in the necessity for unceasing revolutionary activity; they differed in a number of respects. The western Lefts who followed Rosa Luxemburg counted the general strike rather than armed uprising the deciding means of revolu-

---

[21] Quoted in A. Gurevitch, *Zarozhdenie i Razvitie Kommunisticheskovo Internatsionale* (*Origin and Development of the Communist International*), Kharkov, 1926, 14ff.

[22] *Ibid.*, 15.

tionary battle. They were opponents of the centralized party organization which formed the keystone of the Bolshevik articles of faith and led to their split with the Mensheviks in 1903. Unlike Lenin, Rosa Luxemburg held that the encouragement of an oppressed nation to separate from a great power was a reactionary concession to nationalism. According to the Bolsheviks, she placed undue emphasis on the elemental and the spontaneous in mass uprisings, too little on disciplined organization in combat. The Bolsheviks and the western Lefts, nevertheless, found a common language in their battle with opportunism and Revisionism. A close-knit international group of the Left was not really formed until the World War. They managed, however, to exercise some influence on the decisions of the Second International, particularly noticeable in the resolution of the Stuttgart Congress on militarism, in which they succeeded in committing the Congress to use the economic and political crisis called forth by the war to stir up the masses and to hasten the fall of the capitalist ruling class.

The discussions in the congresses of the Second International reveal the fundamental divergencies among the Right, Center and Left Socialists. These differences expressed themselves on a variety of issues, but for the purposes of this study, the attitude toward war and the related question of loyalty to the nation-state are of prime importance.

The problem of war and militarism formed one of the paramount concerns of the Second International. From its earliest days, opposition to militarism and war constituted a principal subject on the agenda of its congresses. In resolution after resolution, wars are denounced as the product of capitalism, and the working class organized on international lines is hailed as the only guarantee of permanent peace. Though all Socialists agreed in denouncing war in the abstract, the logic of their respective positions compelled them to adopt widely disparate attitudes when particular concrete situations presented themselves.

The theory of the Right, that the capitalist state grows by a process of peaceful development into the socialist people's state, that the interests of the proletariat and the state tend to become identical as this transformation takes place, led not to renunciation of love of country, but to a more intimate attachment. Thus even Bebel, who abhorred Revisionism and all its works, could say (in the Reichstag in 1900):

You will find that in case of war with Russia, the Social-Democratic element which you designate as unpatriotic and hostile to the Fatherland, will perform its duty fully. Indeed, if we were attacked by Russia, whom we regard as an arch enemy to all Europe and to Germany especially, since it is upon Russia that the German reaction rests, I myself, old as I am, would be only too willing to shoulder a gun against her.[23]

And Vollmar, on the Right, was even more outspoken when he declared: "It is not true that we have no Fatherland . . . the love of humanity cannot for a moment prevent me from being a good German."[24] In the conflict between patriotism and loyalty to the international proletariat, the Right Socialists demonstrated primary concern for the safety of their own country. Vandervelde, speaking at the Stuttgart Congress of 1907, expressed this point of view when he proclaimed that "Nations, like individuals, have the right of legitimate defense against an attack, or an aggression which menaces their independence."[25] The Right might deplore war, and pass stinging resolutions in condemnation of militarism; when the crucial issue presented itself, national loyalty was stronger than class feeling. Such moderates as Jean Jaurès advocated the general strike as a method of preventing war, but they could not succeed in extracting from their fellow members of the International an express commitment in favor of this anti-war weapon.

The Center betrayed a cloudiness of outlook that proceeded from its uncertain theoretical orientation. In theory it accepted the proposition that war was inherent in capitalism and inevitable. From this proposition the Left drew the conclusion that Socialists could not prevent it and must therefore dedicate their energies to transforming a general war between nations into a revolutionary war which would exterminate capitalism. The Center refused to draw this deduction. Holding that war was a characteristic feature of capitalism, it at the same time acted on the assumption that capitalistic trends could be redirected, and that capitalism could be made to follow peaceful policies by the pressure of the working class. Thus Bebel could reflect, how optimistically only future events disclosed, "Affairs are no longer in such shape that the threads of a war catastrophe are hidden to educated and observing students of politics. Closet diplomacy has ceased to be."[26] In Germany, he assured the Stuttgart Congress, "Nobody in important circles wanted war."[27] The whole dilemma of the Centrist position can be summed up in

[23] See William E. Walling, *The Socialists and the War*, New York, 1920, 223-224.

[24] Lenz, *op. cit.*, 98.

[25] Emile Vandervelde, *Stuttgart Congress 1907, Report*, 387.

[26] Harry W. Laidler, *Socialism in Thought and Action*, New York, 1927, 255.

[27] Lenz, *op. cit.*, 97.

the following quotation from Bebel's speech at the same Congress:

From a certain standpoint a Social Democrat might say that a great European war would further our cause more than a decade of agitation and therefore we should wish for the war. We do not desire such a frightful way of attaining our goal. But if those who are most interested in the maintenance of bourgeois society do not see that by such a war they are tearing up the very roots of their existence, we have nothing against it; then I say: Go your way, and we shall succeed you. If the ruling classes themselves did not know that, we should have had the European war long ago. Only the fear of the Social Democracy has so far prevented them.[28]

Thus the Centrists expressed their opposition to war in agitation against militarism, in refusals to vote money for military expenditures, in demands for democratically controlled citizen armies, and in the mobilization of mass sentiment to combat chauvinism. They refused, however, to sanction the general strike. The opposition to the general strike was particularly strong among the German Social-Democrats. They considered it a tactical error, a provocation which would give the reactionary German government the welcome excuse to prosecute and suppress proletarian organizations. In their eyes the general strike was a weapon of doubtful utility as long as the labor movement was unequally developed in different lands, since in the event of such a strike the nation with the best organized proletariat would be at the mercy of an attack from countries with proletariats less well organized. Thus the Centrist program against the war danger based its hope of success on the growing strength of the labor movement. Had this strength continued to mount for several decades, the hope that socialist propaganda would succeed in transforming the whole psychology of rival states might have been realized. The most charitable estimate of Centrist policy must conclude that its program was better designed to secure the long time triumph of pacifism than to meet an immediate war danger.

The position of the Left has already been briefly indicated. Condemning pacifist illusions and denouncing war as a characteristic feature of capitalism, Rosa Luxemburg and Lenin called upon the International to utilize the war crisis to declare a civil war between classes. At the Stuttgart Congress they even succeeded in forcing the adoption of an amendment to Bebel's anti-war resolution which manifested a clear revolutionary character.

In case war should break out . . . , it is their duty [the duty of the working classes] to intervene in favour of its speedy termination and with

[28] *Ibid.*, 100.

all their powers to utilize the economic and political crisis created by the war to rouse the masses and thereby to hasten the downfall of capitalist class rule.[29]

The resolutions and discussions of the pre-war International reveal that however anxious the Socialists were to prevent war, they could not agree on methods and tactics which would prove most efficacious in attaining that end. The roots of these disagreements have already been explored. A brief review of action taken by the International demonstrates the difficulties.

When the proposal for a general strike was first presented at the Congresses of Brussels (1891) and Zurich (1893), it was summarily rejected. Sentiment in favor of the general strike, nevertheless, grew, and it received the support of the majority section of the Socialist Party of France, led by Jean Jaurès and Vaillant, and was advocated by such leading representatives of British labor as Keir Hardie, J. Ramsay MacDonald and Arthur Henderson. The opposition came chiefly from the German Socialists. This latter group was strong enough to prevent a direct endorsement of the general strike at Stuttgart in 1907, though the way was left open for the general strike as a weapon which national parties might adopt as they saw fit. At the Copenhagen Congress (1910) Vaillant and Hardie proposed the following resolution:

> Among the means to be used in order to prevent and hinder war the congress considers as particularly efficacious the general strike, especially in the industries which supply war with its implements, arms, munitions, transport, etc. as well as propaganda and popular action in their most active forms.[30]

After a warm debate the resolution was tabled and sent to the International Bureau for study. Its further consideration was postponed until the Vienna Congress which was scheduled to meet August 23, 1914. Serajevo anticipated the discussion.

Meanwhile the European horizon steadily darkened. The Agadir incident, the Italo-Turkish war, and the Balkan wars made the danger of a general conflagration seem imminent. When the Balkan war cloud threatened to envelope all Europe, a special Congress of Socialists assembled at Basle (1912) and issued a manifesto, exhorting the workers to unite to secure peace. But again no definite course of action was

---

[29] *Ibid.*

[30] Huitième Congrès Socialiste Internationale, Copenhagen 1910, *Compte Rendu Analytique,* 1911, 202.

mapped out in case of an outbreak. The Socialists still believed, in the words of the Manifesto, that, "The fear of the ruling classes that a revolution of the workers would follow the declaration of a European war has proved an essential guaranty of peace."[31]

The Vienna Congress, scheduled for August 23, 1914, was to mark the fiftieth anniversary of the birth of the First International. Socialist leaders looked forward to it as a fitting occasion for the celebration of past triumphs and the planning of future conquests. Before that conference could assemble a world war had engulfed Europe in its sweep and had revealed the inner weaknesses of the second effort at labor internationalism.

[31] For text of Basle Manifesto see Walling, *op. cit.*, 99-104.

CHAPTER II

INTERNATIONAL SOCIALISM AND THE OUTBREAK OF THE WORLD WAR

In the history of labor and socialist internationalism there is no more fateful chapter than that connected with the failure of the efforts of the Second International to avert the World War. That failure came close to dealing a death blow to the Second International. It prepared the way for the split in the ranks of international Socialists which produced the Third, or Communist, International.

The copious literature which deals with the behavior of Socialists at the outbreak of the World War is noteworthy more for warm partisanship than for historical objectivity. A large part of it is composed of apologias and polemics written under the stress of war-inflamed passions, by actors in the events described, whose prime object was to justify their own conduct as Socialists while denouncing the abandonment of socialist ideals by enemy Socialists. Communist historians and propagandists have utilized the events of 1914 to expose the "moral bankruptcy" of the reformist leadership of the Second International because, they charge, in the emergency, it succumbed to chauvinism and repudiated the international solidarity of the proletariat.

In this flood of mutual recriminations and efforts at self-justification, it is not easy to separate the true from the false. The tangled skein of that period needs to be unravelled thread by thread before any conclusions can be hazarded.

The directives for the conduct of Socialist members of the Second International in the event of the threat of war are contained in the resolution of the Stuttgart Congress (1907) which declared:

if war ever threatens to break out, the working classes and their representatives in Parliament in the countries affected should with the assistance of the International Bureau, strive to take every step possible in order to avoid the occurrence of war. They must use every effort which in their view, according to the political situation and the opposing class interest, will best contribute to the maintenance of peace.[1]

The Socialist International prided itself on its record in mobilizing labor sentiment to maintain peace in periods of international crisis.

[1] Septième Congrès Socialiste International, Brussels, 1908, *Resolutions,* 423-424.

At the time of the Agadir incident (1911) mass demonstrations against the threatened war were held in all the capitals of Europe. German Socialists joined with the French in declaring that "Morocco is worth the bones of neither the French nor the German workmen." These protests may not have been without effect, but theirs is not the major credit for the maintenance of peace at this particular time. Far more important was the determination of the Kaiser and Bethmann-Hollweg not to allow the Moroccan affair to cause a European conflict.[2]

The Socialists, nevertheless, placed great reliance on the influence of these demonstrations. When the Balkan war cloud hung menacingly over Europe, a special Congress of Socialists met at Basle, Switzerland, November 24-25, 1912, to protest against useless bloodshed and to prevent the spread of the conflict. The assembled delegates drew up a resolution calling upon Socialists to exert their influence on the governments to secure peace. Again the localization of the conflict was largely determined by considerations other than Socialist protests, chiefly the unwillingness of the Great Powers to precipitate an open conflict at that time.[3] The apparent success of these efforts, however, gave Socialists renewed confidence, and the feeling was widespread in Socialist ranks that governments would not dare to make war against the solidly massed opposition of the international proletariat.[4] It remained for the events of 1914 to demonstrate the weaknesses of the peace machinery of the Second International.

The assassination of the Archduke Ferdinand and his bride at Serajevo on June 28, 1914, aroused immediate fears in the Socialist press that the peace of Europe was endangered. *Vorwärts,* the official organ of the German Social-Democratic Party, published in Berlin, pointed to Serajevo as a warning that the South Slav question had to be settled if a European war was to be avoided, and pleaded for French, English and German cooperation in solving the problem.[5] As Austria delayed action, the belief that the Austro-Serb difficulties would be settled peaceably began to gain acceptance, although *Vorwärts* on July 16 (♯191) professed alarm at the intentions of the Austrian militarists and war lords

[2] See Sidney B. Fay, *Origins of the World War,* New York, 1930. 2 vols. Second edition, revised, I, 289.

[3] Fay, *op. cit.,* I, 434-438. Also, Walling, *op. cit.,* 99-104 for text of Basle Manifesto.

[4] See *supra,* 25.

[5] Curt Schön, *Der Vorwärts und die Kriegserklärung,* Berlin, 1929, 16. *Vorwärts,* ♯176, July 1, 1914.

and on July 22 (#197) took to task those chauvinistic German news-papers which, by urging Austria to take a stern attitude, were sharpening the tension.

The next day (July 23) the Austrian ultimatum was issued. To the editors of *Vorwärts,* its intent was unmistakable. "They want war, the conscienceless elements which influence and control the Vienna court . . . they want war—the Austrian ultimatum to Serbia makes it clear."[6] Bethmann-Hollweg is accused of backing Berchtold, and the editorial concludes with a threat: "In Berlin there is being played just as dangerous a game as in Vienna," and "highly undesired things" (revolution?) might result for Germany if a European war were to come. The tone of the Vienna *Arbeiter-Zeitung* (July 24) was only slightly less belligerent.[7] All over the world Socialist sentiment was being mustered to avert the new crisis. The German Party Executive meeting on July 25, issued an official proclamation which not only condemned the behavior of the Greater Serbian nationalists, but pointed out that the demands of the Austrian government were "intended deliberately to provoke war." In the name of the class-conscious proletariat of Germany the Party Executive demanded that the

German government use its influence with the Austrian government for the preservation of peace, and if the shameful war cannot be prevented, to abstain from any armed interference. Not one drop of a German soldier's blood shall be sacrificed to the lust of power of the Austrian rulers and to the imperialist profit-interests.[8]

The party membership was called upon to back up this demand at mass meetings.[9] The German deputies of the Austrian Social-Democratic Party, in a long manifesto reprinted in the *Arbeiter-Zeitung* (July 25), washed their hands of responsibility for the war.[10] The trade-union congress in session at Brussels (July 25-27) with a number of foreign delegates in attendance, including Karl Legien of Germany, added its

---

[6] *Vorwärts,* July 25, 1914.

[7] Carl Grünberg, *Die Internationale und der Weltkrieg,* Leipzig, 1916, 86. (This is a reprint of the article appearing in the *Archiv für die Geschichte des Sozialismus und die Arbeiterbewegung,* #6, 7).

[8] *Vorwärts,* July 25, 1914. Extraausgabe.

[9] For an excellent but slightly pro-French review of the action of the German Social Democracy at the outbreak of the World War see Camille Bloch, "Les Socialistes Allemands pendant la Crise de Juillet 1914," *Revue d'Histoire de la Guerre Mondiale,* #4, Oct. 1933, 305-338.

[10] Grünberg, *op. cit.,* 89-91.

protest against the danger of a general conflagration and called upon the Trade-Union International to exert all efforts to prevent "this crime against humanity."

Emphatic protests against the war were also heard in France. *La Bataille Syndicaliste,* the trade-union publication, and *La Guerre Social-iste,* the Socialist paper edited by Gustave Hervé, joined in an appeal for mass boulevard demonstrations against the war. On July 27, from 8000 to 10,000 persons rallied in front of *Le Matin,* sang the "Internationale," and shouted "Down with war," until they were dispersed by the police and by opposing groups shouting "On to Berlin" and "Vive la guerre."[11] On July 28 the French Socialists issued a manifesto appealing for peace and condemning "the aggressive tactics of Austro-Hungarian diplomacy." In the light of future events the manifesto is chiefly remarkable for its declaration that the "French Socialists know that in the present crisis the French Government is most sincerely anxious to avert or diminish the risks of conflict." The government, nevertheless, is asked "to apply itself to secure a policy of conciliation and mediation . . . and to influence its ally, Russia, in order that she should not seek a pretext for aggressive operations under cover of defending the interests of the Slavs."[12]

German mass demonstrations against the war were even more impressive than the French. On July 28 mass meetings assembled in various parts of Berlin—one alone had 70,000 persons in attendance—and adopted resolutions which concluded with the declaration that the "German workers like the French are now confronted with the problem of so dealing with their respective governments as to prevent the sacrificing of these peoples to the desperate tactics of Austria and Russia. Down with the cry for war! Long live the international brotherhood of man!"[13] Similar demonstrations took place in all the leading cities of Germany, and in France, street encounters between the nationalists and the Socialists were frequent.

On July 28 came the Austrian declaration of war on Serbia. The Social-Democratic press of the Empire, muzzled by censorship, took a cautious stand. Without calling for proletarian opposition to the war, the *Arbeiter-Zeitung* bemoaned the sacrifices and bloodshed which wars cause, and faced the possibility that the war might not be localized.[14]

[11] *L'Humanité,* July 28, 1914.
[12] Grünberg, *op. cit.*
[13] *Ibid.,* 57.
[14] *Arbeiter-Zeitung,* July 29, 1914. See Grünberg, *op. cit.,* 93-94.

The Hungarian *Volkstimme* (July 30) called upon the workers not to forget their class loyalties and looked forward to a happier time after the war when the Social-Democrats might continue their battle for proletarian rights. The *Vorwärts* (July 29) was still hopeful of preventing a world war. "The Kaiser can shake war or peace out of the folds of his toga. . . . In the present situation Wilhelm II holds the outcome in his hand." A meeting of the Party Executive and Commission of Control of the German Party was summoned for July 28, and again it was determined that the Party should make all efforts to avert the war. The same day the Socialist representatives in the French Chamber of Deputies met and voted a resolution that the "Bureau communicate with the government in order to acquaint it with the country's desire for peace and to find out its intention on the convocation of Parliament."[15] A committee then waited upon Bienvenu-Martin (who was Acting-Minister of Foreign Affairs during Viviani's visit to Russia) and as a result of the conversation issued a declaration sympathetic toward "unhappy Serbia."[16] Again it was emphasized that France's intentions were peaceful, that she must not be drawn into the conflict by the provisions of her secret engagements, and that she would give her support to the mediation proposals of England. The Executive Committee of the Confédération Général du Travail issued a somewhat similar appeal and called for the intensification of efforts to maintain the peace.[17]

It was not until July 29, one day after the Austrian declaration of war, that the International Socialist Bureau, representing the world's Socialist parties, held its first session at Brussels. Affairs were already in a critical state. Delegates who came without plenary powers confined their efforts largely to speechmaking and resolutions. It was unanimously decided to advance the date of the Congress from August 23 to August 9.[18] On the motion of the German delegates, the place was changed from Vienna to Paris. The chief subject of discussion was to be "War and the Proletariat." The Bureau passed a resolution calling for an intensification of anti-war demonstrations.[19]

[15] *L'Humanité*, July 29, 1914.
[16] *Ibid.*
[17] *La Bataille Syndicaliste*, July 29, 1914.
[18] Grünberg, *op. cit.*, 33.
[19] *Ibid.*, 19. The resolution is as follows: "In assembly of July 29, the B.S.I. has heard declarations from representatives of all nations threatened by a world war describing the political situation in their respective countries. By a unanimous vote the Bureau considers it an obligation for the workers of all nations concerned, not only to continue, but to intensify their demonstrations against the war, in favor of peace and of a settlement of the Austro-Serbian conflict by arbitration."

That evening the leading orators of the Bureau participated in a monster mass meeting in the Cirque Royal, the largest theatre in Brussels.[20] Keir Hardie, speaking for the English workers, sounded the prevailing temper when he said: "Europe is filled with anxiety tonight. The fear of the horror of war is haunting the minds of men, and yet the proletariat of Europe do not desire bloodshed." He appealed to all workers to resist the war fever. Haase of Germany placed the blame on Austria. He declared that the secret treaties between Austria and Germany do not bind the proletariat—even should Russia intervene. Among the other speakers were Agnini of Italy, Troelstra of Holland, Vandervelde of Belgium, Roubanovitch of Russia, and last of all the veteran Jean Jaurès, the most eloquent of all Socialists. In what was destined to be his last speech, he made the significant declaration, "the French government . . . gives Russia counsel of prudence and patience [a statement not verified by later historical research] . . . but if Russia should not take notice, our duty is to say 'we know but one treaty, that treaty which binds us to the human race'." With vast enthusiasm and spontaneous singing of the "Internationale" the mass of workers dispersed. Two days later Jaurès lay dead at the hands of a half-crazed French chauvinist.

With the resolutions drawn up and the oratory concluded, the delegates to the Bureau held no further meetings though the crisis sharpened daily. The delegates had no authority to sanction efforts at direct action. They were, therefore, necessarily limited to resolutions designed to marshal international Socialist opinion. They could only seek to make that opinion prevail on the responsible officials of the respective governments. When the members of the Bureau dispersed, the last international link between the Socialists of the world was broken. True, the International Federation of Trade Unions, through its secretary, Karl Legien, also made efforts to rouse labor sentiment against the war. Rigola of Italy, Jouhaux for France, Martens for Belgium, Appleton for England, Oudegeest for the Netherlands, Schneeberger and Huggler for Switzerland, and Gompers for the United States all sent telegrams to Legien, dated July 31, denouncing the war and calling for a peaceful settlement of outstanding differences, but no attempt was made to agree on a concerted plan of action to avert the catastrophe. There only remained as a last desperate hope an improvised effort at collaboration between the German and French Socialists, which will be discussed in some detail.

The delegates returned from the meeting of the Bureau to find con-

[20] For report see *L'Humanité*, July 30, 1914.

ditions in their home countries increasingly critical. The Russian mobilization order had been issued on July 30. On that day, Haase came back in time to join the German Party Executive in drafting a manifesto to the Party. In the course of the meeting a remarkable scene took place.[21] The telephone rang, and the Party Executive was asked to settle a controversy which had arisen between Ströbel, one of the editors of *Vorwärts*, and Comrade Stampfer, over an article which the latter desired to publish in the Party press. Stampfer's article with which, according to Scheidemann, a large part of the Party agreed, set forth the view that the Social-Democrats would not desert their country in the moment of danger, and that although the Social-Democrats remained opposed to war, if a Russian invasion threatened "we will not have our women and children sacrificed to the bestiality of the Cossacks." The article left the implication that the Reichstag fraction of the Party would vote the war credits. Against this apparent surrender to the war hysteria and effort to commit the Party on the war credits, Haase and his supporters vigorously protested and were powerful enough at this juncture to cause the article to be withdrawn from general circulation though it appeared the next day in a few papers. Excitement in the ranks of the German Party was intense. The special edition of the *Lokal Anzeiger*, a nationalist paper, which issued a premature announcement of German mobilization, caused Ebert and Otto Braun, the Party treasurer, to flee to Zurich.[22] The Party feared that with the outbreak of the war the authorities would arrest members of the Social-Democratic Party Executive and therefore felt compelled to take precautions.

July 31 was a day packed with momentous events. Austria issued its order for general mobilization. Germany proclaimed "Threatening danger of war" and dispatched ultimata to Russia and France. Mobilization was to follow if Germany did not receive from Russia, within twelve hours, a declaration suspending all war measures. France was given eighteen hours to declare "if it intends to remain neutral in a Russo-German war."[23] The same day Great Britain requested both the French and German governments to give assurances that they would respect the neutrality of Belgium so long as no other power violated it.

In the midst of this exciting sequence of events, a joint meeting of the Executive and the parliamentary section of the German Party took

---

[21] Described in Philip Scheidemann, *Memoirs*, New York, 1929. 2 vols. I, 204ff.
[22] *Ibid.*
[23] For texts see Fay, *op. cit.*, II, 528-529.

place.[24] Haase and Ledebour spoke for the rejection of the war credits when Parliament assembled. Scheidemann pleaded for delay until the entire section could assemble. The only definite decision taken at this meeting was to the effect that Hermann Mueller should be sent by the Party to Paris by way of Brussels in order to consult with the French Socialists. It was hoped that identical action by the Socialist parties in the Reichstag and the Chamber of Deputies would exert pressure on world opinion by demonstrating Socialist solidarity in the face of war hysteria. No definite instructions were given Mueller, nor was he empowered to enter into any commitments for the whole Party. Mueller departed at once, although "Threatening danger of war" had been declared and a rigid censorship had been clamped upon all communication with the outside world.

Mueller arrived in Brussels the morning of August 1 and in company with Camille Huysmans and Henri DeMan, who acted as interpreters, immediately departed for Paris. It is necessary at this point to review the events of July 30 and 31 in France, in order to understand the French reception of Mueller's mission. On their return from Brussels, Jaurès and the other French delegates reported the resolution of the Bureau to a meeting of the Socialist members of Parliament, and a resolution was passed invoking further demonstrations against the war.[25] Jaurès called upon the government to remain pacific and when informed that French troops had been ordered to remain out of a zone of ten kilometers from the frontier, in order to avoid any possibility of a clash with German frontier guards, he is reported to have said to a Socialist colleague, Bedouce, "You know, were we in their place, I do not know that we could do any more to assure peace."[26] Jaurès was still hopeful. The next day (July 31) his idealism received a rude shock when news came that *Kriegsgefahrzustand* (Threatening danger of war) had been decreed in Germany, that telephone, telegraph and rail communications with Germany were cut off, that all roads were barred. Still he did not give up hope. He could not believe that *Kriegsgefahrzustand* meant war. Not satisfied with the definitions of the word in the German dictionary belonging to the Chamber, he sought out a larger dictionary and "tortured the syllables in order to give the word a less grave sense."[27] At

[24] Scheidemann, *Memoirs*, 211.
[25] *L'Humanité*, July 31, 1914.
[26] Bedouce, "Le Vendredi Tragique" *L'Humanité*, August 9, 1915.
[27] *Ibid.*

the head of a Socialist delegation, he again made his way to the Quai d'Orsay, where he was received by M. Abel Ferry, Under-secretary for Foreign Affairs. Again Jaurès demanded that the French government should not abate its efforts for peace. In the last of his daily articles in *L'Humanité* he still did not regard the situation as hopeless. Austria and Russia had entered into negotiations. Germany delayed an attack. The peril was great, but not invincible. With "the heroism of patience and the heroism of action," the war danger might still be overcome.[28] That evening Jaurès was assassinated.

Mueller arrived in Paris the next day, when Socialists were grieving the loss of their greatest leader. He was received cordially and held two interviews with the leaders of the French Socialists, one in a room in the Chamber of Deputies, the other in the office of the paper, *L'Humanité*. On that day mobilization decrees were issued in both Germany and France, but Socialists still continued to discuss the possibilities of a peaceful solution. There are divergent reports of the conversations between Mueller and the French Socialists.[29] The accounts of Mueller and DeMan, the Belgian interpreter, corroborate each other on the main essentials, however, and they will be followed here. According to DeMan's account, Mueller began by declaring that he had been sent for the purpose of mutual information. The Executive of the German Social-Democratic Party wanted to inform the French Socialists of the real state of affairs in Germany, and at the same time gather information about the probable attitude of the French Socialist deputies on the vote of the war credits. This was in view of the impending meeting of the Social-Democrat members of the Reichstag which was to precede the full meeting of that body on Tuesday, August 4. Mueller stressed the following points: (1) He could not officially commit his party to any joint declaration since the members of the Reichstag had not yet met when he left Berlin, nor could he give any information on events since his departure because all avenues of communication had been cut off. (2) He believed, however, that the Kaiser and the Imperial Chancellor were sincere in their desires for peace, and had encouraged the anti-war demonstrations of the Social-Democrats, and that, if war came, the decision would lie with Russia. (3) No decision had yet been reached by

[28] *L'Humanité,* July 31, 1914.

[29] Mueller's report is printed in Philipp Scheidemann, *Der Zusammenbruch,* Berlin, 1921. Henri DeMan who acted as interpreter in the conversation has given his version in *The Remaking of a Mind,* New York, 1919, 36-45. Pierre Renaudel presents a French view in *L'Humanité,* Feb. 26, 1915.

the German Party on the question of voting the war credits. He knew that a strong group in the fraction would vote against the war credits, that a part favored voting for the credits if faced with the danger of a Russian invasion, while the question of abstention from voting was also being discussed. It was his personal opinion that the Party would not vote for the war credits.[30] But in a time when everything was in turmoil, he spoke only his own opinion, and he emphasized that he was not empowered to commit the Party to any course of action.

On the French side the important points were several. (1) It was the conviction of French Socialists that France really desired peace; the sincerity of this desire was demonstrated by the promise of the French cabinet to Jaurès to exert influence on Russia to seek a solution of the Austro-Serbian conflict, and by the government order withdrawing the French troops several miles from the frontier in order not to provoke a border conflict. (2) Since France was playing a defensive rôle, French Socialists were in a different position from German Socialists. If Germany attacked France, French Socialists would be bound to vote the war credits. The German Socialists in such a contingency would not be bound to support the aggressor and ought to vote against the war credits. To the contention of Mueller, that the causes of war must be sought in the system of European alliances and rival imperialisms and that therefore the question of who begins the attack is superficial, the French nevertheless maintained that they were bound to defend the free traditions of the French Republic against attack by German imperialism. A section of the French Socialists thought that the Party ought to abstain from voting "to demonstrate their refusal to accept any responsibility for the consequences of a system of competitive armaments which they had always opposed."[31]

The conference arrived at no decision. Mueller had no authority to give or receive pledges. He could only convey information. Each Socialist Party reserved entire freedom of action when faced with the necessity of making the final decision. In the light of the discussion the only hope for uniform voting was abstention in both countries.

Mueller did not return to Berlin until August 3. Meanwhile the German Party had no knowledge concerning his activities or the action of their French colleagues. Events were becoming increasingly critical. Mueller

[30] "Dass man für die Kriegskredite stimmt, das halte ich für ausgeschlossen." DeMan, *op. cit.*, 39-40.
[31] *Ibid.*, 42.

had departed on July 31. On August 1, news reached Germany of the murder of Jaurès. Scheidemann framed a telegram of condolence and sent it to *L'Humanité*.[32] It did not reach Paris. August 1 was Mobilization Day in both France and Germany. At 6 P.M., August 1, came the German declaration of war on Russia. On August 2 the Executives of the German Party and Reichstag section met to consider the action to be taken by the Party when the Reichstag assembled on August 4.[33] According to Scheidemann, Haase and Ledebour were virtually alone in advocating the rejection of the war credits; all the others favored their adoption. For the Party to abstain from voting on the question was held to be impossible. The meeting was tense. "The wise Fischer became so agitated that his nerves failed him during his speech and he began to cry."[34] No decision was reached. It was arranged to meet again at 9 P.M., August 2, in the offices of the *Vorwärts*, to frame a declaration. The majority of the Executive favored voting the war credits; Haase and Ledebour were adamant, and the discussion went on until midnight. There still remained the meeting of the Parliamentary section the next morning to pass finally on the question. At 7 P.M., August 2, the German demands on Belgium were made; at 7 A.M., August 3, came the categorical refusal of Belgium to allow the German advance.

During the morning of August 3, Scheidemann and Haase were summoned to a meeting with the Chancellor for twelve noon.[35] The section met at 10 A.M. and then adjourned until Haase and Scheidemann returned from the interview with the Chancellor. Reichstag representatives of all the parties were present at this interview. The motion to carry the war credits was discussed, and the Chancellor read the speech which he was to make the next day in the Reichstag. When the remarks made indicated that the Chancellor took it for granted that the vote for the credits would be unanimous, Haase and Scheidemann found it necessary to remind those present that the Social-Democratic section had not finally make up its mind. The Social-Democrats reserved the right to make an independent declaration, no matter what the vote might be.[36]

The section resumed its meeting soon afterwards. The discussion was extremely bitter. War with Russia was now a reality. Russian troops

---

[32] Scheidemann, *Memoirs*, I, 211-212.
[33] *Ibid.*, 212.
[34] *Ibid.*
[35] *Ibid.*, 213.
[36] *Ibid.*, 214.

were on German soil. The majority stressed the horror of a Russian invasion, and argued that the Social-Democrats could not abandon their country and allow it to be overrun by hordes of barbaric Cossacks. Prussianism was bad enough, but it was to be preferred to Russianism. It the course of the discussion Mueller arrived from Paris, and his report left the impression that the French Socialists would vote the war credits.[37] Germany did not declare war on France until 6 P.M., August 3, but already there were charges of French hostile acts, and rumors flew thick and fast that the "French had poisoned German water supplies and French airmen had dropped bombs on Nuremburg and Furth."[38] The fact that these rumors were false did not prevent them from being effective. The majority were convinced that the Chancellor had exerted every effort to avert war; they advocated voting the war credits as a measure of self-defense.

Haase, Ledebour, and Liebknecht led the small group of irreconcilables who argued against voting the credits. They were joined by such distinguished Socialist leaders as Karl Kautsky, Rosa Luxemburg and Franz Mehring. They pointed out that the Party section had heard only one side and had taken at face value the information which the government had allowed to dribble through. They considered it a betrayal of socialist ideals to vote military credits and to assume any affirmative responsibility for the war. On August 3 neither group was yet aware of the ultimatum to Belgium and the proposed violation of its neutrality. The final vote was 78 for, 14 against voting the war credits. The fourteen in opposition surrendered to the demands of Party discipline and allowed the vote to be recorded as unanimous.[39] Haase, the minority leader, even consented, though unwillingly, to read the Party declaration in the Reichstag.[40] The history of this inner conflict in the Party did not become

---

[37] *Ibid.*, 215.

[38] *Ibid.*, 220.

[39] Karl Liebknecht in a letter to the *Bremer Bürgerzeitung*, reprinted in Walling, *op. cit.*, 145, reveals the conflict of opinion.

Accounts of the proceedings of the party council of Aug. 3 may be found in: E. Bernstein, *Die Internationale Der Arbeiterklasse und der Europäische Krieg*, Tübingen, 1915. Bernstein sided with those supporting the war credits but later changed his mind.

See also Karl Kautsky, "Die Sozialdemokratie im Weltkrieg," *Die Neue Zeit*, June 11, 1915. Also K. Kautsky, "Die Zersetzung der Reichstag Fraktion," *Die Internationale*, April, 1915. Kautsky was opposed to the war credits.

[40] "Like a coy maiden reluctant against an embrace," said Wolfgang Heine, but the sneer does not do justice to Haase who sincerely detested the office.

widely known until several months later. To the outside world at the time it seemed that the German Social-Democratic Party was a unit in supporting the war.

By the evening of August 3, Germany was at war with France, and the next day the German march through Belgium was underway. On August 4, two meetings of the Reichstag took place. At the first, beginning at three o'clock, Bethmann-Hollweg spoke, and for the first time mentioned the advance through Belgium.[41] The Reichstag then adjourned for an hour. The Socialists had not yet formally approved the war credits although the text of the Party resolution had been handed to the President of the Lower Chamber. The new disclosure did not lead to a reconsideration of the vote. Apparently the Social-Democrats were satisfied with the declaration of the Chancellor that any wrong which had been done to Belgium would be made right. The Czarist menace was more pressing. The Reichstag reconvened and the section voted as a unit in favor of the war credits. One member—Kuhnert—absented himself from the Chamber and did not vote, but his absence was not noticed. Herr Haase read the Party declaration:

> . . . we are menaced by the terror of foreign invasion . . . it devolves upon us, therefore, to avert this danger, to shelter the civilization and independence of our native land . . . we take our stand upon the doctrine basic to the international labor movement, which at all times has recognized the right of every people to national independence and national defense, and at the same time we condemn all war for conquest . . . we do not regard this in the light of a contradiction to our duty in connection with international solidarity. . . .[42]

With this declaration the German Social-Democrats plunged headlong into the World War. The unanimity presented to the world at large was only apparent and concealed some important defections which were to grow and eventually to cause a split in the Party.

The German Social-Democratic Party of Austria promptly followed the lead of their German colleagues. The *Arbeiter-Zeitung* on August 5, in its comment on the Reichstag vote, approved the action of the German Party.[43] As in Germany, however, the Party was not unanimous in giving its support to the war. Dr. Friedrich Adler led a small group of dissenters who became more vocal as the war was prolonged, and did their best to prevent the fragile structure of international proletarian solidarity

[41] Scheidemann, *Memoirs*, I, 220.
[42] Walling, *op. cit.*, 143.
[43] Grünberg, *op. cit.*, 97.

from being overwhelmed in the rising tide of national hatreds.[44] The Czechish and Hungarian Social-Democrats acquiesced in the action taken by the Austrian Party.[45] The Polish Social-Democrats residing within Austria went even further.[46] They welcomed the war with unrestrained enthusiasm as an opportunity to deliver oppressed Poland from the yoke of the Czar and to undermine the most reactionary absolutism in Europe. Josef Pilsudski was delegated to recruit and lead a Polish National Army in a crusade against the Czar.[47]

It is now necessary to turn back and follow the activities of the French Socialist Party prior to August 4. Prominent French Socialists had apparently committed themselves to a war of defense in the conversations with Mueller on August 1. On August 2, a mass meeting was held at the Salle Wagram.[48] News that the neutrality of Luxemburg had been violated by Germany had just reached the gathering. The spirit of the martyred Jaurès hovered over the assemblage. Vaillant, Longuet, Cachin, and Sembat united in a last desperate plea for peace, but all insisted that if France were invaded they would vote to defend their country. Pierre Renaudel in an editorial in *L'Humanité* (August 3) still did not give up hope in spite of the invasion of Luxemburg. He pointed out that Schoen, the German ambassador, was still in Paris. On August 3, a deputation of the socialist parliamentary group called upon the Premier, M. Viviani.[49] The Premier declared that while the hope of peace was slight nothing would be done on the French side to impair the prospect of a resumption of negotiations. Such a resumption was always possible as long as Schoen remained in Paris.[50] The socialist group asked that the French government continue its efforts for peace and that an appeal for mediation be addressed to the British government. M. Viviani promised to bring the request of the deputation before the Cabinet that same evening.[51] This was at 5 P.M. An hour and fifteen minutes later Schoen called for his passports and left behind him the German declaration of war.[52] The break had come.

[44] Ludwig, Brügel, *Geschichte der Oesterreichischen Sozialdemokratie*, Vienna, 1925. 6 vols. VI, 179.

[45] See Grünberg, *op. cit.*, Hungarians, 120ff, Czechs, 116, 313.

[46] *Ibid.*, 107-116.

[47] *Ibid.*, 307.

[48] Reported in *L'Humanité*, Aug. 3, 1914.

[49] Jules Destrée, *Les Socialistes et la Guerre Européenne*, Paris, 1916, 25.

[50] See Joint Manifesto of French and Belgian Socialists after the beginning of the war, reprinted in Walling, *op. cit.*, 175-177.

[51] *Ibid.*

[52] Fay, *op. cit.*, II, 533-534.

The next day, (August 4) *L'Humanité* declared that the French Socialists would vote the war credits unanimously when called upon. The course of events, *L'Humanité* contended, left no doubt that France was the victim of aggression. *La Bataille Syndicaliste* took the same stand. The French socialist deputies gave their consent to the war credits by unanimous vote. The case of the French Socialists was simple. Convinced that their own government desired peace and that they were the victims of German imperialistic aggression, they rallied to the defense of their country. On August 28 the French Socialists authorized two of their members—Jules Guesde and Marcel Sembat—to accept portfolios in the Ministry of National Defense which was then being constituted.[53]

The Belgian Socialists took a similar stand. On August 3, after the German ultimatum, the Council of the Belgian Labor Party voted to abandon anti-war demonstrations and decided that the Socialist Party would vote the necessary war credits. A manifesto was issued which pointed out that "in defending the neutrality and even the existence of our country against militarist barbarism we shall be conscious of serving the cause of democracy and of political liberty in Europe."[54] A few days after the declaration of war Emile Vandervelde, the leading Belgian Socialist and Chairman of the International Socialist Bureau, joined the Belgian Ministry of National Defense.

British Socialists found themselves in a quandary when the war broke out. The sentiment of the working class in the last week of July was solid for peace. After the meeting of the International Socialist Bureau on July 29, the British section issued a manifesto signed by Keir Hardie and Arthur Henderson, urging the workers to strain every nerve to prevent the government from entering the war and cooperating with Russian despotism. "The success of Russia at the present day would be a curse to the world."[55] On August 1 and 2, huge "Stop the War" meetings were held in London and other cities. On Sunday, August 2, 15,000 people assembled at Trafalgar Square. Every shade of socialist and labor opinion was represented. A resolution was drawn up protesting "against any step being taken by the government of this country to support Russia, either directly or in consequence of any understanding with France, as being

[53] Guesde in his statement accepting a cabinet position declared: "I go into the cabinet as an envoy of my party, not to govern but to fight. If I were younger, I would have shouldered a gun. . . ." See Walling, *op. cit.*, 179-180 for complete statement.

[54] Walling, *op. cit.*, 181-182.

[55] A. W. Humphrey, *International Socialism and the War*, London, 1915, 103ff.

not only offensive to the political traditions of the country, but disastrous to Europe," and declaring that "as we have no interest, direct or indirect in the threatened quarrels which may result from the action of Austria in Serbia, the government of Great Britain should rigidly decline to engage in war, but should confine itself to efforts to bring about peace as speedily as possible."[56]

When Sir Edward Grey addressed the House of Commons on August 3, in a speech which indicated the imminence of war, Mr. Ramsay MacDonald, as chairman of the Labour Party, still held out for neutrality. In answer to Grey's appeal to the national honor, MacDonald stated that "whatever may happen, whatever may be said about us, whatever attacks may be made upon us, we will say that this country ought to have remained neutral, because in the deepest part of our hearts, we believe that is right, and that alone is consistent with the honor of the country."[57] *The Daily Citizen,* an organ of the Labour Party, in an editorial of August 4, professed no love for the German autocracy, but reminded its readers that Great Britain in joining France would be fighting to "extend Cossack rule in Eastern Europe." The German invasion of Belgium that journal considered as a good excuse but not the real reason for British intervention.

At midnight, August 4, came the British-German break. The National Executive of the Labour Party meeting the next day (August 5) passed a resolution criticizing British policy in general and the action of Sir Edward Grey in particular, and expressed its aspiration for peace.[58] The same day there took place a meeting of the British Parliamentary group. The chairman, Ramsay MacDonald, proposed that he read the resolution

[56] *Justice,* August 6, 1914.

[57] Humphrey, *op. cit.,* 106.

[58] "That the conflict between the nations of Europe in which this country is involved is owing to foreign ministers pursuing diplomatic policies for the purpose of maintaining a balance of power; that our own national policy of understanding with France and Russia only, was bound to increase the power of Russia both in Europe and Asia, and to endanger good relations with Germany.

"That Sir Edward Grey as proved by the facts which he gave to the House of Commons, committed without the knowledge of our people, the honor of the country to supporting France in the event of any war in which she was seriously involved, and gave definite assurances of support before the House of Commons had any chance of considering the matter.

"That the labour movement reiterates the fact that it has opposed the policy which has produced the war, and that its duty is now to secure peace at the earliest possible moment on such conditions as will provide the best opportunities for the re-establishment of amicable feelings between the workers of Europe."

For text see Walling, *op. cit.,* 160-161.

adopted by the Executive during his speech in the House that evening. The majority of the section refused to consent to this, and Mr. Mac-Donald resigned his chairmanship. The predominant group in the section, feeling that it had exhausted every effort to prevent war, now held that the declaration of war settled the matter and that they, like other people, "had to see it through." With the exception of four of the six Independent Labour Party members—Ramsay MacDonald, Keir Hardie, F. W. Jowett, and Tom Richardson—the rest of the Labour membership in Parliament threw themselves wholeheartedly into war preparations and supported the policy of the government. At the end of August, when a Parliamentary Recruiting Committee was formed, the Labour deputies joined in the appeal for recruits and placed their machinery at the disposal of the Committee. The statement of the National Executive, of August 5, was in effect repudiated by a manifesto signed by twenty-five Labourite members of Parliament, which declared that "if England had not kept her pledges to Belgium, and had stood aside, the victory of the German army would have been probable, and the victory of Germany would mean the death of democracy in Europe."[59]

The British Socialist Party, which as an organization was outside the Labour Party, took the view in the Party Manifesto of August 12 that Germany was the aggressor.[60] Hyndman, the party leader, realized that Britain was fighting on the side of Russian despotism. "As matters stand today it is a choice of evils." Believing that "the victory of Germany would be worse for civilization and humanity than the success of the Allies," he joined the Workers' War Emergency National Committee, and worked side by side with Sidney Webb, the Fabian, only to be cast out, the next year, from the party which he had created when the majority of the membership of the party declared itself anti-war. Most of the trade-unionists supported the war. The only effective opposition came from a group in the Independent Labour Party led by Ramsay MacDonald, Philip Snowden and Keir Hardie, who argued that Great Britain entered the war not to defend the independence of Belgium but in order to fulfill its promises to France, to preserve the balance of power, and to crush a rising commercial rival. "Russia in arms with us to free Europe from an autocracy whether political or military, is a grim joke!"[61] The sup-

[59] Text in Humphrey, op. cit., 112-113.
[60] Text in Justice, Aug. 13, 1914.
[61] See article by Ramsay MacDonald, Labour Leader, Aug. 27, 1914.

porters of this view in England were to increase in number as the war progressed.

Extremely interesting is the attitude taken by the two Serbian socialist deputies.[62] In the sitting of the Skupschtina (Parliament) of August 1, after the Austrian declaration of war, representatives Laptchevitch and Katzlerovitch joined in refusing their support to the government. Representative Laptchevitch, while agreeing that the Austrian note was an outrage, argued that Serbia was partly responsible in having allowed herself to be a pawn in the hands of Russia and France, and in having tolerated the activities of the *Narodna Odbrana* (a Serbian nationalist organization). Therefore, he argued, it did not merit socialist support.

Equally intransigent was the stand taken by the socialist deputies in Russia. Socialists were still bitter at the extreme measures of repression which had been taken by the government to put down the strikes in St. Petersburg from July 17 to 27, 1914, just prior to the outbreak of the war. The position of the Social-Revolutionary Party was set forth in an anti-war manifesto issued soon after the declaration of war.[63] It considered the Russian protection of Serbia the essence of hypocrisy. "Imagine the intervention of the Czar on behalf of poor Serbia, whilst he martyrizes Poland, Finland and the Jews, and behaves like a brigand toward Persia. Whatever may be the course of events, the Russian workers and peasants will continue their heroic fight to obtain for Russia a place among civilized nations."

When the Duma met on August 8 to vote money for the war, Valentin Khaustoff, speaking on behalf of the fourteen Social-Democratic deputies (both Bolshevik and Menshevik), demanded an amnesty for all political prisoners and a policy of conciliation toward nationalities. When these concessions were refused he read a declaration absolving the working class of all responsibility for the war.[64] The socialists then walked out of the Duma without voting for the credits or the resolution of confidence in the government. They were joined by the eleven members of the Labor Party on this occasion, though the latter group, under Kerensky, later supported the government on the ground of danger of invasion. The Social-Democrats continued their policy of opposition, and on November 17, five Bolshevik Duma members were arrested as revolution-

[62] Grünberg, *op. cit.*, 210-213.
[63] English Translation in Walling, *op. cit.*, 188-189.
[64] *Ibid.*, 189.

ists. The plea of Vandervelde, that the Russian Socialists join the battle against Prussian Junkerdom was not heeded. M. Lavin, on behalf of the Mensheviks, declared that "Russian Socialists know their government better than other people do, and they remain the irreconcilable enemies of that government."[65] The Bolsheviks answered that:

the Russian working class cannot under any condition act hand in hand with the Russian government. . . . Today all Socialist journals are stopped, all working class organizations are disbanded, many hundreds of members are arrested, and our brave comrades are sent to exile just as before. Should this war end in victory for our present government, it will become the centre and mainstay of international reaction.[66]

Outside of Russia prominent socialist exiles, among them Plekhanoff, Axelrod and Deutsch, as well as the anarchist Kropotkin, pleaded for an allied victory, but their voices exercised little influence in the councils of the Social-Democratic Party inside Russia.

The attitude taken by the Italian Socialist Party at the time of the outbreak of the World War was of considerable importance, because of its undoubted effect in preventing Italy from aiding the Central Powers. The tremendous general strike of June 1914, while not altogether successful, involved nearly two million workers and gave labor a new consciousness of its power.[67] Toward the middle of July, as the danger of war loomed, *Avanti* threatened another general strike if Italy departed from neutrality.

We do not know what are the secret pacts of this Triple Alliance which was so suddenly renewed by the monarchs against the will of the people, but we know that we boldly declare that the Italian proletariat will break the pacts of the alliance if it is forced to spill a single drop of blood for a cause which is not its own. Even in the case of a European conflagration, Italy, if it does not wish to precipitate its ruin, has but one attitude to take; absolute neutrality.[68]

The Party addressed an ultimatum to the Premier in which it took an extreme anti-German position. "We can assure you that if Italy mobilizes her army and commands it to march to the direct or indirect support of the Germans against the French, that very day there will be no need of any effort on our part to make the Italian people revolt. The insurrection would be unanimous and terrible."[69] The Party took a

[65] S. Dalin, "Russian Socialists and the War," *Labour Leader,* Nov. 19, 1914.
[66] *Ibid.*
[67] On the Italian general strike see Walling, *op. cit.,* 117ff.
[68] *Ibid.,* 121.
[69] *Ibid.,* 197-198.

definite stand in favor of neutrality which was upheld in the joint manifesto of the Party Executive and Parliamentary group on September 21.[70]

Later, as the tide turned and sympathy for the allies became more pronounced, a group within the Party led by Mussolini, the director of *Avanti,* worked for a modification of the Party stand. When Mussolini's resolution was rejected at the meeting of the Executive of October 20, he resigned the editorship of *Avanti* and started an independent newspaper advocating war against Germany and Austria.[71] Shortly thereafter he was expelled from the Party. Anti-Austrian sentiment in the Party, nevertheless, continued to grow.

In the countries which remained neutral at the outbreak of the World War, the influence of the Socialists was generally exerted to maintain that neutrality.[72] In Holland, the Social-Democrats led by Troelstra, voted mobilization funds in the Chamber of Deputies August 1, but only for the express purpose of maintaining neutrality against outside aggression. Troelstra warned the government that the Social-Democrats would resist any aggressive steps which it might take toward participation in the war. The Swiss Socialists sponsored great demonstrations against the war, and joined with Italian Socialists in a conference at Lugano (September 27) which marked the first cooperative step of neutral Socialists to bring "a speedy close to this mass murder of European people." The Socialists of Sweden and Denmark also took a stand for absolute neutrality. In Rumania the Party Executive issued a warning against pro-Russian propaganda which aimed to draw Rumania into the war and appealed for a federated republic of Balkan states as one way out of the dilemma. In Bulgaria the Socialists were divided into two groups—the "narrow" or orthodox Socialists, and the "broads" or opportunists. The eleven members of the "narrow" group declared themselves in favor of a Balkan federation and urged the government to combine with other neutral powers "to bring about the earliest possible end to the bloodshed." The "broad" group which was more nationalistic abstained from this declaration. The Portuguese Socialists at the outbreak of the war demanded strict neutrality, but when Portugal entered the war as an ally of Great Britain they supported the government. The Polish Social-

[70] Humphrey, *op. cit.,* 70-73.
[71] Walling, *op. cit.,* 199.
[72] For stand of neutrals, see Walling, *op. cit.,* Ch. XVIII, "Other Neutral Nations," 203ff.

Democrats residing in Russia opposed the war. The Socialists of the United States also declared their opposition to the war early, and called upon the national government to mediate between the rival disputants in the interests of world peace. Other socialist parties in neutral countries took a similar position in opposition to the war.

In drawing the balance sheet of international Socialism at the outbreak of the World War, it is, of course, the action taken by the Socialists in the belligerent countries which is of chief concern. In only two countries, Russia and Serbia, were the Socialists united in their parliamentary opposition to the war after the war was declared. In the other countries— Germany, Austria, France, Belgium and Great Britain—the great majority of Socialists rallied around the national cause with the declaration of war. The opposition of a forlorn group of irreconcilables—the Haase-Ledebour-Liebknecht group in Germany, the supporters of Friedrich Adler in Austria, the Independent Labourites in Great Britain—only emphasized the completeness of the surrender to the surge of rival nationalisms.

The breakdown of the Second International at the beginning of the war has furnished socialist and other writers with a fruitful topic for speculation and controversy. Harsh words have been spoken concerning this alleged "betrayal" of international Socialism. Much of this criticism arises from a misunderstanding of the nature of the Second International; it proceeds on the mistaken assumption that the Second International was organizationally fitted for the task of averting a war, that it possessed the power to translate its will into action, and that it represented sufficient consensus on theory and tactics to present a united proletarian front against the war measures. None of these assumptions is justified.

The Second International was a weak organization from the standpoint of the opportunities which it held out for International collaboration among the national socialist parties. It was essentially a loose federation of autonomous socialist parties which assembled for consultation with each other at periodic congresses. The International Bureau was little more than an administrative clearing house which handled correspondence, issued appeals and circulars, made arrangements for future congresses, and performed similar duties. The constitutional infirmity of the Second International was its failure to provide for centralized power and authority. There existed nowhere in its scheme of organization any provision for a central body of control which could be summoned together quickly in an emergency and which could bind the constituent membership to a concerted plan of action. The nearest approach was the Bureau, and the scope of its powers has already been indicated. It did not assemble until a day after Austria had declared war on Serbia; its members had no power to act nor to dictate a course of procedure which their party groups would be bound to follow. They could only sponsor protests in mass demonstrations against the war. Before the ponderous machinery of a congress could be set in motion, war was a reality.

No lines of communication existed to coordinate the policies of the national parties after the process of mobilization had begun. After the meeting of the Bureau, the last possibility of effective action lay in collaboration between the German and French socialist parties. The Mueller mission to Paris represented a desperate but feeble attempt to establish agreement on a joint program. But since Mueller had no power to commit his party, the effectiveness of the negotiations was crippled by the cutting off or censorship of all communication between the two parties after mobilization. Mueller's departure from Paris broke the last link, and the only result of his mission was an interchange of views, not a scheme of action. In a time when the movement of events was so rapid, constant communication was absolutely essential if the Socialists were to bring their full international strength to bear. The virtual quarantine in which each socialist party found itself, the dependence of Socialists for information on the facts which the government allowed to reach them, were factors of considerable importance in explaining the inability of the socialist parties to coordinate their policy. Bewildered by the rapid movement of events, they lived in a fog-clouded world, and were buffeted about by storms and winds the direction of which they did not know and the strength of which they could not estimate.

In the next place it is easy to exaggerate the effective force which the International commanded. While socialist strength was growing by leaps and bounds in the pre-war period, nowhere—not even in Germany—were the Socialists strong enough to prevent increased expenditure for armaments. They could record their protests, but their negative votes were futile as long as the party in power secured the adoption of huge military and naval budgets over their heads. An ominous growth in armaments went on side by side with the pacific propaganda of the Socialists. Measured in terms of effective political power, socialist parties prior to the war were still weak minorities, as the attached table indicates:

	Party Vote		Parliamentary Representation	Total Representation in Parliament
Austria	1,000,000	(1911)	82	516
Belgium	600,000	(1912)	39	185
Bulgaria	85,489	(1914)	20	211
Denmark	107,365	(1913)	32	140
France	1,379,860	(1914)	101	602
Germany	4,250,329	(1912)	110	397
Great Britain	370,802	(1910)	42	670
Serbia	25,000	(1912)	2	166
Italy	338,865	(1909)	42	508
Russia	800,000	(1912)	14	442

The possibility of effective international action was made more difficult by the unequal strength of socialist parties in different lands. The degree of resistance which the respective parties could offer might have the effect of placing the nation with the best organized proletariat at the mercy of attack by countries with proletariats less well organized. It was for this reason that the German Social Democracy opposed the general strike as a weapon to avert war. It was felt that its effect would be to invite a Russian invasion. Moreover, even in Germany, where the socialist movement was strongest, leaders pointed out that railroad workers, workers in state factories for the manufacture of military supplies and in private armament establishments were largely unorganized. With these considerations in mind the mass strength of the International becomes less imposing than it seemed at first glance.

While the bulk of the Socialists were opposed to the war and made their protests vocal by mass demonstrations and revolutions, these protests were rendered futile by the overpowering jingoist and chauvinist sentiment which had been aroused by the nationalist press in the days of crisis. The Socialists in the pre-war period were still crying alone in the wilderness, without a reservoir of internationally-minded public opinion to which they could appeal to support their plea for peace.

The principal cause of the inability of the International to function was the lack of consensus on theories and tactics to meet the war danger. The pre-war International was composed of an alliance of fundamentally incompatible elements which were able to maintain a superficial appearance of international proletarian solidarity only so long as a World War could be avoided and competing national loyalties could be prevented from coming into play.

The general agreement among Right and some Center Socialists, that defensive wars were justified, made effective international proletarian solidarity impossible. Faced with the necessity of defining the conditions of defensive warfare, German and Austrian Socialists favored support of the government on the ground that German civilization was threatened by Cossack barbarism; French and Belgian Socialists rushed to defend their native lands against the onslaughts of German imperialism. The same fundamental premise split Socialists into two opposing camps. From that premise each party was able to spin out a logic which destroyed the reality of the international brotherhood which they preached.

Even when Right Socialists continued to do lip service to internationalism, their activity was dictated by a widespread acceptance of the thesis that their own interests were intertwined with the support of their own national economy. The experience of the German Social Democracy furnishes a striking example. The rise of the German Social Democracy synchronized with Germany's growing commercial and industrial supremacy on the continent. Any threat against that supremacy was in an indirect way a stab against the labor movement which fed upon the products of industry and flourished when industry flourished. However much the German government had hampered the rise of the German Social Democracy, it still remained true that the government had allowed that Party to develop the strongest labor and socialist movement in the world. For the German Social Democracy to defy the government was to invite retribution in the form of Party persecutions and restrictive laws which would result in destroying such progress as had been made. The same line of reasoning in somewhat different form was used to justify the allegiance of Socialists to the government in other belligerent countries. In this way Socialists were caught up in the same web of national loyalties for which they so often reproached their opponents. When the crucial test came, international socialism proved powerless. It failed in the greatest task it had set itself—the task of preserving the world peace.

But the socialist surrender to the surge of rival nationalisms was not complete. Even in the belligerent countries where Socialists responded most whole-heartedly to the call of national patriotism, there still remained small dissenting groups which refused to make any compromise with the body of international ideals which they had built up so painfully through the years. From these groups there was to emerge the driving power behind the insistent call for peace during the war years which finally led to the split in the Second International and the creation of the Third.

CHAPTER III

FROM THE OUTBREAK OF THE WAR TO THE
ZIMMERWALD CONFERENCE

The outbreak of the World War came as a great shock to the Socialists. Dazed by the suddenness with which it had descended upon them, they took only feeble steps to avert the catastrophe. When the initial surprise had worn off and the war had become a fact that could not be ignored, they felt themselves compelled to adopt some positive attitude toward it. They turned for guidance to the resolutions passed by the pre-war International Socialist Congresses of Stuttgart (1907) and Copenhagen (1910) which declared that:

if war breaks out, then it becomes their [the working classes] primary duty to bring about its conclusion as quickly as possible, and thereafter to make the most of the opportunities offered by the economic and political crises which are sure to follow the war in stirring up public opinion and hastening forward the abolition of capitalist class rule.[1]

Though the injunction to end the war was clear, Socialists were by no means agreed as to how that object could best be attained. A bewildering variety of programs soon appeared, the effect of which was to increase socialist perplexities rather than to dissipate them.

As opinion among Socialists crystallized, at least three important currents of thought emerged from the chaos.[2] At the Right were those who believed that the cause of international Socialism would be best advanced through a whole-hearted support of the Fatherland and an identification of the interests of the party with that of the nation. The group which took this point of view commanded the support of the largest portion of the socialist movement. It embraced in its ranks such outstanding leaders of international Socialism as Vaillant, Guesde and Sembat in France, Scheidemann, Legien and Südekum in Germany, Vandervelde in Belgium, Plekhanoff in Russia, Hyndman in England and Bissolati in Italy. This group proved most reluctant to inter into a general international socialist conference to end the war as long as the chance for a national victory was bright, though its ardor for peace increased

---

[1] VII° Congrès Socialiste International, *Resolutions*, 423-424.
[2] See R. S. Schuller, *Geschichte der Kommunistischen Jugendinternationale*, Berlin, 1931. 5 vols., I, 94-95.

as the prospect for an immediate victory grew dim. The strength of this group was at its height at the beginning of the war. As the conflict lengthened into a contest of endurance, and war weariness seized the populace, this group suffered numerous defections to the Left and Center.

The Center was much more outspoken in its opposition to the war. It included among its adherents such personalities as Haase, Bernstein, and Kautsky in Germany, MacDonald and Keir Hardie in England, Merrheim and Bourderon in France. As resentment against the war mounted, the opposition of this group expressed itself in a refusal to vote war credits or to support the war affirmatively in any way. Although this group lent its support to all international efforts to end the war, it preferred to operate within the existing framework of the Second International. It called upon the International Socialist Bureau to take more vigorous steps to mobilize socialist strength to stop the bloodshed. Unlike the Left, it hesitated to break its organizational unity with the "patriotic" Socialists of the Right.

The Left wing had as its most extreme spokesman Lenin, the leader of the Russian Bolsheviks. It also claimed the allegiance of the more revolutionary Social-Democrats such as Franz Mehring, Karl Liebknecht, Rosa Luxemburg and others. In the early months of the war Lenin already heralded the collapse of the Second International, condemned the chauvinism of the majority Socialists and called for the organization of a Third International to rally those militant elements which hoped to produce an immediate socialist revolution by transforming the imperialist war between nations into a civil war between classes.[3] This small but intensely active group formed a nucleus around which the Third International was later constructed. In the early years of the war it was relatively insignificant numerically thought it increased in prestige and influence as the war dragged on. In the early days Lenin and his followers in exile were regarded as a band of uncompromising doctrinaires and sectarians whose unswerving adherence to their interpretation of the Marxian dogma had hopelessly split the Russian Social-Democratic Party and who were constitutionally incapable of concerted action with other socialist groups. It remained for the November Revolution to lift Lenin and his followers to the seat of power. These latter-day successes, by a kind of reflected glory, make the activities of Lenin in the early years of the war seem more important than they appeared to contemporaries. To attain perspec-

[3] *Sotzial-Demokrat*, #33, Nov. 1, 1914. V. I. Lenin, *Collected Works*, International Publishers, New York, 35 vols. XVIII, 84-89.

tive it is necessary, therefore, to write the history of the activities of the Left wing against the larger canvas of international socialist history during the war period.

Soon after the beginning of the war, the American Socialist Party took the initiative in efforts for peace. It sent a telegram to foreign socialist parties suggesting mediation by the government of the United States to end hostilities.[4] The invitation proved premature. The belligerents were not yet ready for peace and no action was taken.

Meanwhile the International Socialist Bureau remained virtually paralyzed.[5] At the outbreak of the war the headquarters of the Bureau were located in Brussels, and its Executive was composed of three Belgian delegates—Vandervelde, Anseele, and Bertrand—with Camille Huysmans as secretary. The entrance of Belgium into the war prejudiced the neutrality of the Executive as far as Germany and its allies were concerned. In order to retain the confidence of socialist parties in all belligerent countries, the headquarters of the Bureau were transferred to The Hague, and the Executive was enlarged by the addition of three Dutch representatives—Troelstra, Van Kol, and Albarda—with Vliegen and Wibaut as substitute members. These enjoyed equal rights with the Belgian members. Huysmans was retained as secretary. This arrangement was approved by all the parties represented in the Bureau except the French who did not vote.

In the first months of the war the Executive took no affirmative steps to end the conflict. The Executive at The Hague did, however, maintain a correspondence with individuals in the various socialist parties, but a full meeting of the Bureau was not summoned, since belligerent members declared in advance that they would refuse to sit at the same table with enemy socialists. In the absence of these members, it was feared that any decision which was reached without the concurrence of the rest of the members would lead to a break-up of the International, and this the Executive was unwilling to risk.

The inactivity of the Executive of the Second International was particularly irksome to the representatives of the extreme Left and lent point to their homilies on the moral bankruptcy of the "Chauvinist In-

[4] "In present crisis before any nation is completely crushed, Socialist representatives should exert every influence on their respective governments to have warring countries accept mediation by the United States. This can still be done without loss of prestige. Conferences would be held at The Hague or Washington. Have cabled socialist parties of ten nations urging this action. Wire reply." Walling, *op. cit.*, 405.

[5] Camille Huysmans, *The Policy of the International*, London, 1916.

ternational."[6] In this work of exposing and pitilessly condemning the conduct of the Second International, Lenin led the van. At the outbreak of the World War, Lenin was living in a Galician village situated near enough to the Russian frontier to enable him to keep in close touch with Russian developments. After being arrested and imprisoned by Austrian authorities as a suspected Russian spy, he was released through the intervention of socialist friends and obtained permission to leave Austria for Switzerland.[7] He arrived in Berne on September 5, 1914. In the early days of September he wrote his theses on the war.[8] These contain in skeleton form the central ideas which were to be reiterated and expanded many times in his later discussions of the problem. Their substance may be summarized as follows. The World War is an imperialist conflict in which working men have been duped into slaughtering each other for the benefit of the bourgeoisie. The workers have been betrayed by their opportunist socialist leaders. The Second International has collapsed. It is, therefore, the task of real Social-Democrats to expose the chauvinism of sham Socialists. It is their duty to bring on the social revolution by turning the weapons which are intended to destroy comrades in the working class against the bourgeoisie.

On September 6 and 7 these propositions were presented for approval to a group of Bolsheviks living in Berne.[9] Among those present were N. Krupskaya, G. Zinoviev, F. Samoilov (who was a Bolshevik member of the Duma), G. Shklovsky and G. Safarov. After being adopted in full, the theses were circulated among sections of Bolsheviks living abroad. Samoilov also took the theses back into Russia where they were submitted to the Duma group, the Russian section of the Central Committee of the Party and to the workers of some of the large Petrograd factories. The Russian section of the Party concurred with some modifications, and when Vandervelde made his appeal for allied support to the Duma group of Socialists he received a sharp refusal.[10]

The first international socialist conference after the outbreak of the war took place between Italian and Swiss Socialists at Lugano, Switzerland, on September 27, 1914. According to a report in the *Golos*, the

[6] See articles in N. Lenine and G. Zinoviev, *Contre le Courant*, Paris, 1927. 2 vols. See especially "Le Krach de la II[e] Internationale," I, 143-184.

[7] Lenin, *Works*, XVIII, 494.

[8] Published under the title of *The Tasks of Revolutionary Social Democracy in the European War*. See *Works*, XVIII, 61ff.

[9] *Ibid.*, 407.

[10] For text of reply see Walling, *op. cit.*, 359-360.

daily paper of the international wing of the Mensheviks, the conference was "called at the initiative of some prominent Russian Socialists."[11] Lenin took an active part in the conference preliminaries. His theses on the war were discussed by the conference and influenced the resolutions which were drawn up. Among the participants in the conference were Serrati, Balabanova, Lazzari, Morgari, Turati, Mussolini and Modigliani for the Italian Socialists, and Pflüger, Schenkel, Grimm and Naine for the Swiss.

The resolution adopted by the conference did not go as far as Lenin would have liked.[12] Although condemning the war as "the result of the imperialist policy of the Great Powers," the signers confined their efforts to calling upon Socialists "to uphold the old principles of the International of the proletariat," to fight against the extension of the war, and to exert pressure on their governments "with a view toward a speedy close of this mass murder of the European people." The conference did not accept the theses of Lenin that the war between nations ought to be transformed into a civil war between classes, but it did mark a step forward toward the restoration of international proletarian unity.

The effort to summon a representative international conference of Socialists in the early months of the war encountered numerous obstacles and finally had to be abandoned. On October 11 a conference of Socialist delegates from the three Scandinavian countries decided to convoke a general conference to which all Socialists, belligerents as well as neutrals, should be invited.[13] The unwillingness of the French to participate proved a stumbling block, and it was decided that a conference of representatives of neutral countries alone held out promise of success. The intention was to include representatives of all socialist parties in the neutral countries affiliated with the International Socialist Bureau.

In order to ensure the success of the proceedings, the Dutch and Scandinavian Socialists decided to rule out all controversial issues by not only excluding the belligerent Socialists but also removing from the agenda the discussion of "the conditions which have caused the war," or "the standpoint of the Socialist parties in the various countries toward it. Its only task will be to look for a basis on which Socialists can take action to secure peace."[14] The Spanish Socialists objected to this gingery avoid-

---

[11] Lenin, *Works,* XVIII, 409.
[12] For text see Walling, *op. cit.,* 206-207.
[13] For documents, *Ibid.,* 407-422.
[14] *Ibid.,* 409.

ance of war causes in the agenda of the conference and refused to participate.[15] The decision of Italian and Swiss Socialists not to participate further narrowed the field of effective action. The American Party chose Morris Hillquit as its delegate, but at the last moment Hillquit decided not to go when he discovered that "the Copenhagen assembly had dwindled down to a meeting of Holland and three neighboring Scandinavian countries." These countries had "specific local and sectional interests," and Hillquit felt that the "United States would be out of place" at such a gathering.[16]

When the Copenhagen Congress finally assembled on January 16 and 17, 1915, the only countries represented were those which had issued the invitation. The conference adopted a resolution protesting against "the violation of the law of nations committed against Belgium," and calling upon the socialist parties to request their governments to intervene in order to end the war. The conference stressed the "duty of all Socialist parties to work in the direction of an early peace."[17] Though the conference was without direct practical consequences, it did serve to register a section of neutral sentiment and kept the pot of pacific propaganda brewing.

The first six months of the war served to define more sharply the divergent trends in the socialist movement. They marked the gradual emergence into the open of groups which were opposed to the war and which sought an international expression for their common opposition. These groups were by no means agreed on a program; they were united only by their desire to end the war.

In Germany the fourteen Social-Democrats who had opposed the voting of war credits by the party in the group meeting, formed the nucleus around which the opposition gathered. Within the opposition itself there was division between the Center group led by Kautsky, Haase and Bernstein which was reluctant to break with the majority, and the more extreme group led by Karl Liebknecht, Franz Mehring and Rosa Luxemburg, which wished to make its disagreement with the official position of the party clear. Karl Liebknecht in a letter to the editors of the *Bremer Bürgerzeitung,* of September 3, 1914, revealed the lack of unanimity by which the decision of August 4 had been reached.[18] The beginning of the

---

[15] *Ibid.,* 410.
[16] For text of Hillquit's letter, *Ibid.,* 417-419.
[17] *Ibid.,* 420-421.
[18] Julian Gumperz (ed.), *Karl Liebknecht—Reden und Aufsätze,* Hamburg, 1921, 131.

solidification of the Left opposition was indicated when Liebknecht, Mehring, Luxemburg and Clara Zetkin produced a joint statement under date of September 10,[19] taking issue with the tactics of the German Social Democracy in dispatching Südekum and Fischer to Sweden, Italy and Switzerland to defend the official party policy. In their declaration, Liebknecht and the others said:

> We, and undoubtedly also many other Social-Democrats view the war, its causes, and its nature, as well as the role of Social-Democracy in present conditions, from a standpoint which differs completely from that of Comrades Südekum and Fischer. Martial law deprives us for the time being of the possibility of publicly advocating our views.[20]

The *Bremer Bürgerzeitung*, a Social-Democratic Left wing paper, also came out against the official position of the Party and formed a rallying point for the Bremen Lefts who joined Liebknecht in opposition to the war.

On the question of voting the second war credits on December 2, 1914, the minority in opposition within the group increased to seventeen. Liebknecht alone, however, defied party discipline and cast his ballot against the credits. His vote was accompanied by a declaration denouncing the war as an imperialist adventure on both sides in the interest of the capitalist class.[21] Though Liebknecht was immediately censured by the group for a breach of party discipline, he was not expelled from the Party and was able to carry on his propaganda. In January, 1915, in a speech to a Neuköln gathering he proclaimed his battlecry: "Class War is the solution of the day, not class war after the War, but class war during the War; Class-war against the War."[22] The speech marked an acceptance of the Leninist thesis that the war of nations ought to be transformed into a war of classes.

As the Liebknecht group adopted a more uncompromising position it came into sharp clash with the authorities. In the beginning of February, 1915, the military authorities made an effort to take jurisdiction over Liebknecht because of his enrollment as an "Armierungsoldat," but by invoking parliamentary immunity his release was secured.[23] On February

---

[19] Published in the Oct. 30, 1914, issue of the *Berner Tagwacht*, Swiss Socialist paper.

[20] *Ibid.* See also Lenin, *Works*, XVIII, 416.

[21] For text see Ernst Drahn and Susan Leonhard (editors), *Unterirdische Literatur in Revolutionären Deutschland während des Weltkrieges*, Berlin, 1920, 14-15.

[22] *Ibid.*, 16-17.

[23] Edwyn Bevan, *German Social Democracy During the War*, London, 1918, 46-47.

18, 1915, Rosa Luxemburg was imprisoned. The journal which she and Franz Mehring founded at this time to give expression to the views of the group—*Die Internationale*—was allowed to issue only one number, that of April, 1915, and was then suppressed.[24]

Though the extreme Left wingers were driven underground they did not relax their activity. Their views received wider circulation through an illegal traffic in pamphlets and other means of propaganda. Such incendiary leaflets and brochures as Karl Liebknecht's *The Chief Enemy is at Home* (*Der Hauptfeind Steht im Eigenen Land*) (May, 1915) and the Junius brochure, *The Crisis of German Social Democracy* (*Die Krise der Deutschen Sozialdemokratie*), which was written by Rosa Luxemburg in prison, received wide circulation and did much to inflame revolutionary sentiment among the socialist masses.[25] In the early months of 1915 the persecution of the revolutionary wing of the Party was already lending it an air of martyrdom which had a certain appeal to a portion of the German Social Democracy.

The revolutionary wing of the Party was not the only one which flourished. The Center also increased in boldness and strength. In February, 1915, the Center opposition gained control of the Social-Democratic delegation in the Prussian lower house by a vote of six to four, and in a public declaration read on February 9, expressed its dissent with the majority of the Reichstag.[26] When the imperial budget was voted for the third time the minority was able to command thirty votes against it in the group meeting. Liebknecht again violated party discipline by voting publicly against the budget. This time he was joined by Rühle, another Social-Democrat.[27] The antagonism between majority and minority was rapidly becoming bitter. It agitated the party press and all meetings of party organizations. As the minority grew in strength, the unspoken question on the lips of the German Social Democracy became, how long could party solidarity and unity be preserved.

Opposition to the war in France centered in the ranks of the Syndicalists. In the first flush of the war fever, even such radical leaders as Merrheim "were completely carried off their feet,"[28] and succumbed to the wave of triumphant nationalism. The prolongation of the war pro-

[24] Drahn and Leonhard, *op. cit.*, 17.
[25] Reprinted, *Ibid.*, 21-27.
[26] Bevan, *op. cit.*, 43-44.
[27] *Ibid.*, 44-45.
[28] See declaration by Merrheim, *Report* of the Congrès de Lyon, 1919, Confédération Général du Travail, 170-171.

duced its inevitable reaction, and dissatisfaction with the official policy which supported the war mounted. There were numerous signs of a gathering opposition. In December, 1914, Pierre Monatte, editor of *La Vie Ouvrière*, resigned from the National Committee of the General Confederation of Labor, on the ground that the National Committee had "dishonored itself" by its refusal on December 6 to attend the Copenhagen Congress of neutrals.[29] Monatte led a sizeable minority in syndicalist ranks which demanded peace.

Trotsky and Martov, Russian emigrés, began the publication in Paris, in the autumn of 1914, of the paper *Golos* (*Voice*) which later became *Nashe Slovo* (*Our Word*).[30] Through its columns they fought the "opportunism" of the socialist majority which supported the war. They extended their influence by meeting regularly with some of the more radical spirits in the French labor movement, among whom were Monatte, the journalists Rosmer and Guilbeaux, Merrheim, the secretary of the Union of Metal Workers, "Papa" Bourderon, the secretary of the coopers' syndicate, and the teacher, Loriot. Together they criticized "official Socialism" and cemented the French opposition into a fighting internationalist organization.

In Great Britain, the opposition to the war centered in the ranks of the Independent Labour Party and in the internationalist wing of the Socialist Party which was led by Fairchild and MacLean. At the beginning of the war (August 7) Ramsay MacDonald resigned the leadership of the Parliamentary Labour group in order to have a free hand in criticism. The National Administrative Council of the Independent Labour Party in its manifesto of August 13, 1914, took a definite line against the war. The leaders of the Party—MacDonald, Snowden, Keir Hardie and Jowett—were not extremists. Although against the war, they did not undertake any militant anti-war activity nor were they in favor of a break with the Labour Party which supported the war.[31]

In Russia, the Duma groups of both the Bolshevik and Menshevik wings of the Russian Social-Democratic Labor Party opposed the war.[32] At the Duma session of August 8, the Menshevik, Khaustoff, spoke for both groups in refusing to vote the war appropriations. Yet a distinction needs to be noted. The Mensheviks were largely content to limit their

[29] His statement is reprinted in Walling, *op. cit.*, 413-417.
[30] Leon Trotsky, *My Life*, New York, 1931, 247.
[31] A resolution advocating a break with the Labour Party was rejected at the April 1916 Conference of the Party. See Lenin, *Works*, XVIII, 417.
[32] *Ibid.*, 416.

opposition to parliamentary protests. Some of their leaders—among others, Plekhanoff and Axelrod—came out in favor of an allied victory.[33] The Bolsheviks were intransigent. They seized the disorganization of the war period to renew illegal revolutionary activity on a large scale among the masses.[34] Vandervelde's appeal to the Bolsheviks, to discontinue the revolutionary struggle against Czarism for the duration of the war, was indignantly rejected.[35]

Meanwhile Lenin directed activities from afar. Taking an extreme Left wing position, he pursued his purposes with unremitting energy, and by infusing his fellow Bolsheviks both at home and abroad with the same uncompromising devotion, he sought to kindle the fires of revolution. In Switzerland he was ceaselessly busy lecturing and writing, exposing the chauvinism of the Right, criticizing the Center for its inactivity, purging the ranks of his own party of laggards and doubters, and welding the remnant into a devoted priesthood of revolutionary firebrands. He kept in constant touch with the scattered colonies of Bolsheviks in exile in Europe, and maintained lines of communication with the leaders in the Russian Party and revolutionary elements in other socialist groups.[36]

On November 1, 1914, the *Sotzial-Demokrat*, the central organ of the Party, resumed publication with Lenin as editor.[37] Lenin seized every occasion to flay Plekhanoff for his chauvinism and Martov for his reluctance to break organizationally with the social-chauvinists even though Martov personally opposed the war.

Lenin maintained contact with the Central Committee in Russia, through Shlyapnikov, who made his way from Petrograd to Stockholm in October, 1914. At the Congress of the Swedish Social-Democratic Party meeting in November, 1914, Shlyapnikov, acting on instructions from Lenin, represented the Bolshevik Central Committee and delivered an address condemning the German Social Democracy and appealing for united international action by the proletariat against the war.[38] Branting, the Swedish party leader, argued that "it does not become the convention to denounce other parties," and offered a motion which expressed regret over that part of Shlyapnikov's speech which reflected on the

---

[33] Their statements are available in translation in Walling, *op. cit.*, 363-367.

[34] See E. Jaroslawski, *Aus der Geschichte der Kommunistischen Partei der Sowjet Union (Bolschewiki)* Hamburg, 1929-31. 2 vols. II, 49ff.

[35] For reply see Walling, *op. cit.*, 359ff.

[36] Volume XVIII of Lenin's *Works* is a record of his activities during this period.

[37] *Ibid.*, 420-421.

[38] *Ibid.*, 420.

German party. This motion was accepted, though not without strong opposition from Höglund, the leader of the revolutionary wing of the Swedish Social-Democratic Party.[39] The occasion gave Lenin an opportunity to bring his program before an important party and enabled him to identify his views with the more radical element in that party.

Lenin already envisaged the creation of a new revolutionary International to take the place of the old. In the very first number of the revised *Sotzial-Demokrat* (♯33, November 1, 1914), he intoned the death chant of the old International:

> Overwhelmed by opportunism, the Second International has died. . . . Long live the Third International. The task of the Third International is that of organizing the forces of the proletariat for a revolutionary onslaught on the capitalist governments, for civil war against the bourgeoisie of all countries, for political power, for the victory of Socialism.[40]

The attendance of Shlyapnikov at the Swedish Social-Democratic Convention represented an early effort to enroll in the movement the revoluntionary elements in the Swedish party. Lenin at this time was also keeping in close touch with the revolutionary elements of the Dutch Social-Democratic Party, which included H. Gorter, A. Pannekoek and Roland-Holst, who were grouped around the paper *Tribune*.[41]

On January 10, 1915, the Foreign Bureau of the Central Committee of the Bolsheviks issued a letter announcing a convention of all foreign sections of the Bolshevik Party to assemble at Berne on February 27.[42] On February 14, 1915, nearly two weeks before the scheduled Berne conference of foreign Bolsheviks, a conference of Socialists of the Allied Powers—France, Great Britain, Belgium and Russia—met at London.[43] The invitations were issued by the British Independent Labour Party. The original intention was to make it a general conference with German and Austrian Socialists represented, but when the French refused to attend under such conditions the design was abandoned.[44] Sembat, speaking at a special meeting of the French Socialist Party for the instruction of the delegates, said:

> One must understand that the French and German Socialists cannot be placed upon the same level as to the justice of their cause. The Germans did not pro-

[39] *Ibid.*, 104-105.
[40] *Ibid.*, 89.
[41] *Ibid.*, 424.
[42] *Ibid.*, 490.
[43] *Ibid.*, 425.
[44] *Ibid.*, 140.

test against the violation of Belgian neutrality, which was a wrong. One cannot negotiate with people who deny that. . . .[45]

The agenda of the conference included (1) rights of nations—Belgium, Poland—(2) colonies (3) guarantees of peace. Among those who attended the conference were Keir Hardie and MacDonald of the Independent Labour Party, and delegates representing the British Socialist Party, the Fabian Society, and the Labour Party; Sembat, Longuet, Vaillant, Albert Thomas, Compère-Morel of the French Socialist Party, and Jouhaux of the General Confederation of Labor, Vandervelde of Belgium and Chernov, Roubanovitch and Bobrov (Nathanson) representing the Russian Social-Revolutionaries. The representatives of the Menshevik Organization Committee, Martov, and of the Polish Socialists, Lapinski, were unable to attend because passports had been refused. Maiski spoke for the Organization Committee.

Shortly before the London Conference assembled, the editors of *Nashe Slovo*—Trotsky and Martov—wrote to Axelrod and Lenin, the representatives of the Russian Social-Democrats in the International Socialist Bureau, suggesting "coordinated action by the internationalist elements in the Russian Social-Democrat Labor Party."[46] Axelrod agreed in principle on behalf of the Mensheviks. Lenin replied by attacking the social-chauvinism of the Menshevik Organization Committee and submitted the draft of a declaration which embodied his demands. When the contributors of the *Nashe Slovo,* meeting on February 13, 1915, refused to break with the Organization Committee, union between the *Nashe Slovo* and the Bolsheviks became impossible. The elaborate preliminary negotiations between the rival groups in the Russian Social Democracy to determine the Party position at London were not without their element of grim humor when it developed that the chief representative of the Organization Committee could not attend because he was refused a passport and the Bolsheviks were not even invited. But the latter group could not be turned back so easily.

Maximovitch (Litvinov), the perspi acious London representative of the Bolsheviks, discovered the address of the conference and, in his own words, "without asking for an invitation decided to go in order to read the [party] declaration."[47] Litvinov, after listening to the proceedings for a short time, took the floor and lodged a protest against not being invited.

[45] Walling, *op. cit.,* 423.
[46] Lenin, *Works,* XVIII, 428.
[47] *Ibid.,* 140.

Litvinov's attempt to make a speech was interrupted by the chairman who declared that Litvinov's standing as a delegate had not yet been ascertained, and that the convention had not assembled to hear the various parties criticized. The protest of the Bolshevik delegate was then referred to the Credentials Committee, which decided that he should be allowed to participate. Litvinov gives his own account of what happened next.

I thank the conference for its "courtesy" and wish to continue the declaration in order to make clear whether I can remain. The chairman interrupts me, saying he will not allow me to present "conditions" to the conference. Then I ask permission to declare why I will *not* participate in the conference. Declined. Then, I say, allow me to declare that the Russian Social-Democrat Labor Party does not participate in the conference. As to the reasons, I leave a written declaration with the chairman. I gather my papers and go. The chairman was handed a declaration by the chairman of the Central Committee of the Lettish Social Democracy, Berzin, to the effect that he fully agreed with our declaration. . . .[48]

The declaration itself set in striking relief the differences which separated the revolutionary wing of the socialist movement represented by the Bolsheviks from the "government" Socialists who dominated the London Conference. Before entering into any discussions bearing on the reestablishment of the International, the Bolsheviks demanded:

(1) that Vandervelde, Guesde, and Sembat immediately quit the bourgeois cabinets of Belgium and France.

(2) that the Belgian and French Socialist Parties sever the so-called "national Bloc" which is a renunciation of the Socialist banner and serves to cover up the orgies of chauvinism indulged in by the bourgeoisie.

(3) that all Socialist parties abandon their policy of ignoring the crimes of Russian Czarism, and renew their support of the struggle against Czarism, which is conducted by the Russian workers without fear of any sacrifices.

(4) that in fulfillment of the resolutions of the Basle Congress, it be declared that we extend our hand to those revolutionary Social-Democrats of Germany and Austria who replied to the declaration of war by preparing propaganda in favor of revolutionary action. Votes for military appropriations must be absolutely condemned.[49]

These conditions the conference refused to consider. Though rebuffed at London by the so-called "government" Socialists, the Bolsheviks turned for support to the internationalist elements in the socialist movement. The declaration concluded:

The workers of Russia extend their comradely hand to the Socialists who act like Karl Liebknecht, like the Socialists of Serbia and Italy, like the British

[48] *Ibid.*, 141.
[49] *Ibid.*

comrades from the Independent Labour Party and some members of the British Socialist Party, like our imprisoned comrades of the R.S.D.L.P.

The battle lines between the rival groups were beginning to be more tightly drawn.

The London Conference concluded its work by adopting a resolution which while not ignoring "the profound general causes of the European conflict," declared that:

the invasion of Belgium and France by the German armies threatens the very existence of independent nationalities, and strikes a blow at all faith in treaties; that the Socialists are not at war with the peoples of Germany and Austria, but only with the governments of those countries by which they are oppressed. They demand that Belgium shall be liberated and compensated. They desire that the question of Poland shall be settled in accordance with the wishes of the Polish people (either in the sense of autonomy in the midst of another state or in that of complete independence). They wish that throughout all Europe from Alsace-Lorraine to the Balkans, those populations that have been annexed by force shall receive the right to dispose of themselves.[50]

The Bolsheviks in their analysis of the Conference pointed out that its object was to unite the Socialists of the Allied countries behind the war. It aimed particularly to rally to the Allied cause the still wavering British Independent Labour Party.[51] That this purpose was attained was demonstrated to the satisfaction of the Bolsheviks at least, by that section of the resolution in which the participants declared themselves "inflexibly resolved to fight until victory is achieved to accomplish this task of liberation." That the Bolshevik interpretation of the proceedings was not altogether without foundation is indicated by Sembat's frank admission that his object was "to convince the representatives of British Socialism of the necessity of fighting to a finish."[52]

As a kind of answer to the London Conference, representatives of the socialist parties of Germany and Austria-Hungary assembled in Vienna on April 16 and 17, 1915, to frame a common program and proclaim their solidarity.[53] Like the Allied Socialists, they upheld the policy of the defense of the Fatherland, and declared that it did not constitute an obstacle to the re-establishment of the International. They expressed their will for peace based on the following principles:

[50] See Walling, *op. cit.*, 424ff.
[51] Lenin, *Works*, XVIII, 425.
[52] Raymond Poincaré, *Memoirs of Raymond Poincaré* (1915) trans., and adapted by Sir George Arthur, New York, 1931, 38.
[53] Brügel, *op. cit.*, V, 220-221.

(1) the development of international arbitration courts into obligatory tribunals for settling all differences between nations;

(2) the subjection of all treaties and agreements entered into by states to the democratic parliamentary control of a representative assembly;

(3) the framing of international treaties for the limitation of armaments with a view to complete disarmament;

(4) recognition of the principle of the self-determination of nations.[54]

The "patriotic" Socialists dominated the conference. Though the wish for peace was expressed, no definite terms were advanced. Nothing was said specifically of Belgium or Poland, and the stand of the conference could only be implied from its adherence to the foregoing enumeration of general principles. The delegates sought to preserve the shell of international unity at least by proclaiming their adherence to the Second International "which the war had crippled but not destroyed."[55]

While these meetings of the "official" Socialists of the rival belligerents aimed to cement the allegiance of the rank and file of Socialists to their respective Fatherlands, the revolutionary and internationalist elements in the socialist parties led by Lenin also sought to unite their forces. The Conference of the Foreign Sections of the Bolsheviks which was held at Berne from February 27 to March 4, 1915, was an important step in this direction, because it framed a program for the revolutionary elements in the international labor movement.[56] The conference adopted a resolution condemning the war as "a struggle between England, France and Germany for the division of colonies and for the plunder of the competing countries," and calling upon the proletariat to transform the present imperialist war into a class war.[57]

Representatives of women's organizations affiliated with the Central Committee of the Bolsheviks took the initiative in calling for a conference of Socialist women opposed to the war.[58] As early as November,

[54] *Ibid.*

[55] *Ibid.*

[56] Lenin, Works, XVIII, 426. (Among those present were Lenin, Zinoviev, Krupskaya, Inessa Armand, Lilina, Kasparov, Bukharin, Krylenko, Kharitonov, Shklovsky and others.)

[57] As the first steps in this transformation concrete tasks were outlined. See Lenin, *Works,* XVIII, 426:

"(1) Unconditional refusal to vote for military appropriations and resignation of posts in bourgeois cabinets.

"(2) Complete break with the policy of civil peace (Bloc national, Burgfrieden).

"(3) Creation of an illegal organization wherever the governments and the bourgeoisie abolish constitutional liberties by introducing martial law.

"(4) Aid to fraternization of the soldiers of the belligerent countries in the trenches and on the battlefields in general.

1914, Krupskaya, the wife of Lenin, and others had broached the idea. It was taken up by Clara Zetkin, the secretary of the International Bureau of Socialist Women, who issued an appeal in December, 1914, urging Socialist women to struggle for peace.

The International Socialist Women's Conference finally assembled at Berne on March 26-28, 1915. The significance of this Berne Conference consisted in the fact that for the first time since the opening of the war, Socialists from opposing belligerent nations met together at the same conference. Delegates were present from Germany, France, England, Holland, Switzerland, Italy, Russia, Poland and Hungary.

In the conference a sharp difference of opinion soon disclosed itself between the pacifists led by Clara Zetkin, and the revolutionaries led by Krupskaya.[59] The pacifist resolution which was drafted by Clara Zetkin took a middle-of-the-road position. While condemning the war, it refused to break with the so-called "social-chauvinists" of the Second International. The Russian delegation introduced a far more radical resolution which sharply criticized the position of the majority Socialists and called for an immediate revolutionary struggle. In the final vote the Zetkin resolution was supported by an overwhelming majority of those present, including the representatives of the German, English, French, Dutch and Swiss women. Only the Russian and Polish delegates voted for the Bolshevik motion.[60] Though the action of the majority proved a disappointment to such a thoroughgoing revolutionary as Lenin, the conference at least gave an opportunity for an exchange of views. It marked, moreover, the first organized expression of opposition to the war in which neutral and belligerent Socialists participated.

The Berne Conference paved the way for other international gatherings of Socialists opposed to the war. On April 5-6, 1915, an International Conference of Socialist Youth was held at Berne.[61] The conference was summoned at the behest of Italian and Swiss Socialists after Danneberg, the Austrian secretary of the International Youth Bureau, had refused

---

"(5) Support to every kind of revolutionary mass action of the proletariat. Because of the complete collapse of the 'opportunist' Second International the R.S.D.L.P. must support all and every international and revolutionary mass action of the proletariat; it must strive to bring together all anti-chauvinist elements of the International."
[58] *Ibid.*, 145-149.
[59] *Ibid.*, 192.
[60] *Ibid.*, 192-196.
[61] A full discussion of this conference may be found in Schuller, *op. cit.*, 75-107.

to take action, and majority Socialists had declared themselves opposed to the assembly. Thirteen delegates gathered from nine countries; three from Germany, one from Holland, three from Russia, one from Bulgaria, one from Italy, one from Norway and Sweden, one from Denmark and two from Switzerland.

Lenin showed considerable interest in the proceedings of the conference and appointed the two Bolshevik delegates, Jegorow, and Inessa Armand. The differences of opinion revealed in the discussions of the Youth Congress virtually reproduced the earlier conflict in the Women's Congress. The majority of the Congress followed the lead of Robert Grimm, the Swiss Centrist-pacifist, whose resolution bound the conference to work for peace, to refuse to support the policy of "civil peace" (Burgfrieden), and to put loyalty to class above loyalty to Fatherland. This resolution failed to satisfy the Bolsheviks, who criticized it as inadequate, (1) because it proposed no program for transforming the war of nations into a civil war, and (2) because the resolution did not mark a clean break with the social-chauvinists and did not repudiate the tactics of the wavering Kautskian Center. The Bolshevik substitute proposal received only three votes, two Bolshevik and one Polish Socialist, and the Grimm resolution carried. Thus the Bolsheviks found themselves repulsed again. They prided themselves, however, on having advanced their program with vigor and on having succeeded in impressing its nature on the minds of the participants. Meanwhile they awaited a turn in circumstances to resume the attack.

The Youth Conference concluded its work by electing a new Bureau and providing for the publication of a journal—*Jugendinternationale*—of which ten numbers subsequently appeared. Lenin, Zinoviev, and Karl Liebknecht were among the leading contributors. Their articles gave the columns a revolutionary flavor and helped to account for the strength of the revolutionary ferment in socialist youth circles.

A mere chronological record of events in the international socialist movement in the first nine months of the war is apt to leave a picture of confusion and conflict. Yet the history of that troubled period cannot be oversimplified without opening the way to inaccuracies and distortions. In order to bring some order out of the chaos a summary of the prevailing trends up to May, 1915, may be desirable. Such a recapitulation may serve the useful purpose of setting the rise of the opposition in the socialist movement—both revolutionary and pacifist—in a clearer light.

As has already been indicated, the effect of the war was to divide socialist forces into three broad camps, the Right or patriotic Socialists, the Center or pacifist Socialists, and the Left or revolutionary Socialists. Not all Socialists fitted rigidly into these three categories. Shades of difference among socialist groups more often resemble the gradual merging of the colors of the spectrum than the sharp contrast of black and white. For purposes of convenience the labels are sufficiently accurate. They stand for a fundamental clash of principle.

At the beginning of the war, the patriotic Socialists formed the strongest group. They were in control in Germany, France and England. They dominated the International Socialist Bureau and were responsible for its forced inactivity since the French and Belgian representatives refused to meet with the enemy. They blocked the way to a representative international socialist conference, and all efforts to revive the Second International through a meeting of belligerents and neutrals proved unavailing. The Copenhagen Conference which was originally intended to gather together Socialists of every country found the obstacles insuperable and dwindled down to a regional conference of neutral Socialists. The Socialists of the Right threw themselves into the war, supported their governments, and in the case of Belgium and France even sent representatives into the ministries. The only schemes of international collaboration into which the Right Socialists were willing to enter were those which united Socialists on the same side more closely. The London Conference represented such an effort to promote cohesion among Allied Socialists. The Vienna Conference was the counterblast from the enemy ranks. Both conferences, however, did endorse a set of somewhat vague and tentative principles as a basis of discussion for peace. To this extent they threw the weight of their influence on the side of peaceful settlement. Their efforts were without immediate practical results. The end of the period saw the influence of the Rights diminishing, particularly in Germany.

At the same time, the Center or pacifist Socialists were gaining strength. In England, pacifists dominated the Independent Labour Party, and a large section of the Socialist Party. In France the ideas of the Center permeated a growing minority in the General Confederation of Labor. In Germany, the Kautsky-Haase-Bernstein group increased its parliamentary strength from fourteen votes to thirty in less than nine months and already challenged the hegemony of the majority. Pacifist elements also predominated in the Italian, Swiss, Dutch and Scandinavian parties. At Lugano in 1914, and the two Berne Conferences

(Women and Youth) in 1915, the Centrist elements were powerful enough to dictate the resolutions which were adopted. Although the Centrists denounced the war and opposed all socialist participation in its active support, they preserved their Party connections with the Right. They still clung to the hope that the Second International would be revived and reinvigorated. They refused to accept the counsel of the revolutionaries to embark on immediate class warfare.

The revolutionary wing of the international socialist movement was the weakest in point of numbers. It attempted to make up for this deficiency by the vigor with which it prosecuted its ends. Arguing that the majority Socialists of the Right and Center had betrayed the interests of the proletariat, it called for immediate revolutionary action and the transformation of the war of nations into a civil war of classes. Lenin provided a large part of the driving intellectual force of the movement. He devoted his energies to welding the scattered revolutionary internationalists into a compact fighting organization. To his banner there rallied the supporters of Liebknecht in Germany, the Left wing in the Italian Socialist movement, the Polish Social-Democrats, the Bulgarian Social-Democrats (Narrow), the *Tribune* group in Holland, the followers of Höglund in Sweden and other scattered elements. Lenin allowed no opportunity to escape in which he might expose the chauvinistic weaknesses of his opponents and popularize his own uncompromising program. He participated in the preparatory work of the Lugano conference; his emissary, Shlyapnikov, addressed the Swedish Social-Democrats; Litvinov appeared uninvited at the London conference; Bolshevik delegates advanced the Leninist program at both Berne conferences. In no case was the point of view of Lenin accepted or approved. It did receive consideration, and in most cases it was discussed. The importance of these conferences—particularly those at Berne—consists partly in the fact that for the first time the supporters of Lenin challenged the Centrists for the right to speak for the workers who were opposed to the war. The revolutionaries were defeated, but they were not despondent. Every day that the war continued brought them fresh recruits. The challenge was to be renewed. The next step was Zimmerwald. There the stage was already set for a battle-royal between pacifists and revolutionaries.

CHAPTER IV

THE ZIMMERWALD CONFERENCE

The international conference of Socialists which assembled at Zimmerwald, Switzerland, from September 5 to September 8, 1915, marks an important step forward toward the creation of the Third International. The influence of the conference in hastening the peace was probably negligible. Its significance consists rather in the fact that it assembled in defiance of the Bureau of the Second International. It drove a wedge into the old International which eventually made a split inevitable. The conference was not remarkable for any unanimity of outlook. It was composed of discordant elements which disagreed with each other violently on an affirmative program. They found a common ground in their general dissatisfaction with the policy of the belligerent governments and with the policy of the "patriotic" Socialists who supported these governments.

The Zimmerwald movement was called into being primarily by the inactivity of the Bureau of the Second International. From the very earliest days of the war, the Italian and Swiss Socialists had taken the lead in calling for a meeting of the full Bureau (at Lugano, for example) but without success. The removal of the headquarters of the Bureau to The Hague, and the reorganization of the Executive Committee to include Dutch members to remove any possible charge of partiality had raised hopes that a full meeting of the Bureau might be summoned. But as the belligerent nations, particularly France, proved adamant, the Executive Committee preferred to delay for fear that a premature gathering would mean an open split in the International. Meanwhile the Executive Committee agreed (January-February 1915) to invite various delegations from the belligerent countries to come separately to The Hague for a series of consultations with the object of smoothing the way for a direct meeting later between the belligerents.[1] In the ensuing months a Belgian delegation arrived for consultation, and a German delegation visited The Hague twice. The French Socialist Party, however, replied that the sending of a delegation to The Hague would be considered indirect negotiation with the Germans, which was impossible as long as German armies were occupying French soil.[2] The English expressed

[1] Huysmans, *op. cit.*, 20-21ff.
[2] *Ibid.*

their readiness to come, but for various reasons the delegation was obliged to postpone its visit.[3] Subsequently a meeting in London was arranged. All these negotiations were time-consuming, and meanwhile an international meeting of the Bureau had not taken place.

The more impatient spirits in the Swiss and Italian parties pressed for action. When the Bureau of the International still seemed reluctant to act, the Socialist Party of Italy took the initiative and sent the Italian deputy, Morgari, on a special mission to France. On April 19, 1915, he held a conference with Vandervelde and special representatives of the French Socialist Party, and tried to convince them of the necessity of immediate action.[4] The mission was unsuccessful. Vandervelde and the French majority held that an international Socialist conference would be an obstacle in the war for liberty and justice in which they were engaged. Morgari took the position that "the Bureau should have been convoked the day after war was declared, in spite of the dissensions in the camp of the International."[5] Vandervelde and the French replied by insisting that they could not meet with the German Socialists whom they regarded as traitors to the Socialist cause. Morgari proved equally unshakeable, and then warned that if the Bureau refused to function his party would on its own initiative summon an international conference of all parties and minorities which remained faithful to the principles of Socialism. Vandervelde interrupted dramatically, "We shall prevent it," but in spite of the implied threat, the Italian Socialist Party went ahead with its preparations.[6]

The conference was approved by the Italian Socialists at Bologna on May 15, 1915, and a preliminary conference to consider problems of organization was arranged for Berne, July 11. The organization of this meeting was largely in the hands of the Berne Socialist leader, Robert Grimm, the editor of the *Berner Tagwacht.* To the preliminary conference at Berne in mid-July, came representatives of the Italian and Swiss Socialist parties, Axelrod from the Russian Mensheviks, and Zinoviev from the Bolsheviks.[7]

The crucial question which faced the preliminary conference was the

---

[3] Chief among these was the appointment of Arthur Henderson to the War Cabinet.

[4] Jean Maxe, *De Zimmerwald au Bolchévisme,* Paris, 1920, 27.

[5] *Ibid.*

[6] *Ibid.,* 27-28.

[7] Lenine and Zinoviev, *Contre le Courant,* II, 11ff. Zinoviev, "La Première Conférence Internationale."

problem of the composition of the meeting. What groups were to be invited to come to Zimmerwald? The organizers of the conference were far from agreed on the answer. The official resolution offered by the Italians proposed that an invitation be extended "to those parties or fractions of parties, or labor organizations in general, which have remained true to the principle of class struggle and international solidarity, refuse to vote for war appropriations, and so on."[8] The Bolshevik Zinoviev, fearing that this resolution would allow the participation of non-revolutionary elements, was quick to attack its "vagueness." His criticism did not bring forth any immediate illumination from the supporters of the resolution. The practical question still remained unanswered—was the Zimmerwald Conference to be a union of genuinely revolutionary elements of the Left, as the Bolsheviks hoped, or was its scope to be enlarged to include the so-called pacifist groups represented by the German Center? In June, 1915, Kautsky, Haase, and Bernstein, the leaders of the German Center, had issued a joint manifesto "Against Annexations" which marked a swing toward the Left, and at least one representative of the German Left urged the organizers of the conference to invite them to send representatives, because, as he put it, "We hope to push them to the left."[9] With the drive in this case coming from the Left, there was no difficulty in convincing a large majority of the participants of the necessity of inviting the German Center.

The Bolsheviks offered an alternative proposition—that the final decision on the question of inviting the Center be left with the German revolutionary groups identified with *Die Internationale,* and the radical *Lichtstrahlen,* on the ground that they were best able to judge the sincerity of the German Centrists' change of heart, but this proposal was overwhelmingly defeated. Next the Bolsheviks proposed the convocation of a second preparatory conference to contain representatives from such revolutionary groups as the Dutch Tribunists, the Höglund group in Sweden, the "narrow" Bulgarian Social-Democrats, the *Lichtstrahlen* partisans in Germany, the Lettish Social-Democrats, etc.[10] This attempt to secure Bolshevik domination also failed. It became clear from the temper of the organizers that the Zimmerwald Conference would appeal for the support of all Centrist groups. The sponsorship of the revolutionaries was rejected. Instead of an attempt to unite the most extreme

[8] *Ibid.*
[9] *Ibid.,* 12.
[10] *Ibid.*

Left wing Socialists, Zimmerwald represented an effort to achieve a rapprochement between the Center and the Left, with the Center still discreetly controlling the proceedings and the Left attempting to give the discussions a revolutionary turn but willing to trail along with the Center so long as they both moved in the same general direction.

Although rebuffed in the preliminary skirmishes in the "Vorkonferenz," Lenin and his fellow-Bolsheviks did not withdraw. Lenin still hoped in the time which intervened between the preliminary conference and the real conference to rally the revolutionary elements and make a bid for domination at Zimmerwald. In the event that this strategy failed, Zimmerwald still offered a platform from which to address labor, which the Bolsheviks could ill afford to overlook.[11]

It was not an imposing assembly which finally gathered at Zimmerwald in September, 1915. Trotsky's grim jest that "half a century

[11] Lenin, *Works,* XVIII, 208-210. Lenin's letters to Madame A. M. Kollontai in the summer of 1915 reveal the efforts to unite the Zimmerwald Left into a solid block. Mme. Kollontai, a former Menshevik who took an internationalist position during the war, was then living in Sweden. Through her Lenin hoped to attract the support of the Left wing Scandinavians. In the first letter, Lenin writes:

"It is highly important to attract the Left Swedes (Höglund) and the Norwegians. Be good enough to drop me a line and tell me (1) are we in harmony with you (or you with the Central Committee?) If no wherein do we disagree (2) Will you undertake to attract the Left Scandinavians? . . .

"In our opinion the Left must come forth with a general declaration of ideas which would (1) absolutely condemn the social-chauvinists and opportunists (2) offer a program of revolutionary action (whether to say civil war or revolutionary mass action is not so important after all) (3) repudiate the defense of the fatherland slogan, etc. A declaration of ideas on the part of the Left in the name of several countries would be of *enormous influence.* . . . If you are in disagreement with such tactics let us know in a few words. If you are in agreement, will you undertake to translate (1) the Manifesto of the Central Committee (No. 33 Sotzial Demokrat) and (2) the Berne resolutions (No. 44-S. D.) into Norwegian and Swedish and to communicate with Höglund, ascertaining whether they agree to participate in the preparation of a general declaration (or resolution) on such and such a basis. . . . We must hurry with this."

The second letter praises Mme. Kollontai for her activity:

"We were very glad about the Norwegian declaration, and the trouble you took with the Swedes. A common international appearance of the Left Marxists would be infernally important! . . . It seems that the Scandinavians are overwhelmed by philistine (and provincial kleinstädtisch) pacifism when they reject 'war' in general. This is not Marxian. This has to be fought against, as also their rejection of a militia. Once more greetings, and congratulations upon the Norwegians' declaration."

Thus Lenin fought to make clear the differences which separated the revolutionaries and the pacifists and endeavored to unite the irreconcilable revolutionary Socialists into a fighting organization. See also *Bulletin Communiste,* Dec. 4, 1925, A. Kollontai, "Souvenirs et Mémoires révolutionnaires," 111.

after the founding of the First International it was still possible to seat all the internationalists in four coaches,"[12] was not without its sting. Most of the great names of the Second International were missing. Guesde, Sembat, Renaudel, Longuet, Vandervelde, MacDonald, Plekhanoff, Kautsky, Bernstein and Adler were among the conspicuous absentees. The Bureau of the Second International opposed the gathering to the end; the majority Socialists fought it bitterly. The meeting, nevertheless, took place and became a battlefield in which the Centrists and revolutionary Socialists fought for supremacy.

An analysis of the delegations in terms of the currents of opinion which they represented helps to illuminate the conflicts which took place within the conference. Germany was represented by ten delegates; Kautsky, Haase and Bernstein were not among them, although the preliminary conference had made a determined bid for their participation. At least three distinct tendencies could be distinguished within the delegation.[13] The majority—six persons—had as its spokesman Ledebour, a member of the Reichstag who took a position in the German Social Democracy slightly to the left of the Haase-Kautsky group. Ledebour and his friends did not vote for the war credits. On the other hand, they did not vote against them. In abstaining from voting, they took the attitude that a vote against the credits would create a scission in the Party which they considered undesirable. Ledebour counseled patience and urged his followers to conquer the majority of the Party by boring from within rather than to split it by open defiance. He, therefore, refused to give his consent to any resolution which would obligate his group to cast its vote against the credits.

Another group of three delegates (the so-called Wurtemburgers) were dissatisfied with a simple abstention from voting and felt themselves nearer the position of Liebknecht, whose confinement in prison prevented him from attending the conference. They felt sympathetic toward the adjurations of Liebknecht to utilize the opportunity of the war to carry on revolutionary mass activity, yet like the Ledebour group, they hesitated to break with the official Party.[14]

The third tendency was represented by a single delegate, Julian Borchardt, of the editorial staff of *Lichtstrahlen*. He alone accepted the Liebknecht tactics without reservation and called for a complete

---

[12] Trotsky, *My Life*, 249.
[13] Lenine and Zinoviev, *Contre le Courant*, II, 13.
[14] *Ibid.*

break with the Right and Center, and immediate activity to transform the war between nations into a war between classes. For the Bolsheviks, Borchardt offered the most fruitful possibility of collaboration. They also hoped to bring under their influence the wavering middle group which included Ernst Meyer and Bertha Thalheimer.

France was represented by only two delegates, Merrheim of the Federation of Metal Workers, and Bourderon, the secretary of the Coopers' Union, who together represented that minority in the General Confederation of Labor which opposed the war. The effort of Morgari, the Italian Socialist, to obtain a larger representation, proved unsuccessful. The Center Socialists belonging to the Longuet-Pressemane Parliamentary group refused to have anything to do with the enterprise. The majority Socialists fought it bitterly. Albert Thomas, the Socialist Minister of Munitions, made a personal appeal to Merrheim not to go to Zimmerwald, but his intervention was ignored.[15] Monatte and Rosmer who sympathized with the movement were called to the colors and were thus prevented from going to Zimmerwald. Neither Merrheim nor Bourderon represented the revolutionary wing of the Socialist movement. They came to Zimmerwald as pacifists who desired to put an end to the slaughter and were anxious to help in any program which would secure this purpose. The Zimmerwald Left, nevertheless, made a determined bid for their support, but the French delegates refused to be drawn into the orbit of the Leninist influence.[16]

Great Britain was not represented at the conference. Jowett and Bruce Glasier of the Independent Labour Party and Fairchild of the British Socialist Party planned to attend but were denied passports. Under the

[15] Maxe, *op. cit.*, 37.

[16] Merrheim reports it as follows: "As soon as we arrived at Berne, we were met by the Russian comrades whom Lenin had sent to the station. They conducted us to a room in the People's Hall and there for eight hours on end Lenin and I discussed, toe to toe, the attitude which we should observe at the conference at Zimmerwald. Lenin was all in favor of the immediate creation of the Third International. He added, 'As soon as you are back home after Zimmerwald, you must declare the war of the masses against the War;' I replied to Lenin that we had come, Bourderon and myself, to make heard the cry of a tormented conscience, in order that the people of all countries may rise up internationally in a common action against the War. As for a general strike of the masses. Ah! Comrade Lenin, I do not even know whether I shall be allowed to return to France and describe what has taken place at Zimmerwald; still less am I in a position to pledge myself to call upon the people of France to rise up in rebellion against the War."
(From *Report* at Congrès de Lyon, Confédération Général du Travail, 170-171.)

circumstances they had to limit themselves to sending a declaration expressing their sympathy with the purposes of the conference.[17]

The Russian delegation presented an interesting cross-section of the confused trends in the Russian Socialist movement.[18] At the extreme Left were the representatives of the Central Committee, the Bolsheviks, Lenin and Zinoviev, and Winter, who spoke for the Lettish Social-Democrats. This group called for the immediate creation of a Third International and sought to steer the conference along the straight revolutionary road. The rest of the Russian delegation inclined toward a Centrist position, which enabled them to work in close harmony with the Ledebour majority group in the German delegation. Axelrod and Martov represented the Organization Committee (Menshevik). Of the two, Martov was nearer the Left. The Social-Revolutionaries sent Bobrov (Nathanson) and Gardinin (Chernov). Nathanson took an internationalist position which brought him close to Lenin and eventually caused him to break with Chernov and join the Bolsheviks. Klemansky representing the Jewish Bund had only a consultative voice. Trotsky, the editor of the influential *Nashe Slovo,* also attended the conference and tried to play the rôle of mediator between the two factions by preparing a draft resolution upon which both groups could agree. On the crucial votes his influence was sometimes thrown to the Centrists against Lenin, a fact which was not forgotten by Trotsky's enemies in the bitter struggle for leadership after Lenin's death.

The Italian Socialist Party sent four delegates—Modigliani, Serrati, Lazzari and Morgari. Of these, Lazzari and Modigliani were pacifists and worked with the Center. Serrati and Morgari took a position further to the Left though not identified with the Leninists.[19] The Swiss Socialist Party was represented by three delegates, Grimm, Naine and Platten. Platten threw in his lot with the Zimmerwald Left. Grimm and Naine were Centrists.[20]

The Balkan Federation was represented by two delegates, Kolarov of the "narrow" group of Bulgarian Social-Democrats, and Rakovsky, the leader of the Rumanian Socialist Party. Kolarov was in sympathy with the Bolshevik position, though still unwilling to go to the end of the

[17] Maxe, *op. cit.,* 33.
[18] Lenine and Zinoviev, *Contre le Courant,* II, 15-16.
[19] *Ibid.,* 14-15.
[20] *Ibid.,* 15.

road with them. Rakovsky at this time took a Centrist position and wrote in favor of preserving organizational unity within the Second International.[21]

Höglund and Nerman came from Sweden and Norway. The Swedish Party was divided into two factions; the supporters of Branting, and the Höglund group. Branting, who was closely identified with the Second International, did not come to Zimmerwald. Höglund, who spoke for the remnant of the Party, had been in close touch with Lenin through Mme. Kollontai before the conference and readily identified himself with the Zimmerwald Left. Nerman, who represented the radical youth element in the Norwegian Socialist movement, also threw his support to the Left. Holland was represented by only one delegate, Mme. Roland-Holst, who occupied a median position in the Dutch Party between the Troelstra Right wing and the revolutionary Tribunist group led by Gorter and Pannekoek. The Polish delegation was composed of Lapinski, Warski, Karl Radek and Hanecki. Radek and Hanecki threw their support to the Left.[22]

As this analysis indicates, the rejection of the Bolshevik thesis was a foregone conclusion. Numerically the Zimmerwald Left formed an impotent minority. Out of a total of thirty-five delegates, Lenin could count surely on only seven or eight persons, the two Bolsheviks, the Lettish representative, the representatives of the Polish opposition, the Scandinavians and one German delegate. When both devoted adherents and sympathizers were thrown together his possible top strength on a vote reached ten or eleven. The prospect was not heartening, yet Lenin resolved to give battle.

Though faced with certain defeat, the Bolsheviks were responsible for many a heated argument before the manifestoes and declarations of the conference were finally drawn up. By dint of sheer persistence they managed to impress some of their fundamental principles upon the majority. Even though the resolutions of Lenin were rejected, the propositions which were finally adopted were colored and molded partly by his attacks.

The fundamental conflict began with the discussion of the manifesto and resolution to be issued by the conference. The draft resolution proposed by the Left wing is shot through with the ideas of Lenin. The World War is condemned "as an imperialist adventure waged for the

[21] *Ibid.*
[22] *Ibid.*

political and economic exploitation of the world, export markets, sources of raw material, spheres of capital investment, etc." Instead of a "forced struggle for national independence," the war is an instrument for "the oppression of foreign peoples and countries." The majority of Labor and Socialist leaders "prejudiced by nationalism, rotten with opportunism" are condemned for having "betrayed the proletariat to imperialism . . . the ruthless struggle against social imperialism constitutes the first condition for the revolutionary mobilization of the proletariat and the reconstruction of the International."[23]

The most strenuous objections to the resolution came from the German, French and Italian Socialists. The German Socialists took the position that it was idle to talk of fraternization in the trenches, political strikes, street demonstrations and civil war since it meant inciting the masses to futile revolts. The French also held that the situation in Europe was not ripe for revolution. The French worker was confused and demoralized; as Merrheim said, "he is so over-sated with anarchist and Hervé phrases that he believes nobody and nothing."[24] One of the Italian Socialists took a position against the use of force and direct revolutionary methods in general and argued that the task of the conference was to end the World War rather than to bring on a new civil war.

When the question of submitting the Left draft resolution to the commission was finally voted on, twelve delegates declared themselves in favor and nineteen against. The eight signers were joined in this vote by

[23] Lenin, Works, XVIII, 477-478. See also *Bulletin of International Socialist Commission*, #2, Nov. 27, 1915, 14. The resolution continues:

"It is the task of the Socialist parties as well as of the Socialist opposition in the now social-imperialist parties, to call and lead the laboring masses to the *revolutionary struggle* against the capitalist governments for the conquest of political power for the Socialist organization of society. . . . This struggle demands the refusal of war credits, quitting the cabinets, the denunciation of the capitalist, anti-Socialist, character of the war from the tribunes of the parliaments, in the columns of the legal, and where necessary, illegal press, the sharpest struggle against social-patriotism, and the utilization of every movement of the people caused by the results of the war for the organization of street demonstrations against the government, propaganda of international solidarity in the trenches, the encouragement of economic strikes, the effort to transform them into political strikes under favorable conditions. Civil war, not civil peace—that is the slogan! As against all illusions that it is possible to bring about the basis of a lasting peace, the beginning of disarmament, by any decision of diplomats and governments, the revolutionary Social-Democrats must repeatedly tell the masses of the people that only the social revolution can bring about a lasting peace and the emancipation of mankind."

This draft resolution was signed by Lenin, Zinoviev, Radek, Winter, Höglund, Nerman, Platten and Borchardt.

[24] Lenin, *Works*, XVIII, 347.

Trotsky, Roland-Holst, and the two Russian Social-Revolutionaries. The Zimmerwald Left also submitted a manifesto for the consideration of the conference which cast into more popular and militant form the underlying principles already set forth in the resolution. It met the same fate as the resolution.

The difficult task of arriving at a formula which would retain the support of both pacifists and revolutionaries was entrusted to Trotsky. This unaccustomed and ungrateful rôle of conciliator he discharged with admirable discretion and by steering a careful course managed to prevent the conference from breaking up in a flood of mutual recriminations.

The manifesto adopted by the conference deserves a careful analysis. It begins with the declaration that:

the war which has produced this chaos is the outcome of imperialism, of the attempt on the part of the capitalist classes of each nation to foster their greed for profit by the exploitation of human labor and of the natural treasures of the entire globe. . . . The capitalists of all countries assert that the war serves to defend the Fatherland. . . . They lie. . . . [25]

Responsibility for the war is placed on the

ruling powers of capitalist society who held the fate of the nations in their hands, the monarchic as well as the republican governments, the secret diplomacy, the mighty business organizations, the bourgeois parties, the capitalist press, the church.

The manifesto continues with an indictment of the tactics of majority Socialists[26] and declares the purpose of the conference:

In this unbearable situation we . . . who stand not on the ground of national solidarity with the exploiting class, but on the ground of the international solidarity of the proletariat and of class struggle, have assembled to re-tie the torn threads of international relations and to call upon the working class to recover itself and fight for peace.

[25] *Ibid.,* 474.
[26] *Ibid.,* 475. "Since the beginning of the war, Socialist parties and labor organizations of various countries have disregarded their obligations. Their representatives have called upon the working classes to give up the class struggle, the only possible and effective method of proletarian emancipation. They have granted credits to the ruling classes for waging the war; they have placed themselves at the disposal of the governments for the most diverse services; through their press and their messengers, they have tried to win the neutrals for the government policies of their countries; they have delivered up to their governments Socialist ministers as hostages for the preservation of civil peace, and thereby they have assumed the responsibility before the working class, before its present and its future, for this war, for its aims and its methods. And just as the individual parties, so the highest of the appointed representative bodies of the Socialists of all countries, the International Socialist Bureau, has failed them."

The manifesto concludes with a final appeal to the working classes to restore international solidarity.[27]

A comparison of the manifesto adopted by the Zimmerwald Conference with the proposed Left wing manifesto reveals significant variations. The manifesto approved by the conference is more restrained in its criticism of the tactics of the majority Socialists and, unlike the Left wing document, contains no bill of specifications which indicts individual Socialists by name. Particularly noteworthy is the avoidance of all criticism of the Kautskian Center which the Left considered even more dangerous than the social-chauvinists. It is clear that the majority delegations in the Zimmerwald Conference were not yet ready for an organizational break with their own Socialist parties.

More striking still is the difference in program and tactics for the future. The majority manifesto though couched in impassioned rhetoric is content with a general call for an "irreconcilable proletarian class struggle," without specifying what form that class struggle shall take. The Left wing resolution is specific in its proposals. It calls for the refusal of war credits, quitting the cabinets, open opposition in Parliament, legal and illegal propaganda against the war, street demonstrations, fraternization in the trenches, strikes, and other measures designed intentionally to provoke class warfare.

The vague nature of the majority program was subject to sharp attack from the Left wing and an amendment was proposed binding the participants to vote against war appropriations. Ledebour, speaking for the majority of the German delegation,[28] promptly issued an ultimatum that he would not sign the manifesto unless the amendment were rejected. In order to prevent the conference from breaking up, the Left wing then withdrew the amendment, though it appended a face-saving declaration (signed also by Trotsky and Roland-Holst) that

[27] The manifesto was signed in the name of the entire international Socialist conference, by the following:
For the German delegation: Georg Ledebour, Adolf Hoffmann
For the French delegation: A. Bourderon, A. Merrheim
For the Italian delegation: G. E. Modigliani, Constantino Lazzari
For the Russian delegation: N. Lenin, Paul Axelrod, M. Bobrov
For the Polish delegation: St. Lapinski, A. Warski, C. Hanecki
For the Inter-Balkan Socialist Federation: Rumania, C. Rakovsky; Bulgaria, Kolarov
For the Swedish and Norwegians: Z. Höglund and T. Nerman
For the Dutch delegation: H. Roland-Holst
For the Swiss delegation: Robert Grimm, Charles Naine
[28] Lenin, *Works*, XVIII, 481.

inasmuch as the adoption of our amendment demanding the vote against war appropriations might in a way endanger the success of the Conference, we do, under protest, withdraw our amendment and accept Ledebour's statement in the commission to the effect that the manifesto contains all that is implied in our proposition.[29]

The sharp conflict between the Left and the Center was thus bridged over by the elastic quality of words; their differences were not composed. For the moment both groups declared a truce and agreed on a common formula into which each group read that interpretation which pleased its purpose.

To the intransigent Lefts such tactics smacked too much of compromise and temporizing and had to be explained. Lenin, Zinoviev, Radek, Nerman, Höglund, and Winter insisted on issuing a joint declaration which set forth their position.[30]

Lenin's willingness to bow to political realities and subordinate means to end when expediency dictated is revealed in his defense of the Left wing's signing of the manifesto. Granted that "a struggle for peace without revolutionary struggle is an empty and false phrase, that the only way to put an end to the horrors of war is a revolutionary struggle for Socialism," he still feels "it would be bad military tactics to refuse to move together with a growing international protest movement against Social-chauvinism because the movement is slow, because it takes only one step forward, because it is ready and willing to take a step backward tomorrow, to make peace with the old International Socialist Bureau."[31] Particularly is this step justified, he argues, when the Left wing retains full freedom to broadcast its own views and put them into action.

The issuance of the manifesto did not conclude the work of the con-

[29] Ibid.

[30] Ibid.

"The manifesto adopted by the conference does not give us complete satisfaction. It contains no pronouncement on either open opportunism, or opportunism that is hiding under radical phraseology [a reproach directed at Kautsky], the opportunism which is not only the chief cause of the collapse of the International, but which strives to perpetuate that collapse. The manifesto contains no clear pronouncement as to the methods of fighting against the war.

"We shall continue, as we have done heretofore, to advocate in the Socialist press and at the meetings of the International, a clear-cut Marxian position in regard to the tasks with which the epoch of imperialism has confronted the proletariat.

"We vote for the manifesto because we regard it as a call to struggle, and in this struggle we are anxious to march side by side with the other sections of the International. We request that our present declaration be included in the official proceedings."

[31] Ibid., 343-344.

ference. It also adopted a declaration of sympathy for the war victims and the persecuted in which it did honor to the memory of Jean Jaurès and others who had been subjected to persecution because of their anti-war views.[32]

The French and German delegates also also issued a joint manifesto in which they declared that "this War is not our War,"[33] called for immediate peace, denounced working class collaboration with the government, and proclaimed their firm attachment to the principle of class warfare.

The conference concluded its work by appointing an International Socialist Commission consisting of Morgari, Naine, Grimm and Balabanova. In this Commission which was designed to maintain the permanence of the organization, Lenin saw "a new International Socialist Bureau created against the wishes of the old one, the beginning of a new international."[34] This view the majority of the conference was not yet willing to accept.[35] For them it was to serve rather as a clearing-house for the internationalist elements in the Socialist movement and as a means of binding the protesting minorities more closely together. Arrangements were made by which the International Socialist Commission was to issue a Bulletin to keep the various organizations informed of significant developments.[36] The Zimmerwald Left also appointed a Bureau of its own which published the *Internationale Flugblätter* in November, 1915, and two numbers of the journal, *Vorboten,* the next year.[37] It was this latter group which formed the basic nucleus for the elements which united to form the Communist International in 1919.

The formation of the Zimmerwald Commission marks an important step toward the creation of the Third International. In the early days of the war, rumblings of discontent had come from many quarters. Now for the first time the opposition was organized and functioning.

[32] See Maxe, *op. cit.,* 36-37. The resolution extended "its profound and fraternal sympathy to the Duma deputies exiled to Siberia who are continuing the glorious revolutionary tradition of Russia, to Liebknecht and Monatte, fettered by capitalism, both of whom have taken up the struggle against the civil peace policy of the workers in their respective countries, to Comrades Luxemburg and Clara Zetkin who have been imprisoned for their Socialist convictions, and to all comrades, men and women, who have been persecuted or arrested because they have waged a struggle against war."

[33] *Ibid.,* 34.

[34] Lenin, *Works,* XVIII, 348.

[35] *Avanti* and the *Berner Tagwacht* were among the papers which emphatically rejected this view.

[36] *Archiv für die Geschichte des Sozialismus und der Arbeiterbewegung,* XII, 311.

[37] V. I. Lenin, *Sämtliche Werke,* Verlag für Literatur und Politik, Wien-Berlin, 35 vols., XIX, 545.

It was, to be sure, not a unit. Lefts and Centrists found united action difficult. Yet the fact that, even temporarily, an international organization had been created which offered a rallying point around which discontented groups could gather, held out the ominous threat of a split in the ranks of labor internationalism.

Among the members of the Zimmerwald majority, there was still much vacillation. Its members were in a ferment. They hesitated to break with the Second International and their own Socialist parties. On the other hand, their dissatisfaction with the policies of the patriotic Socialists had not yet crystallized into a willingness to adopt a bold revolutionary stand.

The Zimmerwald Left sought to take advantage of this irresolution. Its tactics were directed toward deepening the gulf which divided the chauvinists and revolutionaries and toward compelling the Center to adopt one view or the other. The willingness of the Left to subscribe to the resolutions of the Center can be explained not only on the principle that a partial victory is better than complete failure, but by the desire to attach those who still wavered and hesitated to the Left position. The Left strategy sought to weed out of the Center the purely chauvinist elements and to absorb the remaining members into its own body.

Zimmerwald considered alone was a temporary rebuff, for certainly the Left did not realize its program. To Lenin, however, who saw history in process, the conference marked a first step toward success. He professed himself highly encouraged. The march of events ensured ultimate victory. Looking back over the year he marked a rising tide:

> In September, 1914 the manifesto of our Central Committee appears to be almost unique. In January, 1915 an international women's conference adopts a miserable pacifist resolution. . . . In September, 1915 we consolidate ourselves into a whole group of the International Left Wing. We promulgate our tactics; we express a number of our fundamental ideas in a common manifesto; we participate in the formation of an International Socialist Commission that is practically a new International Socialist Bureau against the wish of the old one, and on the basis of the manifesto which directly condemns the tactics of the latter.[38]

With this record of growing strength, Lenin regarded the future with more than customary equanimity. He could join Zinoviev in the shout, "The Second International is dead—contaminated by opportunism. Long live the Third International—freed from opportunism."[39]

[38] Lenin, *Works*, XVIII, 344.
[39] Lenine and Zinoviev, *Contre le Courant*, II, 17.

CHAPTER V

FROM ZIMMERWALD TO KIENTHAL

It is a commonplace of the historian that the importance of events may be completely hidden from contemporary observers. The Zimmerwald Conference serves as a particularly apt illustration. Though the movement which it initiated eventuated in the Third International, the Conference itself attracted little attention in the press.[1] The non-Socialist papers largely ignored it. Even the Socialist papers said little. The *Vorwärts*, organ of the German Social Democracy, was prevented from making any comment by the censorship. In France, *L'Humanité*, the party daily, allowed the Conference to go by with only a bare notice. Rosmer, one of the French minority Socialists, charged a conspiracy of silence sponsored by the government censorship and the French majority Socialists and trade-unionists.[2] *Avanti*, the Italian Socialist paper, which gave full accounts of the proceedings at Zimmerwald, took *L'Humanité* to task for its tactics in an indignant outburst:

> In France there is silence. It is not for nothing that Masonry has such deep roots in the French Socialist Party. And the Masonic method is the same as that of the Jesuits, not to disturb things which are quiet.[3]

In England, the *Labour Leader,* published by the Independent Labour Party, and *Justice,* edited by Hyndman, leader of the British Socialists, reprinted the Zimmerwald manifesto in full.[4] The *Berner Tagwacht* edited by the Swiss Socialist, Grimm, gave the most complete account of the proceedings, but its circulation was relatively limited. The great majority of Socialist papers in the belligerent countries were controlled by the so-called "patriotic Socialists," and these commonly dismissed the proceedings at Zimmerwald with contempt or disregarded them altogether.

The Zimmerwald movement, nevertheless, made progress. Its spirit began to penetrate the masses. Minority and opposition groups grew in strength. To some extent the growth was due to the vigorous campaign of propaganda—both legal and illegal—which was directed by the Inter-

---

[1] Maxe, *op. cit.,* 39.
[2] *Lettre aux abonnés de la Vie Ouvrière,* Nov. 1, 1915, 20.
[3] *Avanti,* Sept. 24, 1915.
[4] Maxe, *op. cit.,* 39.

national Socialist Commission and leaders of the opposition groups in the different countries. The manifestoes of the Zimmerwald Left, as well as of the Zimmerwald majority, circulated underground when they could not be distributed openly. Inflammatory tracts, pamphlets, and brochures passed from hand to hand in large numbers. The extent of discontent and opposition to the war which was stimulated by the subterranean traffic in subversive ideas obviously cannot be appraised in mathematical terms. That it was considerable there can be no doubt.[5]

The hardships implicit in war made increasingly large sections of the population receptive to programs which called for an end of the slaughter. After the first wave of patriotic ecstasy which swept the masses into the war had spent itself and sections of the population had time to recover their balance and sense of proportion, doubts began to spring into existence. Food shortages which pressed with especial weight on the laboring masses, the rising cost of living, the mounting toll of dead and wounded, loss of faith in the idealistic ends of the war, and the sobering realities of trench warfare reinforced these doubts and made an increasingly large number of people fertile soil for the pacifist and even revolutionary propaganda of the Zimmerwaldians. The effectiveness of this combination of circumstance and idea in stimulating the growth of the opposition between the first Zimmerwald Conference in September, 1915, and the second conference at Kienthal in April, 1916, is revealed by a survey of developments in the more important countries.

In many respects Germany offers the most interesting picture. In the rapidly growing strength of the opposition, in the variety of views represented within the movement and in the march of events toward a party split there are many dramatic elements that must be passed over with regret.[6] Here the rise of the opposition and its organization can be blocked out only in skeleton form. Two weeks before Zimmerwald (August 20, 1915) the temper of the German opposition was revealed when some thirty members of the Social-Democratic group left the Chamber and refused to vote for the war credits. Their opposition, however, was confined merely to abstention from voting. Karl Liebknecht alone defied party discipline and voted against the war budget. The thirty members of the opposition included elements which were not represented at Zimmerwald. The majority of the Zimmerwald German delegation which represented a Right group at that conference found

[5] Drahn and Leonhard, op. cit.
[6] Edwyn Bevan, op. cit., presents a more detailed account.

itself in the Left fringe of the German opposition movement, midway between Kautsky and Liebknecht.

The deepening of the gulf between majority and minority Socialists is perhaps the most striking development between Zimmerwald and Kienthal. The vote on the war credits at the December, 1915, session of the Reichstag brought matters to a crisis. Before the final vote on December 21, forty-four members opposed voting the war credits in the group meeting, while sixty-six were in favor, making the ratio in favor three to two. Again, the majority insisted on an application of the unanimity rule which demanded that the vote of the group should be cast as a unit, but this time twenty members of the minority voted openly against the war credits, and Bernstein, Haase and Ledebour walked side by side with Liebknecht and Rühle.[7] Twenty-two other members abstained from voting; the other Social-Democrats voted in favor of the credits. The split in the German Social Democracy was now openly exhibited to the world. Ledebour, who at Zimmerwald had refused under any conditions to enter into any commitment which bound him to vote against the war credits, now took such action of his own free will. The logic of events was driving the opposition toward the Left.

The independent action of the twenty Social-Democratic members of Parliament aroused a storm of discussion. The majority censured the twenty for a grave breach of discipline but could not still the discontent.[8] The controversy raged in the party press and in local district meetings. The threat of a party schism loomed more serious. The Emergency Budget of March, 1916, met determined opposition.[9] Seventeen members of the group voted against it while fourteen others absented themselves. Liebknecht and Ruhle also voted against the budget but were no longer numbered in the group.

The majority now took desperate measures. Haase, Ledebour, and the other members of the seventeen were declared to have forfeited their rights as members of the Parliamentary Social-Democratic group through their violation of party discipline.[10] The effect of this drastic measure was to force the minority to constitute itself a separate Parliamentary group—The Social-Democratic Labor Fellowship (Die Sozialdemokratische Arbeitsgemeinschaft) in order to enjoy representation in the

[7] *Ibid.,* 72.
[8] For text of censure, see *Vorwärts,* Jan. 9, 1916.
[9] Eduard Bernstein in *Die Neue Zeit,* April 7, 1916.
[10] Bevan, *op. cit.,* 94.

budget committee and other rights which inhered in party groups only.[11] The seventeen who were later joined by Bernstein to make eighteen, refused to recognize the right of the majority of the group to expel them, and contended that such action must be reserved for a Party Congress. The Social-Democratic Labor Fellowship, nevertheless, continued to function as a Parliamentary group, voted against the Emergency Budget of April, 1916, and by raking the party majority with a steady cross-fire of criticism in press, parliament and country, made a party split seem inevitable.

The most extreme section of the opposition centered around Liebknecht and Rühle. At Zimmerwald, Borchardt alone spoke for this group and cast his lot with the Zimmerwald Left. Meyer and Thalheimer, though identified with the group of internationalists organized by Liebknecht, Luxemburg, Mehring and Zetkin in the early days of the war, still hesitated and voted with Ledebour.[12] Liebknecht had been prevented from attending the Zimmerwald Conference, but in a letter to the gathering he had expressed his complete agreement with the Bolshevik thesis which counselled the transformation of the imperialist war into a civil war. Zimmerwald served to bring into clear relief the differences between Ledebour and Liebknecht, and Liebknecht decided to organize the revolutionary German Social-Democrats for independent action.

On January 1, 1916, adherents of Liebnecht from all parts of the country gathered at his home in Berlin for a conference. Rosa Luxemburg formulated a program, *Theses on the Tasks of the International Social Democracy,*[13] which revealed the group in practical agreement with the Zimmerwald Left on all essential questions. On January 12, the Reichstag Social-Democratic group expelled Liebknecht from its membership on the ground that he "continues to go against the resolutions of the Group and by so doing offends in the grossest way against his duties as a member of the Group."[14] Two days later Rühle voluntarily joined him in coventry, and together they became "Wild Ones," free lances, who belonged to no group in the Chamber and made use of every opportunity to wage a guerrilla warfare against the majority Socialists.

In order to evade the censorship the supporters of Liebknecht were forced to distribute their literature secretly. Revolutionary groups were

[11] *Ibid.,* 94-95.
[12] Lenin, *Sämtliche Werke,* XIX, 570-571.
[13] *Ibid.,* Appendix 538-541 contains text listed as "Leitsätzen über die Aufgaben der Internationale Sozialdemokratie."
[14] Bevan, *op. cit.,* 77.

organized in every corner of the empire, and a vast pamphlet literature was circulated by a carefully chosen list of confidential correspondents. On January 27, 1916, appeared the first of the famous series of "Spartacus" letters which were distinguished by the virulence with which they lashed the majority and Centrist Socialists and by their spirited invocations to revolutionary action.[15] The letters were all signed with the pseudonym "Spartacus" after the leader of a slave uprising in Roman times. The letters enjoyed a wide circulation and made such a profound impression that henceforth the adherents of Liebknecht became known as Spartacists. They worked hand in hand with the Zimmerwald Left, circulated their manifestoes, and exerted every effort to put their program into practice. The strength of the Spartacist group in the early days of 1916 is difficult to estimate. Its parliamentary representation was negligible—only Liebknecht and Rühle. Its most effective work was done underground. That its propaganda found fertile soil was revealed only by future events.

In Austria, too, an opposition group gained strength after Zimmerwald. Dr. Friedrich Adler, in numerous speeches, made vocal the protests of the Austrian Left. At the Party Conference held March 25 and 27, 1916, Dr. F. Adler introduced a resolution approving the work of the Zimmerwald Conference.[16] It was, however, defeated by a heavy vote. The resolution adopted by the Conference expressly condemned any movement designed to split the unity of the old international. Though the Austrian minority was not strong enough to precipitate an open cleavage, the Zimmerwald ideas were a fermenting agent which exercised their influence upon certain portions of the Socialist masses.

The repercussions of Zimmerwald were also felt in France. The minority Socialists who were opposed to the war, grew in strength, captured the Federations of L'Isère, Rhône, Haute-Vienne, and even made a determined bid for control of the Seine.[17] In the Syndicalist movement, Merrheim's Metal Workers' Union was joined by the Fédération des Syndicats d'Instituteurs in adhering to Zimmerwald, and the latter's journal—L'Ecole de la Fédération—became a recognized medium for the propagation of Zimmerwald doctrine. The majority Socialists took steps to arrest this alarming growth. The Commission Administrative

---

[15] These have been collected and published under title of *Spartakus im Kriege*, Ernst Meyer (ed.), Berlin, 1927.

[16] Brügel, *op. cit.*, V. 257.

[17] Maxe, *op. cit.*, 43.

Permanente (C. A. P.) of the French Socialist Party, on November 6, 1915, passed a resolution condemning the Zimmerwald movement,[18] but the injunction of the C. A. P. was not heeded as widely as had been hoped.

At the French Socialist Congress (December 26-29, 1915) Bourderon, a Zimmerwald delegate, boldly introduced a resolution criticizing the party leadership for its opportunism and calling upon the party to renew its efforts for peace.[19] Although the resolution was snowed under by a vote of 2736 to 76, the willingness of the opposition to carry the fight openly into the party convention indicated the more militant spirit which was beginning to permeate it.

On their return from Zimmerwald, Merrheim and Bourderon took the lead in organizing a "Comité pour la Reprise des Relations Internationales" (Committee for the Resumption of International Relations) to coordinate the peace efforts of the minority Socialists and spread the Zimmerwald doctrine.[20] Merrheim became its secretary and enlisted the talents of such French Left wing leaders as Loriot, Rosmer and Monatte. Trotsky worked hand in hand with Merrheim, and Inessa Armand participated on behalf of the Bolsheviks. Lenin worked through Inessa Armand in a vain effort to persuade the committee to break with the old International.[21] The committee conducted a vigorous campaign for peace. Although it criticized the majority Socialists severely, it did not call for a party split nor a revolutionary mass uprising. It reflected the pacifist views of its Centrist organizers, Merrheim and his associates.

---

[18] *Pendant la Guerre—Le Parti Socialiste, la Guerre, et La Paix, toutes les résolutions et tous les documents du parti Socialiste de Juillet 1914 à fin 1917,* Paris, 1918, 128-129.

"In the light of efforts made by two citizens to carry on propaganda in the Federation of the Seine based on resolutions of a conference held in Switzerland at Zimmerwald which they attended without any credentials from the party to confer on the question of peace with other Socialists of neutral and belligerent countries, for the most part themselves without credentials, the C. A. P. recalls that it refused to participate in that reunion as in reunions of a similar sort organized since the beginning of the war.

"In conformity with the decision of the National Council of July 14, 1915, it affirms again that a durable peace can only be obtained by the victory of the Allies and the ruin of German militant imperialism, that any other peace, any premature peace can only be a dream or a capitulation.

"The C. A. P. invites all the Federations and their sections to avoid even the appearance of any kind of participation in propaganda contrary to the interests of national defense, national organization and the Socialist International."

[19] Lenin, *Sämtliche Werke,* XIX, 531.

[20] Maxe, *op. cit.,* 44.

[21] Lenin, *Sämtliche Werke,* XIX, 581.

The movement began to grow in strength. Influential middle-of-the-road Socialists like Jean Longuet and Pressemane now abandoned the majority. At the meeting of the National Council on April 9, 1916, the eve of Kienthal, Longuet and Pressemane introduced a motion demanding the "re-establishment of relations among the various sections of the International, in order to give it force and life."[22] It rallied 960 votes against 1996 votes of the majority. Less than four months before, Bourderon's motion had won only 76 votes. The ominous increase in the French opposition, however, represented a gain for the Center rather than for the Left. The Longuet resolution which called for re-establishment of the Second International, could give little direct satisfaction to the extremists of the Leninist type who called for a complete break with the old International. What satisfaction the Zimmerwald Left could squeeze from this development was confined to the hope that the dissensions within the party opened up the possibility of influencing the minds of wavering Centrists in the direction of scission.

In England also the period between Zimmerwald and Kienthal witnessed realignments within the Socialist movement. Although members of the Independent Labour Party and the British Socialist Party had been denied passports in their efforts to attend the Zimmerwald Congress, the manifesto adopted by the gathering was published in *Justice* and the *Labour Leader*. Its substance was approved by the Independent Labour Party and the international section of the British Socialist Party. These groups found themselves in opposition to the official Labour Party which supported the war, participated in the recruiting campaign, and sent a minister (Henderson) into the War Cabinet. At the Bristol Conference of the Labour Party in February, 1916, these policies of the Party were approved by a large majority.[23] The Independent Labour Party remained predominantly pacifist. The Norwich Conference which took place April 4-6, 1915, passed a series of pacifist resolutions, and a movement developed within the Party for an open break with the official Labour Party.[24]

At the Newcastle Conference of the Independent Labour Party, April 23-25, 1916, this view was rejected by a majority of the Party, but the

[22] *Pendant la Guerre*, 139.

[23] *Report of the 15th Annual Conference of the Labour Party*, Bristol, 1916, 3, 51, 1000.

[24] Lenin, *Sämtliche Werke*, XIX, 549-550. See also the letters of Russel Williams in the *Labour Leader*, Dec. 9 and 23, 1915. The letters expressed this view, already shared by a considerable group within the party.

Party did not abandon its pacifist stand.[25] It continued to maintain connections with the Labour Party because of the advantages of organizational unity.

The British Socialist Party was less successful in reconciling the opposing trends of opinion within its body.[26] One group led by Hyndman, Thorne, Bax and H. W. Lee took a patriotic attitude and supported the government on the ground of national defense. Another section followed E. C. Fairchild and John MacLean in condemning the war as an imperialist adventure for which all the Powers were held equally responsible. This section called insistently for an immediate end to the war. All through 1915, the contest between the two sections raged in divisional conferences. The internationalists dominated the Executive by a slim majority of one. The latter's decision to participate in the Zimmerwald Conference was foiled by the refusal of passports by the government. The conflict within the Party came to a head at the National Party Congress at Salford, April 23-24, 1916. When it became clear that the internationalists were in control, the Hyndman group withdrew and organized a separate National Socialist Party which retained control of the Party organ, *Justice*. The remainder of the British Socialist Party aligned itself with the Zimmerwald movement and started a new paper —*The Call*—through which it conducted a vigorous criticism of Socialist "chauvinism." The remnant of the British Socialist Party contained within its ranks Left wing elements which later found shelter in the Third International.

The most clear-cut support for the Left Zimmerwaldians came from Russia. Although Plekhanoff, Alexinsky, and other Right wing Socialists declared in favor of supporting the allies, a large section of the industrial proletariat followed the lead of the Bolsheviks and internationalist Mensheviks.[27] Toward the end of September, 1915, an attempt was made to enlist workers in defense of the Fatherland by giving them representation in the War Industries Committee. The Bolsheviks decided to participate in the elections in order to expose the designs of the bourgeois sponsors of the idea. At the first Petrograd election the Bolsheviks captured 95 electors to 85 for the Defensists. On the second ballot, the Bolsheviks were again triumphant by a vote of 91 to 81, and then declared themselves in favor of boycotting the War Industries Commit-

[25] Lenin, *Sämtliche Werke*, XIX, 546-547.
[26] Max Beer, *A History of British Socialism*, London, 1921. 2 vols., II, 386ff.
[27] Jaroslawski, *op. cit.*, 57ff.

tee.[28] Subsequently a new election was held, inspired by the Menshevik, Gvosdev. This time 90 of the 153 delegates sided with the Bolsheviks.[29] After these left the meeting, a resolution was passed in favor of entering the War Industries Committee. This action caused the Petrograd Bolsheviks to denounce the "treason" of Gvosdev, and offered them additional ammunition in their campaign against "chauvinist" Socialists.

Bolshevik strength was not confined to Petrograd. Similar efforts were made to organize the workers to boycott the elections in Moscow and other industrial centers, though with less success.[30] Street demonstrations against the war occurred in Moscow as early as September, 1915. Throughout the war, the Bolsheviks carried on organization work secretly among soldiers and workers and attempted to translate the program of the Zimmerwald Left into action.

Food shortages and the hard hand with which the government pressed on the masses stimulated discontent. Spasmodic protest strikes of workers and occasional food riots gave a clue to the underlying unrest. The revolutionary temper of the Russian industrial proletariat mounted as the war worked increasing hardships. The Bolsheviks did what they could to fan the small fire into a blaze. They sought above all to identify themselves with the masses, to share their grievances, and to become their voice. Though the full fruits of their efforts were not finally gathered until the November Revolution their strength was demonstrated early in the factory elections. The prestige of Lenin at Kienthal was increased by his rising influence among the Russian factory workers.

The Italian Socialist Party massed itself solidly behind the resolutions of Zimmerwald. *Avanti,* the official Party paper, gave the Conference its staunch support, and on October 12, 1915, the directorate of the Party, meeting at Turin, officially adopted the Zimmerwald resolution as a basis for action.[31] The predominant opinion in Italy was pacifist rather than revolutionary, and the Zimmerwald Left found only isolated support.

At the Congress of the Swiss Social-Democratic Party, meeting in Aarau November 20-21, 1915, three currents of opinion were disclosed.[32] The Right opposed Zimmerwald; the Center led by Grimm supported the views of the Zimmerwald majority; the group led by Fritz Platten based its program on the views of the Zimmerwald Left.

[28] Lenin, *Works,* XVIII, 493.
[29] *Ibid.,* 440.
[30] Jaroslawski, *op. cit.,* 52-53.
[31] *Avanti,* Oct. 14, 1915.
[32] Lenin, *Sämtliche Werke,* XIX, 587.

By combining forces, Grimm and Platten were able to defeat the Right and pledge the Swiss Socialists to support the Zimmerwald movement. Bolshevik exiles residing in Switzerland contributed to the strength of the Platten group and furnished a large part of its driving power.

This brief survey of developments within the more important Socialist parties in the period between Zimmerwald and Kienthal, serves to reveal the gathering dissatisfaction with the policy of the "patriotic" Socialists. The swelling chorus of pacifism within the Socialist parties of the two most bitter contestants, France and Germany, helps to explain the renewed pressure which was brought to bear on the Bureau of the Second International to become an active force. When that effort failed came the despairing turn back to Zimmerwald and Kienthal. The movement to the Left among Centrists and pacifists generally in this period can be explained not only by the prevailing war weariness and the persistent propaganda of the revolutionary Socialists, but also in part because of the unwillingness or inability of the Bureau of the Second International to take positive steps to end the war.

The Bureau of the Second International fought the Zimmerwald movement vigorously; it was less successful in convincing the "Socialist Center" that it had a workable alternative program which offered any immediate hope for peace. Camille Huysmans, the secretary of the Bureau, speaking at the Extraordinary Congress of the Dutch Party at Arnheim on January 9, 1916, was far from reassuring.[33] He reported that the Bureau was maintaining its relations with the national sections of the International, that it sought to bring about peace on the basis of the four principles to which Socialist representatives of the neutral countries, the Entente nations and of the Central Powers had subscribed in congresses at Copenhagen, London and Vienna—namely, (1) the right of all nations to self-determination, (2) the democratization of diplomacy and the strengthening of parliamentary control, (3) compulsory arbitration in all wars, and (4) reduction of armaments with the ultimate aim of general disarmament. In order to bring about agreement on the concrete application of these principles, the Bureau had invited national delegations to come to The Hague where they might clarify and elucidate their views. The failure of the French Party to send delegates had hindered the progress of negotiations. Rather than hurry matters by calling a conference which would precipitate an open split in the Inter-

[33] Huysmans, *op. cit.*

national, the Bureau counselled patience, placed the organizational unity of the International uppermost, and preferred to postpone activity until a riper moment, that is to say a moment when a spirit of compromise should prevail.

Such a laissez-faire attitude proved unsatisfactory to large numbers of Centrists who felt that the prime purpose of Socialists should be to put an immediate end to the slaughter rather than to quibble over details of the peace. When they could not attain this end at The Hague, the natural tendency was to turn to Zimmerwald to organize their resentment and act to obtain peace.

The majority members of the first Zimmerwald Conference did not contemplate a break with the old International. They sought rather to stir it into action. Soon after the end of the Zimmerwald Conference, the International Socialist Commission which had been elected by the Zimmerwald gathering expressed its readiness to dissolve as soon as the Bureau of the Second International should begin to function.[34] The Bolsheviks were quick to point out that no specific authorization for such a statement was given the commission by the Zimmerwald Conference. It is probable, nevertheless, that the statement registered the prevailing view of the majority Zimmerwaldians at the time when it was issued.

When the Bureau remained inactive, the International Socialist Commission abandoned its provisional character and took steps to coordinate the activities of its member organizations. Contacts with the affiliated party groups were maintained through the official organ, the *Bulletin*, which was issued in English, French and German.[35]

With the growth of opposition groups and the continued inactivity of the Bureau, a more solid and stable Zimmerwald organization was found necessary. A permanent, enlarged Executive Committee was created with all countries adhering represented in its membership. A preliminary gathering of this enlarged Executive was held at Berne, February 5-9,

[34] See Lenin, *Sämtliche Werke*, XIX, 562. The declaration, dated Sept. 29, 1915, appeared in Bulletin #2, (Nov. 27, 1915.) It read:

"Diese Kommission steht dem ISB nicht als eine konkurrenz Organisation gegenüber. Sie trägt nur provisorischen Charakter und wird sich in dem Augenblick auflösen, wen das I. S. B. entsprechend den beschlussen der Kongresse von Stuttgart, Basel und Kopenhagen den Kampf gegen den Krieg durchführt und seine Taktik nicht abhängig macht von der Zustimmung jener sozialistischen Parteien, die in ihren Ländern die Kriegspolitik der herrschenden Klassen unterstützen."

[35] Six numbers appeared in all—#1 Sept. 21, 1915—#6, Jan. 6, 1917.

1916, to make arrangements for a second Congress.[36] The Left wing, though still in a minority, was more heavily represented at this preliminary gathering than at Zimmerwald and therefore played a more important rôle in influencing the character of the resolutions adopted.

The conference opened with reports by the various delegations. A German delegate of the Ledebour camp stressed the rising strength of the opposition in the Party.[37] He reported the circulation of some 600,000 illegal appeals, numerous street demonstrations, and the steady defection of the masses from the majority leadership. He reproached the Liebknecht group, nevertheless, for its deliberate efforts to provoke a party scission and still urged that the real hope of the opposition was to capture the Party machinery rather than to abandon it. This point of view found sympathetic adherents within the ranks of the majority.

The proposition of the Bolsheviks, that the gathering abandon its preparatory character, constitute itself into a congress with plenary powers, and issue a manifesto stating that the time was ripe for revolutionary action by the proletariat, was rejected.[38] Martov and other Centrists fought the proposal on the ground that it would defeat its purpose by antagonizing the French and would be generally useless because the masses would not understand. Finally a compromise measure of Rakovsky's was accepted, which declared that instead of publishing a manifesto to the masses, the committee draw up a round robin circular to the organizations affiliated with Zimmerwald. A committee composed of two representatives of the International Socialist Commission, a German delegate, Rakovsky, Serrati, Martov, and Zinoviev, was appointed to prepare the circular.[39]

The old and seemingly inevitable struggle between revolutionaries and pacifists was now transferred to the Committee. The result was a compromise formula which marked a distinct swing toward the Left. It contained trenchant criticisms of the policies of the "social-patriots" in Germany and France, and of the inactivity of the Bureau. It called for a revival of the class struggle through "the voluntary intervention of

---

[36] Lenin, *Sämtliche Werke*, XIX, 573. Among those who attended this gathering were R. Grimm and Platten from Switzerland; Lenin and Zinoviev, Martov, Ryazanov and Axelrod from Russia; Felix Kon, Lapinski from Poland; Bertha Thalheimer, Hoffmann and Ledebour from Germany; Serrati, Modigliani and Balabanova from Italy; Rakovsky from Rumania and Peluso from Portugal.

[37] Lenine and Zinoviev, *Contre le Courant*, II, 71.

[38] Lenin, *Sämtliche Werke*, XIX, 573.

[39] For text see *Archiv für die Geschichte des Sozialismus, etc.* XII, 327ff.

the working class." It approved strikes and mass demonstrations, votes against war credits, fraternization in the trenches, and it condemned any voluntary participation by workers in institutions dedicated to national defense. Though these proposals testified to the concessions which the Bolsheviks had won, the document still was not completely satisfactory to the Left. It did not go far enough. The Center Socialists were still reluctant to break with their party organizations and create a new International. Though the representatives of the Zimmerwald Left, Lenin, Zinoviev and Radek, signed the circular, they explained in an appended declaration that they did so not because it was satisfactory, but because it marked a step forward from Zimmerwald.[40]

The efforts of the International Socialist Commission to arrange for a second international conference met considerable opposition. The "patriotic-socialists" combined with the belligerent governments to place obstacles in the way.[41] The governments denied passports to Socialists who were suspected of being delegates; the majority Socialists brought pressure to bear on the minority to prevent them from going. Camille Huysmans, the secretary of the Bureau, made special trips to England and France to dissuade the opposition from attending. The Berne Commission matched wits with the secret police by announcing publicly that the conference would take place in Holland while at the same time sending out secret instructions to the delegates to assemble in the remote Swiss hamlet of Kienthal on April 24, 1916. The ruse of the Commission was not altogether successful. A very considerable group of delegates were prevented from attending.[42]

The conference, nevertheless, took place. Ten nations—Germany, France, Italy, Russia, Poland, Switzerland, Serbia, Portugal, Austria and England—were represented in the proceedings by one or more delegates.[43] Forty-three persons in all took part in the Congress. An analysis of their political sympathies has a double value. It reflects the differences of opinion within the ranks of the opposition in the same country; and it illuminates the decisions which were finally made by the Congress.

The seven German delegates represented three distinct tendencies in

[40] Lenin, *Sämtliche Werke*, XIX, 574.
[41] Lenine and Zinoviev, *Contre le Courant*, II, 76.
[42] Among them were ten from Germany, one Austrian, two Englishmen, a Lett, two delegates from the Balkans, a part of the French delegation, and a number of Scandinavian representatives.
[43] Lenin, *Sämtliche Werke*, XIX, 559.

the German opposition. Four, led by the members of the Reichstag—Adolf Hoffmann and Hermann Fleissner—were associated with the Ledebour-Haase group and took a Centrist position. Although this group now formed a separate fraction within the Reichstag and had voted against the war credits, it still refused to risk an open rupture in the Party organization or support the movement for the creation of a Third International. It took the position that it was still an opposition within the Party organization rather than outside of it. The leaders of the new parliamentary fraction, including Haase and Kautsky, had been invited to attend the Kienthal gathering, but had found it politic to refuse on the ground that as official representatives of the German Social Democracy in the Bureau of the Second International, such participation would present some elements of inconvenience.[44] Their cautious stand and unwillingness to make a complete break were reflected in the views of the majority of the German delegation, who were only slightly to the Left of Haase and Kautsky and followed their intellectual leadership.

The standpoint of the Zimmerwald Left was represented by Paul Froelich, who came as a representative of the Bremen Left wing. Between these groups, still somewhat hesitant, but rapidly moving toward the Left, were Ernst Meyer and Bertha Thalheimer, who came as representatives of the International group led by Liebknecht, Luxemburg and Mehring. The members of this group who later developed into the Spartacists had already taken steps which committed them to a complete break with the Party organization and in fact they worked hand in hand with the Left.

France was represented by three deputies, Pierre Brizon, Alexandre Blanc, and Raffin-Dugens, and the Left Syndicalist, Henri Guilbeaux. The three deputies were pacifists, rather than revolutionaries. They followed the leadership of the Longuet-Pressemane opposition group which confined itself largely to demanding the re-establishment of the Second International. And like the majority German group, they had not voted against the war credits. They expressed, though somewhat vaguely and uncertainly, the rising dissatisfaction with the official leadership of the French Party. They were not yet ready for the drastic steps proposed by the Zimmerwald Left. Guilbeaux who published the journal, *Demain*, in Switzerland, offered more fertile soil for the latter group. A larger representation from Left wing Syndicalists and the "Committee for the

[44] Lenine and Zinoviev, *Contre le Courant*, II, 77.

Resumption of International Relations" was prevented by the refusal of the government to grant passports.[45]

The Italian Socialist Party was represented by seven delegates—Morgari, Modigliani, Lazzari, Prampolini, Musatti, Serrati and Dugoni.[46] The majority of the delegation belonged to the group styling themselves "reformers of the Left." They adhered to a Centrist program, sought to revive the Second International, and placed their faith in courts of arbitration, democratic control of the conduct of foreign relations, and progressive disarmament. The minority led by Serrati, the editor of *Avanti*, was much closer to the Zimmerwald Left.

Five delegates came from Switzerland. Of these, three—Platten, Nobs and Robmann—adhered to the Zimmerwald Left. The remaining two—Naine and Graber—took a Centrist position.

The Russian delegation was composed of three representatives of the Bolshevik Central Committee—Lenin, Zinoviev and Petrova (Inessa Armand); two Mensheviks, Martov and Axelrod, who were identified with the Zimmerwald majority; one delegate—Nathanson (Bobrov)—who represented the international wing of the Social-Revolutionary Party and supported the Zimmerwald Left, and two other unidentified delegates from the Social-Revolutionary Party who masqueraded under the pseudonyms of Saveliev and Vlassov. One of these was probably Chernov.[47] This last group allied itself with the Mensheviks.

Poland was represented by five delegates. Of these, three—Radek, Bronski and Dombrowski—belonged to the Zimmerwald Left. One, Warski, though a Centrist, supported the Left on a crucial vote on the question of the convocation of the Bureau of the Socialist International. The fifth, Lapinski, was closer to Martov and attempted to mediate between the Left and Center. Serbia was represented by one delegate, the deputy Katzlerovitch, who wavered in his allegiance but showed some tendency to support the Left. The Portuguese delegate—Peluso—took a similar position. The Austrian delegate—Koritschoner—was identified with the Center. An anonymous English delegate acted apparently only as an observer. Radek was entrusted with the mandate for the Revolutionary Socialists of Holland who had been prevented from attending the conference. Zinoviev performed a similar function on behalf of the Lettish Social Democracy. Robert Grimm and Angelica

[45] Maxe, *op. cit.*, 43.
[46] Lenin, *Sämtliche Werke*, XIX, 559.
[47] *Ibid.*

Balabanova took part in the proceedings as representatives of the International Socialist Commission. Willy Münzenberg, the secretary of the International Socialist Youth organization which was rapidly moving toward the Left, also attended the Congress.

This enumeration reveals three streams of opinion in the conference— an extreme Left revolutionary group, a vacillating Left fringe, and the pacifist majority.[48] Out of the total of 43 delegates, 12 now belonged to the Zimmerwald Left—three Russians, Lenin, Zinoviev and Petrova; three Germans, Froelich, Meyer and Thalheimer; three Poles, Radek, Bronski and Dombrowski; and the three Swiss, Nobs, Platten and Robmann. In addition there were at least seven other delegates who, though not identified with the Left, sympathized with it and were prepared to support it on crucial votes. This group included Serrati, Bobrov, Warski, Peluso, Katzlerovitch, Guilbeaux and Münzenberg. The combined strength of those two groups totalled nineteen votes, only three short of a majority. The rest of the delegates were Centrists whose opinions ran the gamut from those who sought to prod the Bureau into renewed activity by mild exhortations to others who not only criticized the policy of the Bureau, but even called for an open break with the Right wings of their own party organizations.

The great increase in Left strength goes far to explain the more radical cast of the Kienthal resolutions. The original group of eight "intransigents" had mounted to twelve; the total strength which they commanded had increased from twelve or thirteen to nineteen. Though they still lacked a majority, they were in a position to exercise a much more important influence in the deliberations. The majority was divided and uncertain. The pressure of circumstance was forcing the Centrists toward the Left. Nowhere was this more strikingly revealed than in Germany, where the Zimmerwald majority after threatening to bolt the first Zimmerwald Conference if a resolution were passed binding participants to vote against the war credits, had returned to Germany to find that the gathering popular unrest made imperative a vote against the war credits. It is against this background of solidarity and increasing strength on the Left, of uncertainty and vacillation in the Center, of rising mass dissatisfaction which the Centrists sought to make vocal, that the proceedings at Kienthal assumed their true perspective.

[48] For a Bolshevik analysis see G. Zinoviev. "Zimmerwald et Kienthal" in Lenine and Zinoviev, *Contre le Courant*, II, 75-89.

The published agenda of the Conference included the following items:

1. The fight to end the war.
2. The attitude of the proletariat toward the question of peace.
3. Agitation and Propaganda
   A. Parliamentary activity
   B. Mass Action.
4. The question of the calling of the International Socialist Bureau at The Hague.[49]

The Zimmerwald Left came into the Conference with a carefully prepared program. The Central Committee of the Russian Social-Democratic Labor Party under the leadership of Lenin had drawn up a set of theses on all the questions listed in the agenda which was freely distributed among the delegates at the Conference. Consequently, the Left entered the Congress with a tactical advantage. By assuming the offensive, it forced the majority to yield concessions. It offered a definite and concrete program which could be used as a basis of discussion. Into the details of this program it is unnecessary to go.[50] It is sufficient to indicate that it followed the same revolutionary line already set forth in the exposition of the proposals of the Zimmerwald Left, namely, the transformation of the war into a civil class conflict through revolutionary mass activity, a complete break with the "social-chauvinists," and the creation of a new Third International.

The question which excited the liveliest and most bitter discussions in the Congress was the problem of the relation of the Zimmerwald-Kienthal organization to the Bureau of the Second International.[51] The question was in some ways the most important before the gathering for in the answer to it was bound up the whole destiny of the Third International. It will be recalled that soon after the adjournment of the Zimmerwald gathering, the International Socialist Commission had issued an official communication that it would dissolve as soon as the Bureau resumed activity. Since no specific authorization to make such a statement had been given the Commission at Zimmerwald, the Left promptly protested and challenged the validity of the act.[52] At Kienthal, Grimm, the representative of the Commission, was forced to make an explanation which qualified the original declaration by stating that "it

[49] *Archiv für die Geschichte des Sozialismus etc.* XII, 340.
[50] Lenin, *Sämtliche Werke*, XIX, 65.
[51] Lenine and Zinoviev, *Contre le Courant*, see note 48.
[52] *Ibid.*, 75.

is applicable only in the case of the I. S. B.'s renouncing its policy, and actually placing itself in the position of Zimmerwald."[53] The Bolsheviks then insisted that this explanation be recorded in the procès-verbal of the Conference, and this was done. It marked a Left victory in the preliminary skirmish.

The Bolshevik Central Committee in its proposals came out flat-footedly for a repudiation of the "bankrupt" Second International and the social-chauvinists who dominated its policy. In the ensuing debate this proposal was energetically attacked by the majority. Axelrod led the onslaught. In an eloquent plea for the preservation of socialist unity, he argued that party scissions would not aid the socialist cause. He recognized that the Bureau of the Second International was remiss in its duties and that patriotic Socialists had allowed patriotic sentiments to warp their socialist faith, but he pointed out that these Socialists had become patriots with mass approval and that with changing mass sentiment they could be led back to international socialist principles. He called not for the art of the surgeon but for that of the healer; not for a rending of the party organization but for a remolding of its policies from within. As he saw it, the task of Kienthal was to appeal to the masses to reveal to the party leaders their true wishes and to demand the immediate convocation of the full Bureau. Such mass pressure the Bureau would not dare disregard. He therefore called upon the assembled delegates to organize this campaign of mass propaganda and agitation.[54]

The majority of the Italian delegation and Hoffmann, the representative of the moderate German opposition, took a somewhat different tack. They argued that it would be bad practical politics to organize a new International since the opposition either had or would have enough votes to control the activities of the Bureau when it was summoned.[55] Buttressing this argument was the undoubted fact that the opposition was rapidly gaining strength, but the question which was still left unanswered by the proponents of this view was the problem of how a full meeting of the Bureau could be forced with the Executive unwilling to take action. Those who advanced the Italian proposal were compelled to fall back on Axelrod's argument that the masses must be aroused to demand the meeting and that when such a demand existed the "social-chauvinists" would not dare defy it.

[53] Ibid., 75n. "Elle se rapportait seulement au cas ou le B.S.I. renoncerait à sa politique et se placerait en fait sur le terrain de Zimmerwald."
[54] Ibid., 82.
[55] Ibid., 82-83.

These arguments did not satisfy the Left. They reiterated their demands that no compromise be made with opportunism; that the patriotic Socialists be branded as traitors and be excommunicated from the socialist family; that the Bureau and all the Bureaucracy of the Second International be abandoned as useless and outworn pieces of machinery which no longer served the purpose of a militant fighting organization of revolutionary Socialists.

Scission versus Unity—so the battle raged. Between the two views tenaciously held, no reconciliation was possible that did not involve a yielding of ground on one side or the other, or on both. Continued debate only intensified the bitterness on both sides, and in order to avoid a deadlock, a search began for a formula. The conference appointed a committee of seven members to work out a satisfactory resolution.[56]

The committee mirrored the conflict of opinion in the Congress. It divided into two groups. The majority composed of Lazzari, Naine, Hoffmann and Axelrod favored agitation for the convocation of the Bureau; the minority composed of Lenin, Warski and Meyer was opposed to the convocation and stood for a severing of all relations with the Second International.

The majority made the first gesture toward a compromise. A resolution was offered which, while calling for the convocation of the Bureau, severely criticized the policy of the Bureau during the war, demanded the replacement of the old Executive Committee by a new one from which Huysmans was excluded, and insisted that government Socialists —that is, Socialists who had entered coalition cabinets as ministers, such as Sembat, Guesde, Thomas, Vandervelde and Henderson—be ousted from the Party.[57] The minority resolution took the extreme position already outlined. The proposals were then thrown back on the floor. The majority proposal proved too extreme for some of the Right and not extreme enough for the Left with the result that it received only ten votes. The minority resolution mustered the full strength of the Zimmerwald Left—twelve votes.

With a deadlock still threatening, other proposals were made from the floor in an effort to reach a compromise. A project of Hoffmann's which provided merely for the convocation of the Bureau received only two votes. The Pole, Lapinski, then offered a resolution which severely criticized the policy of the Bureau and left open the question of participa-

[56] *Ibid.*, 83-84.
[57] *Ibid.*, 84.

tion in the work of the Bureau or agitation for its convocation. This received fifteen votes. Another resolution proposed by Serrati repeated the main outlines of the majority committee resolution and like it received only ten votes. A proposal of Zinoviev's, that if a meeting of the Bureau be convoked, the Zimmerwaldians reassemble to examine the situation and decide their attitude toward it, won nineteen supporters. The Congress was still in an impasse.[58]

At this stage it was determined to refer all the resolutions back to the committee, which was now enlarged by the addition of two members of the Left, Zinoviev and Nobs.[59] The balance was now thrown to the Left in the committee, though the Centrists still commanded a majority in the Congress. After continued manoeuvering in the committee, the Left declared that they were willing to support the Lapinski resolution in order to facilitate a compromise. This cleared the way for action, and a resolution was framed combining the proposals of Lapinski, Zinoviev, and a last minute proposal of Modigliani's which came as an ultimatum from the Italian delegation and insisted on the recognition of the right of each party which so desired to call for the convocation of the Bureau. This *pot pourri* was accepted by an overwhelming vote. Only the Italian, Dugoni, voted against it. Axelrod abstained from voting.

The resolution of the Kienthal Congress on the International Socialist Bureau which was finally adopted, therefore, offers an interesting study in compromise.[60] The resolution begins with a bitter criticism of the war policy of the Executive Committee of the Bureau and declares that the International can only become an effective force when the proletariat frees itself of imperialist and chauvinist influences and takes its stand on a program of class warfare. In the event that a full meeting of the Bureau is summoned it calls upon delegates who support the Zimmerwald-Kienthal movement to expose the treachery and opportunism of the patriotic Socialists. Should the Executive Committee summon a meeting of the Bureau, the International Socialist Commission is empowered to call a meeting of the enlarged Executive to instruct its representatives on the attitude to be taken toward the proceedings. At the same time the right of each national section affiliated with the International Socialist Commission to call for a full meeting of the Bureau is reserved.

[58] *Ibid.*
[59] *Ibid.*, 85.
[60] For text see *Archiv für die Geschichte des Sozialismus,* etc. XII, 350-351.

The resolution is in many respects a triumph in ambiguity. It is difficult to award the palm of victory to any particular group in the Kienthal gathering. Both Centrists and revolutionaries found elements of consolation in the resolution. Neither obtained complete satisfaction. The Centrist majority could console itself with the reflection that each party group had the right to work for a convocation of the Bureau, and that no competing International had been created. Less satisfactory was the thought that collaboration with patriotic Socialists in the rehabilitation of the Second International was made practically impossible by the extremely critical tone of the resolution. Disturbing too was the reflection that a full meeting of the Bureau had to be approved by a preliminary conference of Zimmerwaldians, which still left possible a break with the Bureau even after it had been convoked.

The minority derived their solace from the sharpness with which the resolution criticized the Bureau, the hope that such criticism would precipitate an open break, and the fact that they had delayed an immediate commitment of the Kienthal Congress to the policy of resurrecting the Second International. They failed in their objective of erecting a new International. They regarded with some dismay the possibility of defection from the Zimmerwald movement which opened up out of the right of the national sections to work independently for the convocation of the Bureau. The Zimmerwald Left on the whole professed itself satisfied with the result. It saw in the resolution a step forward toward the creation of the Third International.

The attitude to be adopted toward the question of peace received considerable attention in the conference. At Zimmerwald, a resolution had been adopted calling for immediate peace and condemning the "social-chauvinists" who had invoked the slogan of "national defense" to trick the masses and enroll them under the banner of rival imperialistic powers. At Kienthal under greater pressure from the Left, a much more radical position was taken. The Kienthal resolution not only condemned the "social-chauvinists"; it went much further and openly ridiculed as visionary Utopians those pacifists who placed their hopes for peace in compulsory arbitration, disarmament, and democratization of foreign politics. Only by revolutionary mass action, the resolution contends, can peace be attained. Socialists are called upon to struggle against a policy of annexations and oppression of weak nations and minority groups, to defend the right of self-determination of peoples, to place the burden of the war on the possessing classes rather than on the worker; and to support mass movements against the high cost of living, new taxes, unemployment and political reaction in order to direct mass unrest into socialist channels.[61] Thus the resolution went far toward embodying the demands of the Zimmerwald Left. The proposed resolution of the latter group differed from the resolution adopted only in singling out the Independent Labour Party of Great Britain and the German Center for special opprobrium as social-pacifists, and instead of inciting the masses to action in general terms, it called upon them to turn their arms against the common foe, the capitalist régime.[62]

A significant omission in the resolution on the question of peace which the Conference adopted was the failure even to mention voting against the war credits as one of the methods to be used. The omission was not accidental; it was due to the position of the three French deputies, Blanc, Brizon and Raffin-Dugens, who still argued that the special position of France as the victim of attack made support of the war budget necessary. Nineteen members and sympathizers of the Zimmerwald Left issued a separate declaration in which they condemned the attitude of the French Parliamentary minority as absolutely inconsistent with Socialism and the struggle against war.[63]

The Conference also issued a May Day Manifesto in which it called upon the masses to take up the struggle against the war, and after the fashion of May Day manifestoes, closed with three stirring slogans: Down with War! Long live Peace, peace without annexations! Long Live International Socialism![64]

When the resolutions adopted at Zimmerwald and Kienthal are compared, a steady drift toward the Left is clearly apparent. It is not only that the numerical strength of the Left has increased. The Center itself began to adopt the tactics of the Left. The Party scissions which the Center regarded with such horror at Zimmerwald had become a fact in the British Socialist Party, were rapidly approaching in Germany, and with the rise of a strong opposition even threatened in France. The mass weariness generated by a war of attrition was forcing the Center to take desperate measures. The sharp tone of the Kienthal resolutions, the trenchant criticism of the dilatory tactics of the Executive Bureau of the Second International, the impatience with pacifist yearnings for

[61] Lenin, *Sämtliche Werke*, XIX, 522.
[62] *Ibid.*, 525.
[63] *Ibid.*, 527. "für absolut unvereinbar mit dem Sozialismus und dem Kampfe gegen den Krieg."
[64] *Ibid.*, 520.

peace, the emphasis on mass action and class war—all reveal a growing revolutionary coloring not apparent at Zimmerwald.

Yet the decision to break with the Second International had not yet been taken. The majority at Kienthal still hesitated at the cross-roads. The Left beckoned one way, and called for an open split, and sought with every resource at its command to give a firm revolutionary direction to the movement. The Right—the majority Socialists—still remained aloof. What would happen if the Right began to bid for the support of the Center? Would the Center grasp the bait of reconciliation and come back into the fold of the old International? It was still too early to answer that question. But it was already clear that it might be a question which would have to be answered when and if the Second International was reconstituted.

The hopes of the Zimmerwald Left ran high. The foundation of the Third International had been laid at Zimmerwald. It had added height at Kienthal. It remained for the future to reveal whether it could weather the storm when the full strength of the Right was turned against it.

CHAPTER VI

KIENTHAL TO THE RUSSIAN REVOLUTION

The history of Socialist internationalism in the period between Kienthal and the Russian Revolution is a complex tapestry of interweaving strands that does not lend itself easily to chronological treatment. For purposes of convenience, the thread of events may best be disentangled under the three following heads: (1) the activity of the Executive Committee of the Bureau of the Second International during this period; (2) the ever deepening gulf between majority and minority Socialists and concomitantly the rising strength of the opposition in various countries; (3) the fortunes of the Zimmerwald Left.

The impending Kienthal Congress, it will be recalled, prodded the Executive Committee of the Bureau into renewed activity. Different reasons were given for this reawakening. According to one explanation, the Executive Committee bestirred itself primarily because it deemed the time ripe for renewed preliminary discussions in preparation for a full meeting of the Bureau. The Zimmerwaldians contended that the object was rather to solidify the ranks of the majority Socialists against the menace of Kienthal. Both factors probably entered into the calculations of the Bureau.

During the last week of March, 1916, Vandervelde, the chairman of the Bureau, in company with Huysmans, the secretary, visited Paris and held a series of conferences with leaders of the French Socialist Party.[1] What transpired at these meetings was not reported. That these emissaries did not convince the French majority Socialists that an immediate meeting of the Bureau ought to be called is indicated by the fact that at the April meeting of the National Council of the Party, the Renaudel motion calling for an adjournment of the meeting of the Bureau was carried by a vote of 1996 to 960.[2]

On April 1, Vandervelde held conversations with the Parliamentary Committee of the National Council of the Independent Labour Party of Great Britain.[3] The representatives of the I. L. P. took a different tone. They emphasized their desire for an immediate meeting of the

[1] *Labour Leader,* April 6, 1916.
[2] *Pendant la Guerre,* Resolution of National Council, April 9, 1916, 139.
[3] *Labour Leader,* April 6, 1916.

Bureau and expressed the willingness of the I. L. P. as previously notified, to the Commission appointed by the Zimmerwald Conference, to take any steps in any bona-fide attempt to bring about international action in the interests of peace.[4] Mr. Ramsay MacDonald, in an article on "Socialists and the War," suggested as a practical way to end the deadlock (1) that the Bureau obtain from the various Socialist parties—especially the belligerents—a statement of their intentions—"why they support their governments, what they are fighting for, what they are afraid of, what they can agree on;" (2) that the Socialist parties continue to make demands on their governments for accurate statements and precise definition of war aims.[5]

The statement made by Huysmans on his return to The Hague summarized the results of the visits to France and Great Britain as follows: (1) the French and British recognize the Bureau at The Hague as the center of the international Socialist movement; (2) the French and British parties approve the attitude of the Executive Committee; (3) the majorities in these countries do not judge the moment opportune for a meeting of the Bureau; (4) there are, however, minorities who desire such a meeting; (5) all are in accord that the Executive Committee shall not act in the face of the wishes of parties; (6) the parties in France and Great Britain are in accord concerning the necessity of exercising influence on the terms of peace; (7) the results of the conferences are a complete condemnation of the Zimmerwald Conference which is recognized by neither the French, British, Germans, nor Austrians.[6]

Avanti, the Italian Socialist daily, promptly challenged the accuracy of Huysmans' statement so far as it seemed to imply that Zimmerwald had been condemned by the I. L. P. and the British Socialist Party. As for the rest, it said:

A declaration from Huysmans was not necessary to inform us that official parties of France, Germany, and Austria were opposed to the deliberations of the Congress of Zimmerwald. These official parties have ranged themselves with the nationalists and only their minorities, which are increasing so eloquently, have initiated that action which will reconduct the International movement along those paths indicated at the Socialist Congresses of Copenhagen and Basle.[7]

[4] *Ibid.*
[5] *Ibid.*
[6] *Ibid.*, May 11, 1916.
[7] Reprinted in *Labour Leader*, May 11, 1916.

Ramsay MacDonald also took occasion to set forth the policy of the Independent Labour Party in an "Open Letter to the International Socialist Bureau," which for all its politeness contained a threat of defection.[8] The manifesto issued by the Bureau in reply, defended its attitude of prudence but, nevertheless, tried to conciliate complaints by pointing to the achievements and plans of the Bureau.

We ask all affiliated parties, without exception to examine with as little delay as possible the whole of the political problems which in their opinion ought to find a solution in the terms of peace.... With a view to instituting a preliminary inquiry we have called a conference of delegates of the Socialist and Labour Parties of neutral countries, which is to meet at The Hague on June 26. This date has been fixed at the request of the United States and Argentinian delegates.[9]

Because of delays the Conference of Neutral Socialists did not open until July 31. The Zimmerwald Left exerted its influence to prevent Zimmerwaldians from participating except with instructions to expose the hypocrisy of the organizers of the Conference.[10] This action was taken because the Left feared that the Conference constituted the beginning of efforts to reconcile the Right and Center and to seduce the Center away from Zimmerwald.

Following the Kienthal Conference a meeting of the Enlarged Executive was held (May 2) to determine the attitude of Zimmerwaldians toward the projected conference.[11] Two points of view were represented, that of the Zimmerwald Left which has already been set forth, and the view of the majority, that each neutral country be left to make the decision of participation for itself. The latter view triumphed, qualified, however, by the proviso that the Zimmerwald adherents should partici-

[8] *Ibid.,* May 18, 1916.
"I hope you have watched the growing revolt against your apparent inactivity which has resulted in the Zimmerwald Conference and which if allowed to go on will turn the supporters of that conference into an independent organization and so split the international movement. To such a split the I.L.P. has given no countenance. It was not for that purpose that it was prepared to send delegates to Zimmerwald or that it expressed sympathy with that meeting. But there is a limit to your inactivity. . . .
"My friends, you must come into activity. There is not much time left to you to make your choice. The action of the German minority has forced your hands. The minorities in all the countries look to you to lead as they pass on to their great work of liberating Europe. If you lose touch with them, your international will be a thing of the past."
[9] *Ibid.,* May 25, 1916.
[10] Lenine and Zinoviev, *Contre le Courant,* II, 88-89.
[11] *Archiv für die Geschichte des Sozialismus,* etc., XII, 356-357.

pate on the basis of the resolutions adopted at Zimmerwald and Kienthal on the question of peace.

The neutral conference was attended by nine delegates from Holland, Denmark, Sweden, the Argentine, and the United States. The German authorities at first refused passport visas to the delegates from Luxemburg, Switzerland, and the Scandinavian countries, but eventually granted them, too late, however, for the delegates to reach the Congress in time to participate in the deliberations. The Spanish delegates were prevented from attending because of the difficulties of transportation. As a result the Congress was not as fully representative as had been expected.

The Congress adopted resolutions fixing the responsibility for the war on the capitalistic system, unanimously condemned "projects that had been formed with the object of prosecuting after the War a systematic policy of economic warfare" (reference to the Paris Economic Conference); advocated free trade; declared the situation favorable for peace negotiations, and offered as the basis for peace the recognition of the right of peoples freely to decide under what government they will live. It urged the re-establishment of Belgium and Serbia as independent states, autonomy for Poland, and negotiations between the German Social-Democrats and French Socialists on the question of Alsace-Lorraine.[12]

Highly significant was the resolution on the International Socialist Bureau. The Conference declared that it earnestly deprecated any movement that would tend to break up already existing organizations and concluded:

Finally the Conference invites the Executive Committee to continue its efforts to reestablish international relations, and it declares itself favorable to the summoning of a full meeting with the object of settling existing differences and promoting common action for peace on the basis of the resolutions of the International.[13]

The Conference thus indirectly rebuffed the more extreme Zimmerwaldians. In the vote of confidence given the Bureau and in the implied promise of a meeting of the full Bureau in the near future it tried to bind majority and Center Socialists together against the threat of a split in the International.

The growing demand for a full meeting of the Bureau was reflected in

[12] *Labour Leader,* August 24, 1916.
[13] *Ibid.*

the actions of the Socialist parties in various lands. At the August 6 meeting of the National Council of the French Socialist Party, the minority which favored calling an international conference and renewing relations with German and other enemy Socialists was able to muster 1075 votes against the 1824 of the majority.[14] The Independent Labour Party of Great Britain grew more insistent in its demands. Its National Administrative Council, meeting in September, 1916, issued a report in which it declared:

> While we welcome the issue of the Manifesto of the Executive of the Bureau as an indication of its desire to maintain communication with the parties, and though we realize the difficulties of travel, we persist in demanding that the International Bureau should meet and call a conference of all the national sections, and that the conference be held irrespective of the refusal of any particular section to take part in its proceedings.[15]

The British resolution failed to spur the Bureau into action.

Meanwhile, the National Council of the French Socialist Party had, on August 6, voted the calling of a second Congress of Inter-Allied Socialists to meet in Paris in order (1) to

> influence the policy of the respective countries in a direction which excludes during the war and after the war any thought of conquest and annexation, (2) to bring their governments to avoid in their economic agreements, during and after the war, anything which would mean an increase of exploitation for the international working class or anything which would contain germs of future conflicts between the nations, thereby risking that these agreements, in themselves so desirable, will be made the instruments of prolonged war.[16]

The technical organization of the Conference was confided to the secretary of the Bureau who was instructed to provide that "the traditions of the International Congresses be scrupulously maintained in so far as the repartition of votes is concerned." The last fact—the use of the secretariat of the Second International—inspired the hope in some circles that the Congress might be a stepping-stone toward the revival of the International. The date of the Conference was tentatively fixed for January, 1917. Later events compelled a postponement.

In order to give the conference a completely representative character, the participation of Italian and Russian Socialists was necessary. The fact that these groups had participated in the Zimmerwald-Kienthal movement made it questionable whether they would join in an Inter-

[14] *Pendant la Guerre*, 146.
[15] *Labour Leader*, Oct. 12, 1916.
[16] *Ibid.*, August 24, 1916.

Allied Conference. The Parliamentary group of the Italian Socialist Party first decided on September 18, to accept the invitation of the French Socialists in order to give the Italian Socialist Party an opportunity to explain its attitude of opposition to the War and to advance the project for a speedy convocation of a general international conference of Socialists.[17] The Bolsheviks (December, 1916) replied with a categorical refusal to participate in any congress sponsored by the "agents of the French bourgeoisie," as it labelled the majority of the French Socialist Party. The Bolsheviks refused to recognize divisions like Socialists of the Entente or Socialists of the Central Powers, since they proclaimed themselves international Socialists. The reply concluded:

At the same time we turn to the International Socialist Commission of Berne with the proposal that a conference be convened of the Zimmerwaldian (international) organizations invited to the conference of the Entente in order that such Zimmerwaldian organizations may adopt a common action in opposition to the Congress of the Entente.[18]

The last proposal revealed the efforts of the Bolsheviks to bring about a clear break. While no preliminary Zimmerwaldian conference was held, the blunt Bolshevik refusal to participate had its effect in influencing the Italians to follow suit.[19]

It is probable that an additional factor which influenced the Italian Socialist Party in its decision was the action of the French Socialist Congress (December 25-30, 1916) in again voting against the convocation of the International Socialist Bureau though this time by a reduced majority of 1537 to 1407.[20] This fact combined with the rejection by the British Labour Party in its Manchester Conference of January, 1917,

---

[17] *Ibid.*, Oct. 5, 1916.

[18] For text see Lenin, *Sämtliche Werke*, XIX, 541-544.

[19] *Labour Leader*, March 15, 1917. The Italian Socialist meeting at Rome, Feb. 26, 27, 28, 1917, passed the following resolution:

"The Congress, affirming its unshakeable intention of maintaining during the war, as before, relations with all the sections of the International, and having confirmed the fact that the adhesion of the Italian Executive Committee to the Paris Congress has as its sole object the persuasion of the Allied Socialists to agree to a complete conference of all sections of the International.

"And considering that such laudable initiative would be frustrated (1) by the non-participation of the Russian Socialist Party and (2) by the intention manifested by the French section of the International Socialist Bureau to invite (contrary to the rights of the Italian Socialist Party to the disposition of the votes assigned to it by International congresses) to take part in the (Paris) congress persons expelled from the Italian Socialist Party and outsiders, the Congress votes that the Executive decides not to take part in the Congresses of Paris."

[20] *Pendant la Guerre*, Resolutions of National Congress, 152ff.

of a similar resolution calling for a reconstitution of the International made the attainment of the Italian objective, an immediate meeting of the Bureau, virtually hopeless.[21] Participation in the Inter-Allied Conference by the Italians, therefore, seemed fruitless because two of the major participants stood committed beforehand against the only policy which the Italian Socialists were anxious to further.

With the Bolsheviks and the Italian Socialist Party boycotting the conference and an eleventh-hour decision on the part of the British Labour delegates not to attend, it was found expedient to postpone the Inter-Allied Socialist Conference to some later date.[22] Originally scheduled for some time in January, then postponed to March 19, it was now indefinitely postponed only to be resurrected again under changed circumstances.[23]

A review of the activity of the Executive Committee of the Bureau between Kienthal and the Russian Revolution reveals two chief tendencies: first, a determined effort to arrest the rising influence of the Zimmerwaldians, and second, an attempt to impress the majority Socialists of the Allies—especially the French—with the necessity of convoking a full meeting of the Bureau at the earliest possible opportunity in order to prevent a threatened split in the International.

[21] See *Report of the 16th Annual Conference of the Labour Party,* Manchester, 1917.

[22] *Labour Leader,* March 15, 1917.

[23] *Ibid.,* January 4, 1917. Meanwhile another possibility for the revival of activity by the Bureau opened up. Vandervelde, on behalf of the Belgian workers, appealed to the Bureau to exert its influence to prevent the deportation of Belgians from occupied areas for compulsory work in Germany. On the invitation of the Bureau, Scheidemann and Ebert, leaders of the majority Socialists, came to The Hague, and expressed their determination to take steps to curb the practice. As a result of this incident, the Bureau in its reply to Vandervelde and the Belgians, made the following suggestion:

"If the parties of the principal belligerent countries each nominated a delegate to constitute at The Hague a commission which would work under the direction of the Executive Committee of the Bureau, we should thereby have a central bureau which would furnish to the Socialist representatives in the various Parliaments the necessary documents in order to obtain from their governments the suppression of numerous abuses. This idea has been received with sympathy by the delegates of the German section of the International, and we recommend it to your consideration."

This overture received little encouragement from the Socialists of the Allied countries and eventually proved abortive. It reveals, nevertheless, that the Executive Committee of the Bureau was making sincere if limited efforts to urge the Socialists of the belligerent countries to come together in some kind of a scheme to preserve the international solidarity of the Socialist movement.

The outbreak of the March Revolution found the Executive Committee still pursuing these objects and making slow but perceptible progress toward its goal. The greatest obstacle to a full meeting of the Bureau remained the French majority Socialists, but even in France the trend of the votes indicated that the minority Socialists were rapidly gaining strength. The Executive Committee confined by the limitations of the framework within which it operated and motivated by the desire not to antagonize such an important party as the French, preferred to let time go by in the hope that a transformation of party policy would come from within through the growing influence of the minority. The danger implicit in this policy—stressed by the British Independent Labour Party—was that the Zimmerwaldians, even the less extreme Zimmerwaldians might refuse to wait, might disown the Bureau, and organize an independent international organization of their own composed of elements in opposition to the policy of the French majority Socialists. With this danger, the Executive Committee had to take its chance. It could only hope that the French majority would relent its attitude or that the triumph of the French minority Socialists would come before the opposition groups in other lands were driven to withdraw from the Bureau and take their stand with the Zimmerwald Left for the creation of a Third International. The Executive Committee found itself the somewhat helpless spectator of a dramatic race with time in which the life of the old International was at stake. The issue was drawn, but the result of the race was far from clear when the Russian Revolution introduced a new imponderable into a situation already remarkable for its tangled complexity.

In order to see the events between Kienthal and the Russian Revolution in more accurate perspective, it is useful to turn back and follow another thread of development—the growth of the opposition and the widening chasm between majority and minority Socialists, in the more important countries.

To enter into an exhaustive treatment of the general causes of dissatisfaction with the policies of the majority, or patriotic, Socialists would make necessary a study of the effects of prolonged warfare on the psychology of peoples. Such a study is not here attempted. It is enough here to indicate that the losses of life, the lack of food and clothing, the prolonged sacrifices, the war weariness, and the other hardships which war entailed, implanted a longing for peace in the heart of the masses and drove increasing portions of the proletariat to withdraw their allegiance from Socialists who supported the war, and to transfer it to Socialists who promised to end the war.

One factor deserves special emphasis. The peace movement of the winter of 1916-1917 which was initiated by President Wilson's note of December 18, calling upon the belligerents to state "terms upon which the war might be ended," aroused soaring hopes among people on both sides of the trenches that peace was in sight. The frustration of these hopes which resulted from the unwillingness of the belligerents to come together brought despair to the rank and file of Socialists. Their disillusionment vented itself not only in criticism of the policy of their governments, but also in attacks on the "government" Socialists who continued to vote war credits and support those governments.[24] The result was to strengthen the pacifist minority and to widen the gap between war and anti-war Socialists.

In Germany the mounting dissatisfaction was most apparent. Even before Kienthal the Social-Democrats in the Reichstag had divided into two groups, the majority retaining the party name and the minority styling itself the Social-Democratic Labor Fellowship. The fiction of party unity to which both groups subscribed was belied not only by the independent action of the groups in the Reichstag, but by the contest between the groups to capture the local party machinery. Although majority and minority joined forces in opposing the budget of June 7, 1916, because of general discontent with the policy of the government, the groups split again on the question of voting an extraordinary credit of 12,000 million marks for the prosecution of the war. As usual, the Social-Democratic Labor Fellowship and Rühle voted against the credits; twenty-two members of the group left the chamber before the vote took place; the rest voted for the credits.[25]

The conflict between majority and minority also extended to a fight for the control of the party press. *Vorwärts,* the Central Party organ, which was edited by a board in which the minority predominated, tormented the majority with its constant criticism. The majority took steps to eject the editorial representatives of the minority and to censor the contents of the paper.[26] As a result, revolt seethed in Berlin, which was a minority stronghold, and which had a special voice in the management of the paper since *Vorwärts* served the double purpose of a local paper

[24] *Ibid.,* Feb. 8, and Feb. 22, 1917.
[25] Bevan, *op. cit.,* 110.
[26] *Ibid.,* 112-113.

and a general party organ. In June the new Party Directorate chosen in the Berlin district recorded a minority triumph.

To arrest the growing disorganization, the majority began to advocate a Parteitag, or convention. The minority fought the project bitterly on the ground that no truly representative congress could be held while so many Socialists were in the trenches. Feeling ran high. "The enmity of the different nations to each other," said the majority weekly, *Die Glocke,* "is child's play compared with the mad fury which at the present time excites German Social-Democrats against German Social-Democrats. If we have not yet turned machine guns on to each other, it is not for want of will!"[27] The Party Committee meeting on July 20, postponed the congress, but decided instead to call a conference of delegates from the local party branches all over the Empire.

The Conference was summoned to meet September 21-23 in the Reichstag building in Berlin. A contest for delegates began immediately.[28] From the ranks of the minority came complaints that the system of representation was unfair to them since their strength was located in the large cities, and the system of voting adopted gave undue representation to small branches. Though the more extreme representatives of the minority demanded that the conference be boycotted altogether, more moderate counsel prevailed, and the minority leaders determined to participate in order to state their views, even though they could exercise no real influence on the determination of policy.

The test of minority strength came on Haase's motion that the conference was not competent to pass resolutions on questions of policy. This motion was rejected by a vote of 276 to 169.[29] The vote of the minority included not only Haase and his Labor Fellowship group and the extremist sections, but also those who had refused to vote for or against the credits. Although the majority succeeded in passing a motion approving its own action in voting the war credits, the conference revealed a significant growth in minority strength which could not but be disturbing to the adherents of party solidarity.

The events of the next few months indicated that the conference had not healed the breach. After the suppression of *Vorwärts* by the government censorship on October 8 (for ten days) the condition of its reappearance was made a complete change in staff. As a result, *Vorwärts*

[27] *Die Glocke,* July 15, 1916.
[28] Bevan, *op. cit.,* 128-129.
[29] *Ibid.,* 133.

became a majority organ. The *Leipziger Volkszeitung* now became the principal minority voice in the Socialist press. As a result of the *Vorwärts* incident, the minority charged that the majority was openly a government party. Minority agitators urged their supporters to withdraw dues and contributions to the party chest. On December 2, the minority Social-Democrats of Bremen voted to stop payments, an action which was virtually equivalent to secession. Other local organizations followed suit.[30]

On January 7, 1917, the minority held a conference of its own in Berlin.[31] The conference was dominated by the Haase-Ledebour group, though representatives of the more extreme Spartacists and International Socialists were also present. The latter groups explained that they would not be bound by the decisions of the conference. A resolution was passed denouncing the seizure of the party press by the majority, defending the collaboration of the opposition elements, and calling upon the opposition when in the minority "to work indefatigably within the framework of the Party Statutes for the dissemination of their views." The resolution to withhold contributions from the party chest was defeated. It was clear that the predominant sentiment of the conference did not yet sanction a party split.

The majority refused to take this view of the matter. On January 18, 1917, the Party Committee voted 29 to 10 that the action of the minority in holding the conference constituted a party schism. On January 20, the Party Directorate declared that all those who supported the resolutions passed by the opposition were no longer members of the party. Minority Socialists were ordered ejected from locals where majority Socialists were in control. Where minority Socialists dominated, the local representatives of the so-called majority were ordered to withdraw and form distinct organizations.

This action virtually made the split inevitable. In the middle of January the Social-Democratic group in the Prussian lower chamber divided into two sections. In the election to fill the seat left vacant as the result of Liebknecht's imprisonment, the majority Socialists put up a candidate to oppose Franz Mehring, an extremist who in this case was supported by the Haase-Ledebour group. Though the minority still sought to preserve what vestige of unity remained, the break now became unavoidable. In April, 1917, at the famous Gotha conference, a separate organi-

[30] *Ibid.*, 142.
[31] *Ibid.*, 145.

zation—the Independent Social-Democratic Party of Germany—was formed by a union of the Labor Fellowship and the Spartacist group. With this action the cleavage between the majority and minority Socialists was complete.

In Austria the split was not so evident. At the national party conference of March 25-28, 1916, Dr. Friedrich Adler's anti-war resolution received only 15 votes.[32] The war policy of the party which was defended by the elder Adler (Victor) was overwhelmingly endorsed by the party. The dramatic spectacle of son arrayed against father served to disclose the intensity of the conflict. The brutal policy of repression which the government adopted in its treatment of Socialist organizations and the refusal to convoke Parliament drove Friedrich Adler to shoot and kill the Premier, Count Stuergkh. Though the minority gained strength through 1916 and the early part of 1917, the majority still remained in control, and no open split developed.

In Bulgaria, the Socialist movement divided between the "broad" and the "narrow" Socialists. The former acquiesced in the government's war policy and stood toe to toe with the German majority. The "narrow" Socialists endorsed the resolutions of the Zimmerwald Conference and suffered greatly from the persecutions of civil and military authorities.[33]

Three currents of opinion divided the French Socialist movement after Kienthal. The majority Socialists led by Sembat and Renaudel still stood for uncompromising support of the war and no dealings with enemy Socialists. A Center group which followed Longuet, Pressemane and Paul Louis, while voting for the war credits was internationalist in its outlook and favored the immediate reconstitution of the International. More to the Left was a third group centering around the "Comité pour la Reprise des Relations Internationales" (Committee for the Resumption of International Relations) which included in its ranks not only pacifists of the Merrheim-Bourderon stamp but also revolutionary Socialists such as Guilbeaux, Rosmer, Monatte and Loriot. The Longuet-Pressemane group constituted the only effective Parliamentary opposition.

Its rising strength was reflected in the votes of the party councils. At the meeting of the National Council of the Party in April, 1916, the Pressemane resolution demanding a full meeting of the International Socialist Bureau at the earliest possible moment, received 960 votes to 1996 for the Renaudel resolution favoring the adjournment of the meet-

[32] Brügel, op. cit., V, 251ff.
[33] American Labor Year Book, 1917-1918, 235.

ing.[34] Although this marked a considerable increase in strength over previous votes, the minority pointed out that its real power was not reflected in the vote since at least 800 majority votes were cast by war refugees from the occupied regions who could not claim a real representative character.[35]

In June, 1916, three Socialist deputies, Raffin-Dugens, Blanc, and Brizon, all members of the Kienthal Conference, for the first time refused to vote in favor of the war credits. At the August 6 meeting of the National Council the minority resolution calling for an international conference and renewal of relations with German and other enemy Socialists commanded 1075 votes against the 1824 of the majority.[36] Votes from the invaded territories were divided as follows: 689 for the majority; 29 for the minority. Again the minority challenged the validity of these majority ballots.

Meanwhile the minority Socialists were conducting an active campaign for popular support. New opposition weekly organs appeared in great profusion and were widely read. *Le Bonnet Rouge* had been founded in June, 1915. *Le Populaire* appeared in May, 1916. It was joined in its critical attitude toward the majority Socialists by *Le Populaire du Centre, Le Midi-Socialiste, Droit du Peuple* and others. A veritable rash of reviews, with such picturesque titles as *Les Humbles, La Veilleuse, La Caravane, Demain, La Forge,* etc., helped to swell the voice of protest.[37] Victories for the minority Socialists in the local federations revealed the drift of the tide.[38]

The French Socialist Conference which assembled from December 25 to 30, 1916, found the majority and minority factions fairly evenly balanced. Feeling ran high, and the proceedings were enlivened by frequent outbursts of hot passion.[39] The opposition jeered when the Socialist ministers made their appearance. Even Vandervelde, who had been invited to address the Congress as a guest, was heckled frequently and had to forego his speech after he found it impossible to subdue his assailants. The evenness of strength in the convention was indicated by the vote on the minority resolution demanding the immediate convocation of the Bureau of the International. This time the minority rallied

[34] *Pendant la Guerre*, 139.
[35] *Labour Leader*, May 18, 1916.
[36] *Pendant la Guerre*, 146.
[37] See Maxe, *op. cit.*, 71ff.
[38] *Labour Leader*, Dec. 14, 1916.
[39] *Ibid.*, January 11, 1917.

1407 votes to 1437 for the majority.[40] The minority was strong enough now to demand and obtain representation on all party committees and on the editorial staff of *L'Humanité*. The representation of the minority in the Central Committee increased from 8 to 11; the representation of the majority decreased from 17 to 14.

With the increase in minority strength, the dissension within the French Socialist Parliamentary group assumed a collective character.[41] Thirty-six deputies adhering to the minority now met separately and determined to present independently an interpellation respecting the objects of the war. Though this motion was easily defeated by a record vote of 437 to 45, the action of the minority was highly significant. For the first time the French "minoritaires" had dared to adopt an independent attitude in Parliament. The majority and minority groups now regularly held their meeting separately. Although an open split was avoided, the outbreak of the Russian Revolution found the breach between majority and minority Socialists in France rapidly widening.

The attitude of the British Socialist parties after Kienthal remained practically unchanged. The Independent Labour Party, which took a pacifist position in opposition to the war, nevertheless, vetoed the resolution proposed at the Newcastle Conference, April 23-25, 1916, to withdraw from the Labour Party. While adhering to the position of the Zimmerwaldians, its activities in the realm of international affairs were devoted largely to attempts to spur the Bureau of the International into action. The British Socialist Party which had split into two sections continued to agitate against the war under the official party name while the Hyndman group, styling itself National Socialist, supported the government.

The Labour Party at the Bristol Conference in February, 1916, had taken a pro-war stand and approved the participation of its representatives in the War Ministry. The next party conference meeting at Manchester in January, 1917, did little to indicate a change in attitude. The resolution of Bruce Glasier, an Independent Labourite, which called for the reconstitution of the International, was rejected by a vote of 1,498,000 to 696,000.[42]

[40] *Pendant la Guerre*, 152ff.
[41] *Labour Leader*, Feb. 8, 1917.
[42] *Report of the Sixteenth Annual Conference of the Labour Party at Manchester, 1917*. The I. L. P. representatives contended that these figures did not truly reflect the minority strength because of the bloc system of voting by which each labor union cast all its votes as a unit, regardless of the strength of the minority in the

The Italian Socialist Party, which from the first opposed all participation in the war, continued its opposition even after the entrance of Italy. The Party participated in both the Zimmerwald and Kienthal congresses and was critical of the inactivity of the Bureau of the Second International. At the Party Conference in Rome, February 26-28, 1917, it again demonstrated its anti-war solidarity by renewing its demands for peace and for the reconstruction of the International.[43] Its refusal to participate in the Inter-Allied Socialist Conference demonstrated its impatience with the majority "government" Socialists and a disposition to make common front with the Bolsheviks. In Italy, the Reformists, products of a Socialist Party scission during the Tripoli crisis of 1912, took a pro-war attitude and participated in the ministerial reorganization of May, 1916. This group, however, was no longer identified with the Italian Socialist Party.

The spirit of schism in Socialist ranks extended into the parties of neutral countries. In Sweden there was conflict between the so-called Young Socialists who adhered to the Zimmerwald Left, and the majority of the Socialist Party. When it appeared as if Sweden might be drawn into the war, the Young Socialists met at Stockholm on March 18-19, 1916, and took an extreme anti-war position, attacking the majority in the Socialist Parliamentary group and supporting revolutionary action.[44] The majority replied with a counter-attack in which they called upon the party membership to combat the opposition movement. As a result, three members of the Executive Committee who adhered to the opposition, resigned. The convention of the Swedish Social-Democratic Labor Party, meeting at Stockholm on February 22, 1917, supported the majority viewpoint and set forth conditions which the radical faction was unwilling to accept.[45] The outcome was a party split and the formation of a new Swedish Socialist Party on lines of the Zimmerwald and Kienthal resolutions.

The Swiss Socialist Party was also faced with internal defections. At the Congress of Aarau (November, 1915), the Zimmerwald resolutions had been approved, and a reorganization of the Party was decided upon which involved a complete merger with the affiliated Grütli Union. The

---

union. Under this system, the miners, cotton workers and engineers, controlling over a million votes, were a unit against the resolution although very sizeable minorities in each of these federations favored the proposal.

[43] *Labour Leader,* March 15, 1917.
[44] *American Labor Year Book,* 1916, 216-217.
[45] *Ibid.,* 1917-1918, 278-279.

Grütli Union was given the choice of disbanding or joining the Party. Though some members joined, the great majority seceded and took a more nationalist position.[46] In Switzerland, as in Italy, the rôles were reversed. The so-called minority view dominated the Party; the "patriotic" Socialists were forced out.

In the Socialist Party of the United States, a difference of opinion developed between a minority which justified preparedness measures as part of a program of national defense, and the majority view which uncompromisingly condemned war, or any preparation for war. In 1915, a referendum of the Party membership approved the expulsion of any elected official of the Socialist Party who gave a vote in favor of war or war credits.[47] The omission of the national convention in 1916 postponed a definite declaration of policy until the special convention which assembled at St. Louis, in April, 1917, to define the war policy of the Party and dispose of other pressing business. The majority report which took a position opposing the war, won an overwhelming victory.[48] As a result, a number of influential pro-war Socialists, including John Spargo and Charles Edward Russell, withdrew from the Party. The American Socialist-Labor Party, like the Socialist majority, took a firm anti-war position.

As this survey indicates, the period between Kienthal and the Russian Revolution witnessed a growing cleavage between pro-war and anti-war Socialists and a distinct rise in the strength of those elements which were opposed to the war. The German Party split. The French Socialist Party rapidly approached an open rupture. The Socialists of Italy, the Independent Labour Party of Great Britain, and the larger part of the British Socialist Party continued to oppose the war. The American Socialists took a similar stand. Anti-war minorities grew in Austria and Bulgaria. A schism threatened in Sweden. Perhaps the most significant feature of the period was the fact that the elements in opposition which were drifting toward an open party schism included not only revolutionary Socialists but moderate pacifist groups like the Haase-Ledebour group in Germany and the Longuet-Pressemane group in France. The question which still remained unanswered was whether the Left wingers could impress their revolutionary spirit upon the more moderate elements which were being driven into their arms. To the activity of the Left wing in this period, attention will now be turned.

[46] *Ibid.*, 281-282.
[47] *Ibid.*, 1916, 126.
[48] *Ibid.*, 1917-1918, 373-374.

The Zimmerwald and Kienthal congresses revealed that the revolutionary opposition was rising in power. At Zimmerwald this group had included the Bolsheviks and sections of the Polish, Lettish, Swedish, Norwegian, Swiss and German opposition. At Kienthal additional recruits had come from the Serbian Social Democracy, the Swiss Socialists, and the Bremen Left wing radicals in Germany.[49] A Bureau consisting of Lenin, Zinoviev and Radek, had been established to coordinate the work of the Zimmerwald Left. At Kienthal, the increasingly truculent tone of the resolutions revealed that the Left had made considerable progress in winning over the Center to its views, though very marked differences still separated the two factions.

The rising strength of the revolutionary Left caused great concern to both pro-war Socialists and the official authorities. The pro-war Socialists feared that the poisonous doctrine of civil war and the proposal for a new International which were being advanced by the Left, would spread to the Center and wean the wavering groups of pacifist Socialists away from the parent organizations. The attempt to put the machinery of the International Socialist Bureau into motion represented a partial if unsuccessful answer to the threat of the Left. The belligerent governments, too, saw in the activity of the Left a treasonable challenge to their authority which had to be exterminated at all costs.

The meeting of the Kienthal Congress was a signal for the intensification of government efforts to stamp out the Left wing opposition. In almost every country the Left wing found its propaganda hindered by government persecutions. Its newspapers were suppressed; its meetings were disbanded; its leaders and prominent adherents were confined in prison. In Germany, Karl Liebknecht was arrested for taking part in a demonstration in the Potsdamer Platz in Berlin on May Day, 1916. Although a member of the Reichstag and entitled to immunity from arrest, the Reichstag refused to intercede for him. He was sentenced at first to thirty months imprisonment, and on appeal the sentence was increased to forty-nine months. Rosa Luxemburg, Clara Zetkin and Franz Mehring—all prominent leaders of the Left—had to serve prison sentences for "disturbing the peace." Many less prominent supporters were confined to "Schutzhaft" and were kept under guard until the end of the war.

In Austria the government met peace demands of the Socialists with brutal repression. The refusal of the government to convoke Parliament

[49] Lenin, *Sämtliche Werke*, XIX, 591.

or to take steps toward peace drove the otherwise gentle Dr. Friedrich Adler, the scholarly editor of *Der Kampf*, to assassinate Count Stuergkh, the Austrian Premier. He was first condemned to death, but as the result of widespread agitation, the sentence was commuted to life imprisonment.[50]

The heavy hand of government censorship also fell upon the opposition in France. *Nashe Slovo*, the journal edited by Trotsky, was suppressed as the result of Russian protests. Trotsky was expelled from the country. Many of the leaders of the Left—among them Monatte and Rosmer—were forced to do military service. In Rumania, Dr. Rakovsky, the moving spirit of the Socialist Party, was arrested with a number of his supporters, and kept incommunicado.

In Great Britain many members of the Independent Labour Party and the Socialist Party found themselves behind prison bars because of their opposition to the war. One of the most notable cases was the long term imprisonment of MacLean, leader of the radical "Clyde-siders" who later became a prominent supporter of the Communist International. In Sweden the leaders of the Young Socialists came to blows with the authorities in their effort to give the Socialist movement an anti-war bias. Höglund, member of Parliament, and two other leaders of the minority, Heden and Oljelund, were arrested, convicted of high treason and sentenced to long prison terms. The International Socialist Commission of Berne, in special manifestoes issued May 1 and July 1, 1916, described Europe as a "pesthouse of reaction" and called upon all Zimmerwaldians to protest against these continued persecutions.[51] Though the sentences of the Swedish Socialists were reduced on appeal, partly as a result of widespread protests, the Left wing Socialists were compelled to wage their battle against both mass inertia and implacable government hostility. The German Social-Democratic majority urged that the régime of repression defeated its purpose, that governments only advertised revolution by making martyrs of revolutionaries and thus drove the masses to more extreme measures.[52] But these arguments had little effect on governmental policy. Persecutions continued, and the Left wing found legal propaganda increasingly difficult.

With open propaganda hindered by legal restrictions, the Left wing Zimmerwaldians turned their energies into illegal channels. Secret meet-

---

[50] *American Labor Year Book*, 1916, 164.
[51] *Archiv für die Geschichte des Sozialismus*, etc. XII, 357-362.
[52] Bevan, *op. cit.*, 105.

ings, privately printed pamphlets of an incendiary character, circulated from hand to hand, surreptitious propaganda conducted in factory, workshop and army, all supplemented and helped to inspire more open expressions of discontent such as mass demonstrations, food riots, and strikes. In spite of repression, the Zimmerwald Left increased in strength.

In Germany, three distinct groups adhered to the Zimmerwald Left: the Bremen Left Radicals whose spokesman was Paul Froelich; the International Socialists of Germany (I. S. D.) who were led by Julian Borchardt, the editor of *Lichtstrahlen*; and the largest of the groups, the Group Internationale led by Liebknecht, Luxemburg, Mehring and Zetkin, which eventually became known as the Spartacist group. Of the three, the Spartacists were by far the most important, and though less extreme than the other two, they accepted the revolutionary program of the Zimmerwald Left.[53] They had not yet abandoned all contacts with the chief party groups. At the Reichkonferenz of the Social Democracy, held in September, 1916, Kate Duncker represented and spoke for the Spartacists. The Spartacists also participated in the Conference of the Opposition held in Berlin, January 7, 1917.[54] Of the 157 delegates, 35 adhered to the Spartacist group, and the International Socialists claimed 7. The two extremist groups qualified their participation in this conference, however, by declaring that they would not be bound by any resolutions which the Congress should adopt unless satisfactory to them. While willing to sanction the resolution providing for criticism of the majority position, they divided with the rest of the conference on the question of continuing contributions to the party chest. The extremist groups opposed this resolution which was carried by the majority of the conference.

At the beginning of 1917, the Spartacist group formed by far the most powerful current in the stream of German revolutionary thought.[55] The Bremen Left Radicals worked in close harmony with them. The Spartacists took a prominent part in the strike movements of 1916, led mass demonstrations, and perfected an unusually successful underground system for the distribution of revolutionary literature in order to escape the censorship. The Spartacus letters appeared at irregular intervals and contained trenchant criticisms of the policies of the majority and Centrist Socialists.[56] An illegal party organ—*Spartakus*—

[53] Ernst Meyer (editor) *Spartakus im Kriege*, Berlin, 1927.
[54] Bevan, *op. cit.*, 145.
[55] Lenin, *Sämtliche Werke*, XIX, 572.
[56] Meyer, *op. cit.*

edited by Leo Jogisches, fired damaging shots at the ramparts of the majority faction.[57]

The tactics pursued by the Spartacists were based on the necessity of transforming the war between nations into a class war. Like the Bolsheviks, they pressed for the establishment of a new militant International to replace the inactive Bureau. At the end of March, 1917, however, when the split between majority and minority was clear, and the Spartacists were faced with the alternatives of adhering to the minority or of welding the three radical parties into an independent revolutionary organization, they decided on the former. In participating in the Gotha Conference of April, 1917, when the Independent Social-Democratic Labor Party was organized, the Spartacists did insist on retaining complete freedom of action on questions of policy, and thus showed that the alliance was for them at least largely a union of convenience rather than of principle.

In France the revolutionary Socialists were relatively weak. Yet Trotsky in his letter to Guesde before leaving France, testified to their increasing strength.[58] The Zimmerwald group—both Left and Center—clustered around the Committee for the Resumption of International Relations, which had been established by Merrheim and Bourderon after the first Zimmerwald Conference. Inessa Armand, a Bolshevik who worked with the Committee, tried in vain to give its work a revolutionary direction, and finally had to report that "In France the Socialists do not wish to consider a split."[59] In the autumn of 1916 the Committee replied to the attacks of the majority Socialists by issuing a pamphlet called *Les Socialistes de Zimmerwald et la Guerre,* in which it not only denounced the majority Socialists but severely criticized the Longuet-Pressemane Center for its wavering indecision.[60] The pamphlet declared that there was no hope for a rebirth of the International as long as Socialists subordinated their ideals to the politics of the rival imperialist powers and called upon labor to repudiate this alliance with the government.

On the whole, the revolutionary Socialists in this period were not a strong factor in the political situation. They constituted a ginger group on the Left fringes of the Longuet-Pressemane Center and tried unsuc-

[57] Lenin, *Sämtliche Werke,* XIX, 572.

[58] "The opposition grows," he wrote, "the group of *Nashe Slovo* reflected as incompletely as the Censorship permitted the voice of the French section of the new International arising out of the horrors of fratricidal war. . . ." See Maxe, *op. cit.,* 60.

[59] Lenin, *Sämtliche Werke,* XIX, 581.

[60] *Ibid.,* also Maxe, *op. cit.,* 64.

cessfully to drive the Center to take a more uncompromising position against the majority.

The English situation was even less promising for the Zimmerwald Left than the French. The Independent Labour Party and the British Socialist Party were identified with the Center. Left wingers existed in each organization, but formed uninfluential minorities. The Clydesiders led by MacLean offered the most fertile field for revolutionary propaganda. Bolshevik emigrés residing in London, among them Chicherin and Litvinov, did what they could to spread the Leninist gospel but without notable conversions either in quality or number.

Russia remained the stronghold of the Zimmerwald Left. Most of the outstanding Socialist leaders were in exile, but agitators to work in Russia were not lacking. Encouraged by the comparative laxness of police espionage, they conducted a very effective underground propaganda throughout the war. They took advantage of the régime of repression, the food shortages, the war weariness, and the general inefficiency of the government to awaken revolutionary ardor. The Bolsheviks, in particular, worked among the industrial proletariat of Petrograd and other large industrial centers and impregnated a large number of workers with the spirit of class warfare.[61]

Revolutionary groups grew in strength in the neutral countries as well. In Sweden the Young Socialists led by Höglund adhered to the Zimmerwald Left and waged an energetic campaign to exclude from the Party all Socialists who desired the entrance of Sweden into the war. The Young Socialists sponsored the Peace Congress of February, 1916, and when their leader, Höglund, and others were jailed by the authorities, the Young Socialists continued an energetic protest campaign through their journal, *Politiken*. In May, 1916, three members of Parliament who supported Höglund withdrew from the Parliamentary group. This marked the beginning of the split which ended in May, 1917, with the creation of a new Left Socialist Party.[62]

The Youth also led the revolt in Norway. Through their organ, *Klasse-Kampen,* they conducted a vigorous campaign of propaganda and reprinted the pamphlets of Lenin and Zinoviev. Under pressure from this group the party leadership declared its sympathy with the principles proclaimed by the Zimmerwald and Kienthal congresses, though not formally joining in the Zimmerwald organization.[63]

[61] Jaroslawski, *op. cit.*, 57ff.
[62] Lenin, *Sämtliche Werke*, XIX, 594.
[63] *Ibid.*, 596.

In Denmark it was the Youth Group again which attempted to give the Socialist movement a revolutionary turn. At the Party Congress of October 1, 1916, they opposed, though unsuccessfully, the participation of Stauning, the Socialist leader, in a coalition ministry. Led by Trier and Sundbo, the Left conducted an active campaign of propaganda. In Holland, the Tribunists took a Left position. Their leaders were Roland-Holst and Anton Pannekoek.

The Zimmerwald Left formed a strong group in the Swiss Social Democracy under the leadership of Fritz Platten. This group worked in close collaboration with the large colony of Russian exiles led by Lenin and Zinoviev. At the conference of the Social Democracy held in Zurich on February 11, 1917, the Left won a decisive victory.[64] There was even the beginning of a Left tendency in the United States, represented by a portion of the Socialist-Labor Party and the more extreme Left Socialists. *The Internationalist*, the organ of the Socialist Propaganda League, which began to appear in January, 1917, echoed the views of this group.

The work of coordinating, uniting and directing the activities of the Zimmerwald Left fell largely to the Bureau composed of Lenin, Zinoviev and Radek. In November, 1915, after the first Zimmerwald Conference, the *Internationale Flugblätter* which contained the manifestoes and resolutions of the Zimmerwald Left, made its appearance, and in translation these documents were broadcast throughout the Socialist world. In January, 1916, a more theoretical organ—*Vorboten*—made its appearance and served as an open forum for the discussion of the program of the Left.

Under the direction of the Bureau the work of organizing the revolutionary elements proceeded with great vigor. The International Youth Organization and its organ—*Jugend Internationale*—which opened its columns to Lenin, Zinoviev, Radek and other representatives of the Left, played a significant rôle as the activity of the Socialist Youth in the Scandinavian countries demonstrated.[65] Papers in various lands helped to disseminate the gospel.[66]

[64] *Ibid.*, 595.
[65] Schuller, *op. cit.*, I, 120-152.
[66] Lenin, *Sämtliche Werke*, XIX, 592. These other papers in Germany included *Lichtstrahlen, Spartakus, Arbeiter Politik, Kampf,* the *Bremer Bürger-Zeitung,* and *Volksfreund,* and a host of pamphlets including the famous Spartacist letters. Outside of Russia the Bolsheviks edited *Sotzial-Demokrat, Sbornik Sotzial-Demokrata,* and the *Kommunist,* copies of which were regularly smuggled into the country. The Swiss journals included *La Sentinelle, La Voix des Jeunes,* and *Freie Jugend.* In Sweden *Politiken* and *Stormklockan* helped to stir unrest. *Die Tribune* helped to

The articles of Lenin and Zinoviev on Socialists and the war were translated into German, French and Norwegian and were widely read among the Left. Switzerland was transformed into a miniature revolutionary printing press, and a steady stream of Left wing propaganda poured over the borders into Germany, and France, to be distributed to every part of the country.

Lenin, who even at this early date was the directing genius of this network of propaganda, sent special emissaries to whip up the fighting spirit of the Left. The Bolshevik colonies which were dispersed in various parts of Europe were used as avenues of communication. Karl Radek took a leading rôle in linking Lenin with German and Polish comrades. Litvinov and Chicherin operated in London; Inessa Armand in Paris. Bukharin and Piatakov established headquarters in Stockholm; Alexandra Kollontai and Shlyapnikov kept in touch with the Norwegian Left. Later Bukharin and Kollontai journeyed to the United States where they continued their activity.[67]

To the Bolsheviks in the Scandinavian countries fell the heaviest responsibility. They not only collaborated with local revolutionaries, but they served also as a link between Lenin and the Bolshevik organization in Russia. They smuggled letters and propaganda over the border of Finland and tried to keep Lenin completely informed of developments in Russia. To read the letters of Lenin of this period couched because of the censorship in the Æsopian language of pseudonyms and fabulous countries is to appreciate the difficulties which were faced and to marvel at the ingenuity with which they were evaded.[68]

The effort of Lenin to coordinate the activities of the Zimmerwald Left and to weld the disparate groups into a fighting revolutionary organization with a common program was not a complete success. Lenin's only effective instrument of control was his power of persuasion, and that weapon did not suffice. The chief bone of contention was the attitude to be adopted toward the majority Zimmerwaldians or Centrists. Should the Left break with this group or should it continue to work side by side with it? At Zimmerwald and Kienthal the Left had justified its cooperation with the majority Zimmerwaldians on the ground that while

---

spread Left propaganda in Holland; *Klassenkampen* served Norway. *Gazeta Robotnicza* was smuggled into Poland. *The Internationalist* was published in the United States.

[67] See extracts from Lenin's Correspondence, *Works*, XVIII, XIX.

[68] See "Brief an Schlyapnikov," Lenin, *Sämtliche Werke*, XIX, 341-345.

the majority did not go as far as the Left, at least both groups were going in the same general direction. It was the hope of the Left that the majority Zimmerwaldians would become permeated with a revolutionary ideology in time.

This expectation seemed doomed to disappointment. While the Left could not but be pleased by the party split in Germany and the signs of an approaching scission in France and other countries, the pleasure was mixed with some misgivings. It was becoming increasingly evident that the Haase-Kautsky-Ledebour group in Germany and the Longuet-Pressemane-Merrheim-Bourderon group in France and other countries had no revolutionary orientation, that while they desired peace, they were not ready to precipitate a class war.

Should the Left continue to work in close cooperation with these groups? The Bolsheviks answered in the negative, and were as critical of pacifists as of "patriotic" Socialists. In Germany, however, the Spartacists maintained a united fighting front with the Kautsky-Ledebour group. The French Revolutionary Socialists worked side by side in the Committee for the Resumption of International Relations with Merrheim and his associates.

For Lenin such a permanent union was unbearable. It was not the path toward the Third International. The Zimmerwald majority which he had hoped to convert to revolutionary Socialism had failed him. In a letter to Mme. Kollontai of March 3, 1916, he confessed his disappointment with the Zimmerwald majority.[69] For Lenin it was already apparent that the Left would have to purge itself of all non-revolutionary connections, that a break with chauvinist Socialists was not enough, that even the Zimmerwald movement would have to split. The Spartacists were not yet convinced of the necessity for this break. They were still willing to give the Center a qualified support in its contest with the majority Socialists. Thus even within the ranks of the Left Zimmerwaldians all was not unity. A clear-cut policy had not yet emerged. Only one thing was certain—fundamental differences of principle separated

---

[69] *Ibid.* 510. "Denn 'Zimmerwald' hat offensichtlich bankrott gemacht, und ein guter Name dient jetzt wieder zur Verhüllung von Fäulnis! Die Zimmerwalder Mehrheit—als da sind Turati und Co., Kautsky mit Ledebour, Merrheim—ist geschlossen in das Lager des in Kienthal so feierlich (und so nutzlos!) verdammten Sozialpacifismus übergegangen. Das Manifest Kautsky's und Co. vom 7 Januar 1917, eine Reihe von Resolutionen der italienischen sozialistischen Partei, die Resolutionen Merrheim, Jouhaux und Longuet-Bourderon . . .—ist das nicht der bankrott Zimmerwalde?"

the Center and the Left, and any pooling of strength was founded on expediency rather than similarity of program.

The situation in the international Socialist movement in the spring of 1917 was full of perplexity and confusion. It was still impossible to predict with any degree of inevitability the emergence of the Third International. Yet certain drifts and tendencies were apparent which made that a reasonable outlook. The International Socialist Bureau showed only the feeblest signs of life. Every attempt to arouse it into activity met the determined, if weakening resistance of the French. There were numerous evidences of disintegration in the Socialist parties which constituted the staunchest support of the old International. The German Party had split; the French Party was drifting toward a split. Similar tendencies were apparent in Sweden and other neutral countries. The Independent Labour Party of Great Britain, the Italian Socialist Party and other Centrist groups criticized the inactivity of the Bureau severely.

On the other hand, there were signs that the Bureau might still emerge from the crisis whole. Though the last-mentioned parties called for the immediate reconstitution of the old International, they still waited more or less patiently for the Bureau to take action and were unwilling to sponsor a break. The fact that the French minority was rapidly growing seemed to indicate that the way would soon be clear for a full meeting of the Bureau and for the resulting trial of strength between Left and Right for the support of the Center.

To the Zimmerwald Left the last was sad music. Their hopes rested on the expectation that the Center would be driven to adopt a revolutionary position and help in the formation of the new International. Zimmerwald and Kienthal had convinced them that the tide of events ran their way. The events after Kienthal seemed to demonstrate that the Center was not prepared to go the full distance of a new International until every possibility of reviving the old one was exhausted.

Meanwhile the Zimmerwald Left went on with its plan of consolidating the scattered revolutionary groups into a united organization. Cooperation with the Center was not wholly abandoned. The entrance of the Spartacists into the Independent Social-Democratic Party of Germany represented the most conspicuous example of the continuation of the Entente. At the same time there was an increasing conviction among the leaders of the Left—particularly Lenin—that no real compromise was possible, that all hopes of a union with the Center were doomed to disappointment, and that the Third International would emerge only from the fighting group of revolutionaries who formed the Zimmerwald Left.

In the spring of 1917 the Zimmerwald Left still constituted a small and obscure minority. It remained for the Russian Revolution to lift them to the front page of history. Like a catalytic agent in muddy waters, the Revolution precipitated a new realignment of forces which upset all calculations and had its reverberations in the inner history of every Socialist party of the world.

CHAPTER VII

STOCKHOLM

The Russian Revolution of March, 1917, galvanized Socialists into action. The important rôle which the Russian Socialists played in the first revolution was a signal for Socialists in other countries to assume the aggressive and give expression to their collective will for peace. The Russian Revolution provided an impetus to the movement for an international Socialist conference which even the most patriotic Socialists could not afford to disregard.

In Socialist ranks the Russian Revolution aroused tremendous enthusiasm. The reaction of the Independent Labour Party of Great Britain was typical. The National Council of the Party and the Party members in Parliament joined in a resolution of congratulation.[1]

The impact of the Russian Revolution was also felt in Germany.[2] The majority Socialists who had declared a truce with the government for the duration of the war took on a more militant tone. The collapse of the old régime in Russia weakened the hand of the German bureaucracy and Junkerdom. The victory of the Revolution in Russia reinforced the demand for democratic reform in Germany. For the first time the threat of a German revolution loomed large if the popular clamor were disregarded. At the same time the military found some comfort in Russian events. The disorganization of the Russian army made the burden of warfare easier. The war weariness of which the Revolution was a partial expression raised the hope in Germany that Russia would be ripe for the negotiation of a separate peace, or in any event, would exert its influence on the allies to obtain peace on terms more favorable to Germany than those to which the old Russian régime had been willing to consent.[3]

[1] *Labour Leader*, April 5, 1917. "To their fellow Socialists," the Independent Labourites sent "their warm and wholehearted congratulations on the magnificent achievement of the Russian people in their long struggle against serfdom, official tyranny, and persecution, and in favor of democracy and political liberty. It expresses the strong conviction that the revolution in Russia and the overthrow of despotic Czarism will be a great liberating force throughout Europe, and will everywhere help forward the cause of the people and of Socialists and of international solidarity, and will hasten the coming of a peace based, not on the dominance of militarists and of diplomats but on democracy and justice."

[2] Scheidemann, *Memoirs*, I.

[3] *Ibid.*, 366ff.

The foreign offices of the Allied Powers viewed the Russian Revolution with mingled feelings. There was some satisfaction in the knowledge that a democratic Russia made a more acceptable ally against the "militarist Junkerdom" of the Central Powers and provided a more reasonable basis for the participation of the United States in the war "to make the world safe for democracy." There was the hope that the citizens of a free Russia would be stirred into patriotic fervor, would throw off their apathy and repel the invader from the land which had become theirs in a new sense. Yet there was also misgiving in the chancellories. Would the new government continue to be bound by the treaty obligations of the old? Had the accumulated discontent of the masses reached such a pitch that the government would be forced to enter into negotiations for a separate peace with Germany or bring pressure to bear on the Allies to obtain peace at any price? The knowledge that the Soviet of Soldiers' and Workers' Deputies which was dominated by Socialists exercised a strong influence on the policy of the Provisional Government only increased these misgivings. The policy of the Allied diplomats was directed toward keeping Russia in the war and the Eastern front intact, if possible with secret treaty obligations unchanged, but if necessary with such modifications of war aims as the Russian situation made absolutely indispensable.[4] To secure this object it was essential to obtain the support of the Socialists who controlled the Soviets as well as the formal approval of the Provisional Government. The regular diplomats were unequal to the task. The delicate work of convincing the Russian Socialists of the necessity of remaining in the war was therefore entrusted to patriotic Socialists from the various Allied countries who arrived in Russia soon after the Revolution, ostensibly to bring greetings to their Socialist comrades.

Meanwhile, among the Socialist masses on both sides of the battlefield the Russian Revolution released the yearning for peace which had been suppressed through two and one-half years of continued bloodshed. The call for peace came with a vigor that could not be denied. The victory of the Russian masses over their government forced the conviction that peace would only come by a direct appeal by Socialists to the people over the heads of the governments. The spontaneous demand for an end of the war reinforced by the success of the Russian Revolution raised

[4] See George Buchanan, *My Mission to Russia and Other Diplomatic Memories,* Boston, 1923. (2 vols.) II, 142ff. Also, Maurice Paléologue, *An Ambassador's Memoirs,* London, 1925, (3 vols.) III, 218ff.

hopes that the time at last was ripe for a successful international conference of Socialists of all shades and complexions.

The movement for an international conference came from three
sources—the Zimmerwaldians, a committee of neutral Socialists identified with the International Socialist Bureau, and the Petrograd Soviet.
The latter two organizations finally merged in the call for a conference
at Stockholm.[5]

The convocation of an international Socialist conference by the Bureau
of the Second International had been discussed ever since the beginning
of the war, but without result. At the second conference of neutral
Socialists at The Hague, July 31, 1916, Troelstra of Holland, Branting
of Sweden and A. Lee of the United States had declared themselves in
favor of a meeting of the full Bureau. But the time was not yet judged
opportune. The problem at the beginning of 1917 still remained that of
conquering the resistance of those Socialists who were still not convinced
of the necessity and utility of a general conference. The Russian Revolution supplied the drive. Socialists regained confidence in themselves. At
last the time seemed ripe for a determined effort to break down the
opposition of French and Belgian majority Socialists.

The Danish Socialists took the initiative.[6] At the beginning of April,
Stauning, one of the leaders of the Danish Socialists, wrote the Executive
of the International Socialist Bureau that if the Executive were not willing to act or could not act, an international conference of Socialists would
take place without them. The members of the Dutch delegation on receiving this letter decided to go to Stockholm, acting, however, not as
members of the Executive Committee of the International Socialist
Bureau, but as representatives of the Dutch Socialists. Huysmans, the
secretary of the International, shipped as a steward on a Dutch boat
bound for Stockholm and set up headquarters there. Immediately,
Branting, the Swedish Socialist, insisted that the convoking of the full
conference should not be left to the sole initiative of the Dutch delegation. It was decided to organize a committee composed of Dutch and
Scandinavian Socialists with which the Secretariat of the International
Socialist Bureau would collaborate.

The real reason for this broadening of the organizational base of the

---

[5] The story of the relations of the Zimmerwald organization to the proposed Stockholm conference will be reserved for the next chapter. Here attention will center
on the fate of the conference summoned by neutral Socialists and the Petrograd Soviet.

[6] Emile Vandervelde, *Three Aspects of the Russian Revolution*, London, 1918,
210-211.

conference was to avoid all suggestion of partiality. Already the more vehemently nationalistic press of both the Allies and the Central Powers denounced the organizers of the Stockholm conference as tools of the enemy.[7] The Allies charged the conference was German-inspired because of the alleged pro-German sympathies of Troelstra, leader of the Dutch Socialists. The Germans claimed that it was an Allied venture because of Branting's pro-Entente views. The inclusion of both elements helped to deflate criticism on this score.

On April 22, 1917, Camille Huysmans, the secretary of the Bureau issued the following invitation:

> The Dutch delegation of the Internationalist Socialist Bureau charges me to announce to you that it has taken the initiative, in accord with numerous sections, in the convocation at Stockholm on May 15 and the days following of an international conference of all affiliated sections. . . .[8]

On May 3, the Dutch-Scandinavian Committee was organized to prepare for the conference.[9]

After an unofficial canvassing of opinion neutral Socialists recognized that the convening of an international conference was still far more difficult than anyone had imagined. The National Council of the French Socialist Party on receiving Huysmans' telegram announcing the convocation of an international conference for May 15 refused to recognize the right of the Dutch delegation to speak in the name of the International, though it held out hope for a resumption of international relations when German Socialists would repudiate their imperialist aims.[10] The Belgian Socialists, speaking through Vandervelde and Louis de Brouckère said that they considered it "impossible to participate in a plenary assembly with Socialists who supported the imperialistic policies of the Central Powers."[11] The British Labour Party still showed no signs of reversing the stand taken at the Party Convention of Bristol.

Faced with opposition from these quarters, the neutral Socialists decided that the collaboration of Russian Socialists was necessary to cause

---

[7] *Comité Organisateur de la Conférence Socialiste Internationale de Stockholm (Documents)*, Stockholm, 1918, iv. (Hereafter referred to as *Comité Organisateur.*)

[8] *Ibid.*, viii.

[9] *Ibid.*, ix. Its composition was as follows: Netherlands—Troelstra, Albarda, Van Kol (alternates Vliegen and Wibaut); Sweden—Branting, Moller and Soderberg; Denmark—Stauning (alternate Bang), Vidnes; the Secretariat—Huysmans and Engberg.

[10] *Pendant la Guerre*, text, 162.

[11] *Comité Organisateur*, ix.

French, Belgian and English Socialists to retract their objections. From that moment the Dutch and Scandinavian Socialists directed their efforts toward attracting the Russian Socialists into playing an active rôle in the organization of the proposed international conference.[12]

Russia now became the focal point of interest. Borgbjerg, member of the Danish Social-Democratic Party, arrived in Petrograd in April, 1917, and transmitted an invitation to the Petrograd Soviet to send representatives to the international conference planned for Stockholm.[13] Borgbjerg's mission to Russia was not solely devoted to the cause of the international conference. Before leaving for Russia, he met with Scheidemann and Ebert, German majority Socialists, who reported that Stockholm represented the great hope for peace in Germany.[14] Borgbjerg was instructed to tell the Russians that "we wish for peace without compulsion." To demonstrate the sincerity of Germany's willingness to negotiate a separate peace, Scheidemann reported in his *Memoirs,* "I asked Borgbjerg and strictly authorized him to tell the Russians that no offensive from the German side would be undertaken against Russia."[15] These remarks were reported by Borgbjerg to the Petrograd Soviet.

When asked "Is the Chancellor in agreement with what Scheidemann and his colleagues have told you?" he replied, "I cannot say but I think so." Though these gestures toward a separate peace were without immediate results, the proposal for an international conference was received favorably, and Borgbjerg was told,

Your mission has succeeded. The Workers' and Soldiers' Council has decided to issue invitations to a conference. It will be easier for the English and French to take part, and a clashing with the other conference is then out of the question.[16]

Meanwhile some of the Allied nations decided to send Socialist missions to Russia in order to rally the Russian Socialists to the support of the war. The missions were entrusted to patriotic Socialists. Great Britain sent two Labour Party members, O'Grady and Thorne, and later Arthur Henderson, the Labour member of the War Cabinet. France dispatched three Socialist deputies, Cachin, Lafont and Montet, and later followed these with Albert Thomas, the Socialist Minister of Muni-

[12] *Ibid.*
[13] Lenin, *Works,* XX, Part One, 377.
[14] Scheidemann, *Memoirs,* I, 362ff.
[15] *Ibid.,* 363.
[16] *Ibid.,* 367.

tions. Belgium sent Emile Vandervelde who was accompanied by Louis de Brouckère and Henri DeMan. Charles Edward Russell, the American Socialist, accompanied the Root mission to Russia. These missions had important if unintended effects on the fate of the Stockholm Conference.

The primary object was not concealed. Mr. Bonar Law on being interpellated as to the reason for the journey of Thorne and O'Grady to Russia answered "These gentlemen are going with the one object of encouraging, so far as they can, the present Russian government in the prosecution of the war."[17] Lord Robert Cecil in a telegram to Buchanan, the British ambassador to Russia, informed the latter that the War Cabinet was sending Henderson to create a more favorable attitude among Russian Socialists toward the War and to rectify the false impression inculcated in Russia on Allied war aims.[18] The three French Socialist deputies told the French ambassador that their main anxiety was to know "whether Russia is capable of continuing in the war and if we can still rely on her for an effort which will enable us to secure our terms of peace."[19] Vandervelde revealed that the Belgians desired

(1) to join our efforts to those of Thomas, Henderson, and other Socialists from the Allied countries against the tendency which seemed to exist in certain circles in favor of either a separate peace or of bringing pressure to bear on the Allies to obtain peace at any price, (2) to bring before our Russian comrades the case of Belgium and the situation of the Belgian workmen, to appeal to their solidarity in this struggle that we are carrying on against German imperialism, (3) to take up a definite attitude on the subject of the proposed conference at Stockholm.[20]

From the very beginning a fundamental difference in outlook separated the Allied and Russian Socialists. The Allied Socialists were patriotic and anxious to see the war to a victorious conclusion. The majority of the Russian Socialists had participated in the Zimmerwald movements. Those who were not committed to a revolutionary class war stood on the manifesto of the Petrograd Soviet of March 27, that "the time had come to begin a resolute struggle with the predatory aspirations of the governments of all countries, the time had come for the peoples to take the matter of war and peace into their own hands."[21] Under pressure from the Socialists the Provisional Government had been forced

[17] *Labour Leader,* April 12, 1917.
[18] Buchanan, *op. cit.*, II, 142-143.
[19] Paléologue, *op. cit.*, III, 297.
[20] Vandervelde, *op. cit.*, 199.
[21] Lenin, *Works,* XX, Part One, 362.

(March 9) to re-define the aim of the war as "not the domination over other peoples, not the rape of their national territory, not the violent conquest of foreign territories, but the establishment of a permanent peace on the basis of the right of self-determination of peoples."[22]

When, therefore, the Allied Socialists came to whip up the fighting spirit of the Russian Socialists, they received a frigid reception. "Instead of being received as friends," reported Cachin, "we were put through a regular cross-examination and in such a tone that I could see the moment coming when we should be obliged to retire."[23] The scarcely concealed contempt of the Russian Socialists for their erstwhile comrades began to work a subtle transformation in the attitude of the latter. Cachin and his fellow Socialists came to the conclusion that it would be necessary to revise the peace terms in order to adapt them to the ideas of the Russian democracy and to galvanize the Russian Socialists into action. It would be necessary "to throw out ballast."[24] Cachin now informed the Russians that the French Socialists instead of demanding the unconditional restoration of Alsace-Lorraine to France were willing to subject its fate to a plebiscite in accordance with the principle of the self-determination of peoples.

The Allied Socialists were captured by the revolutionary milieu. They had come to do the convincing. They remained to be convinced. Especially was this evident in the reception given to the proposal for an international socialist conference. The opposition which had heralded the conference while under neutral sponsorship began to melt when the Russian Socialists took up the idea.

On May 15 the Executive Committee of the Petrograd Soviet issued an appeal "To the Socialists of all countries." After denouncing the war as inspired by the imperialists of all countries, the Russian Revolution is hailed not only as a national revolution but as the first stage of the international revolution that will put an end to the war. The appeal sounds the call for a

general peace on a basis which is acceptable to the toilers of all countries who do not want conquests, do not strive for plunder, and are equally interested in the free expression of the will of all peoples and in the destruction of the power of international imperialism . . . the program of peace without annexations and indemnities on the basis of self-determination of peoples.

[22] *Ibid.*, 366-367.
[23] Reported in Paléologue, *op. cit.*, III, 300.
[24] *Ibid.*, 299.

To secure this end

the Petrograd Soviet of Workers' and Soldiers' Deputies has decided to take the initiative in calling an international conference of all Socialist parties and fractions of all countries . . . not a single fraction of the proletariat must fail to participate in the common struggle for peace. . . . Proletarians of all countries, unite![25]

This appeal was issued independently of the action of the Dutch-Scandinavian Committee, though the two movements later merged.

The first reaction of the Allied Socialists in Russia to the proposal of the Soviets' was one of opposition. Albert Thomas, Vandervelde, and Arthur Henderson—the three most important Allied representatives in Russia, announced their joint refusal to take part in the conference.

More than ever are we convinced that a meeting to which would be admitted those who supported the present policy of the majority Socialists in the Central Empires would be useless and dangerous; useless because such a meeting of contrary views could not end in action; dangerous because it would give rise to misunderstandings and would lead the working and peasant classes to think that a just and durable peace is possible before aggressive imperialism is destroyed. As long as by a public declaration made without reticence or reservation in their own country on the responsibility of their own working classes, the Socialists of all nations interested have not renounced their associations with an aggressive imperialism we hold that an international Socialist conference would be impossible.[26]

If the object of the Allied Socialists in issuing this proclamation was to nip the proposed conference in the bud, the effort proved a failure. As the Russian Socialists continued to make preparations for the conclave, the Allied Socialists felt called upon to revise their attitude. As Vandervelde put it,

Although many Socialists in France and Great Britain judged this conference to be undesirable, it had in certain diplomats open partisans especially preoccupied with humoring the Russians. They were afraid of their meeting with the Germans only. The opinion was expressed that Socialists of the Allied countries ought also to attend this conference to plead energetically the cause of the Western democracies.[27]

In addition to this practical motive, other less tangible but pervasive influences were at work. The war weariness of the Russian masses and the peace hunger of the Russian Socialists infected the Allied Socialists

[25] Lenin, *Works*, XX, Part One, 315.
[26] Vandervelde, *op. cit.*, 217.
[27] *Ibid.*, 215-216.

and revived their socialist faith. Albert Thomas, reported Paléologue, was caught up in the contagion of the Russian Revolution.[28] The more staid Mr. Henderson responded to the pressure of the demand for Stockholm and bowed to the inevitable.[29] Montet, one of the French Socialist deputies, journeying back to France with Cachin and Paléologue, the French ambassador, revealed the soul searching which his experience in Russia had entailed in his conversation with Paléologue:

> Fundamentally, the Russian Revolution is right. It is not so much a political as an international revolution. The bourgeois, capitalist, and imperialist classes have plunged the world into a frightful crisis they are now unable to overcome. Peace can only be brought about in accordance with the principles of the Internationale. I have come to a very clear conclusion. I've been thinking about it all night: The French Socialists must go to the Stockholm conference to summon a full assembly of the International and draw up the general scheme of peace terms.[30]

The members of the Allied Socialist missions to Russia thus became an important factor in the Stockholm movement. They had come to dissuade the Russian Socialists from participating in conferences with the Socialists of the Central Powers. They remained to be converted to the ideas of their Russian comrades. They had tapped the feelings of the Russian masses, and considerations of expediency joined with more idealistic motives in dictating participation in a general international conference. They returned to their native lands to spread the gospel of Stockholm.

Meanwhile, preparations for the Stockholm conference continued. While the Russian Socialists were influencing the French and English representatives in Russia to withdraw their objections, the neutral committee used the interval to prepare for the general conference. May 15, the suggested date, seemed premature. The committee decided that be-

---

[28] Paléologue, *op. cit.*, III, 309.

[29] He explained his position in a Parliamentary debate: "It seems to me that there are two positions we [British Socialists] can take up. The one is, if we conclude that the conference is inevitable—a conclusion that I have already reached—we can say we will remain away, that we will not even go to state the British case. That is a perfectly plain understandable position. But as we have always claimed we have nothing to fear by a clear definite frank statement of the position in which we stand, the aims for which we entered the War, and for which we are continuing the War, it seems to me that at the close of a Conference consisting of neutrals and enemy countries only, the position of Great Britain and France if they were not represented, would be very seriously prejudiced." (August 1.) See *Official Report Fifth Series, Parliamentary Debates Commons,* 1917. Vol. XCVI, July 16-August 3, 2195.

[30] Paléologue, *op. cit.*, III, 343.

fore a general conference could be gathered together, it was necessary to hold a series of preliminary conferences with the various delegations to enable them to define their views. A communiqué was issued stipulating that the delegations which accepted the idea of separate conferences would preserve their complete freedom as to participation in a general conference.[31] The conference was postponed until June 10 to enable the series of conferences to take place.

Coincidentally, the Soviet on its own volition determined on May 9 to call for an international conference in a neutral country.[32] Thus two parallel movements were at work to obtain an international conference, and it became necessary to adjust and correlate them. The Dutch-Scandinavian Committee declared itself anxious to confer on the subject with Russian delegates who had just arrived at Stockholm. They met. May 10, and organized their work the next day. Three decisions were taken.[33] First, a series of dates were fixed for the visits of the separate delegations. Second, the text of the questionnaire to be submitted to the various delegations was agreed upon. Third, on May 18, a manifesto was issued.[34] This manifesto explained the intentions of the committee.[35] It pointed out that the Stockholm conference had been organized to reestablish the International and to create through it the foundations of a general peace. It set forth the aim of the preliminary conferences as that of defining with more precision the attitude of the separate parties, and it attempted to placate the hesitating by affirming that in coming to Stockholm they undertook no commitments to participate in the general conference.

While the Dutch-Scandinavian Committee was meeting in Stockholm, Vliegen departed on a mission to Paris.[36] He arrived May 11, and had several interviews with French Socialists in order to explain the purpose of the proposed conference. On May 6, the French minority had held a conference which had decided almost unanimously to reject the view of the majority and to send a minority delegation to Stockholm.[37]

[31] *Comité Organisateur* x.
[32] Lenin, *Works*, XX, Part Two, 315.
[33] *Comité Organisateur* x.
[34] The questionnaire was arranged under the following heads: I. Terms of peace. II. Principles of International Relations. III. Practical Realization of these Aims. IV. Action of the International and of Democracy. V. General Socialist Conference under the last of which was embraced the readiness to take part in a general conference.
[35] *Comité Organisateur* xii.
[36] *Ibid.*
[37] *Labour Leader,* May 10, 1917.

Vliegen's visit represented an effort to swing the majority over to the minority position.

On May 18, the Organization Committee of the Russian Social-Democratic Party (Menshevik) took steps to ally itself with the proposed conference.[38] With the promise of collaboration from the Menshevik section of the Russian Social Democracy assured, at least one section of the Russian socialist movement was committeed to the success of the Stockholm conference.

The possibility of a full meeting at Stockholm now depended on two factors: (1) the formal adhesion of the majority Socialists of France and the Labour Party of Great Britain; (2) the granting of passports to the delegates by the respective governments. Of the two, the second proved the chief stumbling block. The capitulation of British and French Socialists was already foreshadowed by the changed outlook of the Allied Socialist leaders who had visited Russia.

The first skirmish came in France. The National Council of the French Socialists assembled on Sunday, May 27, to determine its attitude toward the proposed conferences. The account of the correspondent of the *Manchester Guardian* in the issue of June 2, 1917, captures the drama of the situation:

When the council met . . . the two sections of the party held to their old positions. The minority led by Jean Longuet, Pressemane, etc., advocated participation in the Stockholm conference and the majority led by M. Renaudel, Sembat, Guesde, etc., opposed any international gathering during the war. But on Sunday afternoon the council had a dramatic surprise. Mm. Marcel Cachin and Montet who arrived from Petrograd only Sunday morning appeared quite unexpectedly at the council. . . . Mm. Cachin and Montet who before they went to Petrograd were among the staunchest opponents of the revival of the International during the war have returned convinced 'minoritaires.' Their speeches on Sunday afternoon made a profound impression on the council and shattered the unity of the 'majority.' Their speeches were received with enthusiastic applause by the minority, but the majority was at a loss how to act. The Council adjourned at 7 P.M. without arriving at any decision . . . finally a resolution that the question of Alsace-Lorraine could only be settled rightly by plebiscite of people was accepted, and the minority at once presented a motion accepting both the invitation to Stockholm and that of the Russian Socialists. Renaudel swung over and the resolution was carried unanimously.

While the council was sitting the Place de la République was a scene of great animation. A crowd began to collect early in the afternoon . . . and gradually increased until at about 6 P.M. it numbered several thousands. As time went

[38] *Comité Organisateur* xvi. The following telegram was dispatched to the Dutch-Scandinavian Committee:

on the crowd became impatient and raised cries of "Go to Stockholm; down with the War!" . . . At about 7 P.M. we heard in the room where the council was sitting a distant refrain:

> C'est la lutte finale
> Groupons nous—et demain
> L'Internationale
> Sera le genre humain.

The crowd was singing the Internationale; it was the first time that it had been sung in the sreets of Paris since the war. During the suspension Mm. Longuet, Brizon, and Rappaport went down and addressed the crowd. Longuet said: "We are going to Stockholm to make peace," and the declaration was received with tremendous cheers.[39]

The party was won over, and mass enthusiasm was strong, but the voice of the government was yet to be heard on the question of granting passports to Socialist delegates to Stockholm. The question of the passports agitated and divided the Foreign Offices of the Allied Powers even before the about-face of the French Socialist Party. In England, Lloyd George inclined to the opinion that English Socialists of every shade of opinion ought to be allowed to go to Stockholm.[40] He feared that if the Allied cause were not represented at Stockholm, a bad impression would be produced on the Russian Socialists and the latter would respond more readily to the overtures of the Germans; moreover, he hoped that a direct meeting between Allied and German Socialists might result in inserting a wedge between the German Socialists and their government by pointing out that the absolutist governments of the Central Powers were the greatest obstacle to peace. These considerations were conveyed to Ribot, French Foreign Minister, by Lloyd George at a private meeting in the

---

"The organization committee of the Social Democratic party of Russia greets the Socialist parties of neutral countries who have taken the initiative in convoking an international Socialist conference at Stockholm, and we are all ready to participate and collaborate energetically toward its success. It asks you to transmit immediately by telegram the following address to all Socialist parties:

"The most pressing task of the moment is the convocation without delay of an international Socialist conference where all Socialist parties, majority and minority, will be represented. This conference must set forth a Socialist program for peace as well as an international campaign plan to realize this Socialist peace. To attain this end, the organization committee asks you to take the necessary steps to assure that your party will be represented."

[39] *Manchester Guardian,* June 2, 1917; for text of resolution favoring adherence to Stockholm see *Pendant la Guerre,* 167.

[40] Alexandre Ribot, *Lettres à Un Ami—Souvenirs de ma Vie Politique,* Paris, 1924, 257-258.

last days of May, but Ribot reserved the decision of the French government until it was faced with the necessity of taking action.[41]

The determination of the French Socialists to go to Stockholm forced the Foreign Office to define its attitude. On May 31, the National Council of the French Socialist Party named Longuet and Renaudel to go to Petrograd to consult with the Soviet on the conditions of the projected conference. They were also instructed to stop in Stockholm to talk with Branting and the Dutch-Scandinavian Committee.[42] The applications of Longuet and Renaudel for passports raised the problem in an acute form. To Ribot the issue presented itself in such a fashion that if the French government granted the passports, it would be held responsible for what would be decided at Stockholm.[43] Ribot was not prepared to accept the terms of peace which would be dictated by an international conference of Socialists, and he therefore directed his efforts toward preventing that gathering from meeting. The Council of Ministers decided unanimously that the passports should be refused. The decision was announced in the Chamber of Deputies on June 1, and was approved by a large majority.[44] But the question was not buried, and the French Socialists continued to make strenuous efforts to convert Ribot to their view.

On the same day that Ribot announced the refusal of passports, the Dutch-Scandinavian Committee launched another appeal to the socialist parties and trade-unions of the world to assemble at the international conference at Stockholm.[45] The date of the conference was again postponed to July 8. Meanwhile the series of separate conferences was being held at Stockholm. By the beginning of June, delegations had come from Bosnia, Bulgaria, Finland, German Austria, and Hungary. The German majority Social-Democrats came a few days later. The full list of dates and delegates is found below.[46]

[41] *Ibid.*, 259.
[42] *Pendant la Guerre,* (for decision of C. A. P. May 31, 1917) 169.
[43] Ribot, *op. cit.,* 261.
[44] *Ibid.*
[45] *Comité Organisateur* xviii.
[46] A list of the visits of the more important delegations:
  May 19—Bosnia—Glumac and Markie.
  May 21, 22—Bulgaria (Broad Socialists)—J. Sakasoff, K. Pastouchoff; N. Sakaroff; P. Djidoff; I. Ianuloff; A. Zankov.
  May 23, 24—Finland—K. Wiik; I. Sirola.
  May 25, 26—German Austria—Dr. V. Adler; Ellenbogen; Renner; Hartmann; Seitz; Hueber.
  Bohemian Centralists—V. Stein; E. Burian.

The British government granted passports to MacDonald, Jowett and Fairchild, who had been invited to Russia by the Soviets, but the action of the Seamen's Union prevented them from undertaking the journey.[47] On the instruction of Union officials, the seamen refused to man the vessels on the ground that MacDonald and his companions in their statement of war aims at the Leeds Conference of Socialists had not given sufficient recognition to the seamen's demands for indemnity for sailors drowned or maimed by submarines or mines.

The French delegation was delayed by the refusal of passports. The National Council of the French Socialist Party addressed a letter to the Soviet—June 25, 1917—in which it suggested another postponement, on the ground that the tentative date—July 8—did not allow an opportunity for preliminary discussion between French and Russian Socialists.[48] The National Council and the Socialist Parliamentary group named a commission consisting of Cachin, Longuet, Mistral, Montet, Renaudel, Valiers, and later Thomas and Louis Dubreuil. This commission sent three telegrams—one to the Soviet in care of the London Russian Embassy, asking the Soviet delegates to come to Paris for an interview, the second to the Labour Party at London asking that the English Labour Party delegates accompany the Russians to Paris, and the third to Huysmans and Branting at Stockholm insisting that the mode of representation be based on the rules of the International Socialist Bureau and not on the Berne Zimmerwald Commission.[49]

The Russian delegates arrived for an interview at Stockholm, July 4. As a result of the discussions it was decided on July 11 to replace the

---

May 29, 30—Hungary—L. Weltner; E. Buchinger; D. Bokanyi; E. Garami; S. Jassai; Dr. Kunfi.

June 7-13—German—Social-Democratic Party (Majority)—Ebert; Scheidemann; H. Mueller; Molkenbuhr; Sassenbach; G. Bauer; K. Legien; R. Fischer.

June 20, 21—United States (S.L.P.)—M. Goldfarb; B. Reinstein; D. Davidovitch.

June 22-25—Germany—Independent Social-Democrats—Bernstein; Haase; Herzfeld; Kautsky; Stadthagen; Hofer; Ledebour; Wengels; O. Cohn.

June 30—Belgium—Emile Vandervelde; Louis de Brouckère.

July 4, 6, 9-11—Russia—Axelrod; H. Erlich; J. Goldenberg; M. Panin; W. Rosanoff; N. Rousanoff; A. Smirnov.

July 26—Poland—H. Diemand; I. Daszynski.

Oct. 15, 16.—Serbia—D. Popovitch; T. Katzlerovitch.

[47] *Labour Leader*, June 14, 1917.

[48] *Pendant la Guerre*, Letter of June 25, 1917, 176.

[49] *Ibid.*, 177-178.

Dutch-Scandinavian Committee by a "Comité-Russe-Hollande-Scandi-nave."[50] The Dutch-Scandinavians had performed the useful function of conducting the separate conferences. But the double origin of the call for the general conference was confusing, and it was decided to merge the two in the new committee which was to take the initiative in the second project, the calling of a general conference.[51] The committee yielded to the French demand for postponement of the general confer-ence and in a manifesto of July 11 fixed August 15 as the date.[52] The manifesto also expressly invited trade unions to attend although they had never been excluded in previous invitations. The Russian delegates proved to be especially interested in ways and means to terminate the war, and insisted on the necessity of refusing any collaboration with a govern-ment which was unwilling to indicate its war aims or renounce imperi-alist pretensions. To rally the hesitant, the Russian delegates decided to undertake a circular trip through the Allied countries to complete the work begun in France and Belgium by Wibaut in 1916 and 1917, and Vliegen in France at the beginning of 1917.[53]

The attitude of the British Labour Party toward the proposed con-ference still remained an enigma. The Manchester resolution of Febru-ary, 1917, was hostile to the idea of a general conference, and in the in-tervening months there was no official indication of a change of attitude. As in the case of France, the visit of the British Labour and Socialist Mission to Russia worked a transformation. Arthur Henderson who had just returned from Russia explained the situation to the Executive Com-mittee of the Labour Party on July 3. He argued that opposition to the idea of a general conference could no longer be defended in the light of Russian developments, and he proposed participation in a consultative capacity. The Executive Committee of the Labour Party approved Hen-derson's stand by a vote of 9 to 4, and instructed him to accompany the Soviet delegation to Paris with Wardle and MacDonald for a joint con-ference with the French Socialists.[54]

[50] *Comité Organisateur* xix.
[51] The composition of the committee was as follows:
    Holland—Troelstra, Van Kol, Albardi, with Vliegen and Wibaut as alternates.
    Sweden—Branting, Moller and Soderberg.
    Norway—Vidnes.
    Denmark—Borgbjerg (in place of Stauning) with Mme. Bang as alternate.
    Russia—H. Erlich, J. Goldenberg, W. Rosanoff, Rousanoff, and Smirnov.
See *Ibid.*, xx.
[52] *Ibid.*
[53] *Ibid.*
[54] *Ibid.*, xx-xxi.

On July 29, the British representatives telegraphed the Secretariat at Stockholm that after an interview with the Russian delegation it had been decided that it was advisable to postpone the conference again.[55] This time the date was fixed for August 22. The reason given was that on the initiative of the Executive Committee of the Labour Party the British section of the International had convoked a conference of all Labour and Socialist parties of the Allied countries, and in order to permit the Americans to participate, this conference could not take place before August 8 or 9. This Inter-Allied conference was to be followed by a special conference of the Labour Party which would examine the resolutions of the Inter-Allied conference and the vote of the Executive Committee of the Labour Party to accept the invitation to go to Stockholm.

The National Council of the French Socialist Party met with the English and Russian delegates on July 31, and adopted a set of resolutions regulating the conditions of their participation in the proposed conference. The conferees asked that all organizations affiliated with the International be invited to participate in the conference. "When since the beginning of the war, the organizations have been divided, the minority as well as the majority must be invited, particularly where the minorities are grouped in distinct parties."[56] This represented a strategical move to ensure representation of both wings of the German Socialist movement. The assembled delegates requested another delay in the conference setting the date forward to September 9-16. If practical difficulties stood in the way of an assembly at Stockholm, the transfer of the assembly to Christiania or some other spot was suggested. The conference also decided on the initiative of the English delegates, to hold the preliminary Inter-Allied Socialist conference at London, August 28-29.[57] The organizing committee of the conference replied to these resolutions by expressing a desire to see French and British Socialists accept September 3 as the definitive date for the conference, but this was declared out of the question because of a conflict with the Inter-Allied Socialist Conference of August 28-29, and the British Labour Party Congress of September 9.[58]

While the preparations for the general conference went slowly ahead, the willingness of the Allied governments to grant passports to Socialist delegates to the Stockholm conference still remained a moot question.

[55] *Ibid.*, xxi.
[56] *Pendant la Guerre,* text of resolution, 181ff.
[57] *Ibid.*
[58] *Comité Organisateur* xxii.

Sir George Buchanan, ambassador of Great Britain to Russia, in a dispatch of August 2, reported on the attitude of the Russian Provisional Government:

I have reason to believe that the non-Socialist members of the government would much prefer that the Stockholm conference should not take place for fear that peace talk might have a bad influence on the army. They will not, however, place any obstacles in the way of the attendance of Russian Socialists, but they will not consider themselves bound by the decisions which the conference may take. They are anxious that it should be attended by Socialists of other Allied countries so that Russia should not be left tête-à-tête with Germany.

My personal opinion is that it would be a mistake to leave the Germans a clear field at Stockholm, more especially as it would render our attitude open to misconstruction here. As we have no intention of being bound by the conference's decisions, I do not see how the attitude of British Socialists can prejudice our interests.[59]

As has already been indicated, Lloyd George was at first also inclined to take this view of the situation. Two factors were influential in changing his mind. First, the attitude of his Allies, and second, his view that the change in government in Russia signified a willingness to prosecute the war more vigorously and to reject pacifist makeshifts. The United States set the pace in refusing passports.[60] Influenced by the determined anti-war stand of the American Socialist Party and the opposition of Samuel Gompers, the head of the American Federation of Labor, to the proposed conference, the State Department denied passports to the American delegates, Morris Hillquit, Victor L. Berger, and Algernon Lee. Baron Sonnino, the Italian Foreign Minister, who had had to contend with the bitter opposition of Italian Socialists throughout the war, took a similar position. The French stood adamant on the previous declaration of Ribot against the granting of passports. In the light of this united opposition, Lloyd George felt it necessary to modify his stand.

The decisive factor was the alleged change of attitude of the Russian government toward the conference. Lloyd George pointed out that he had been officially informed that "Although the Russian government does not deem it possible to prevent Russian delegates from taking part in the Stockholm conference, they regard this congress as a party concern and its decision in no way binding on the liberty of action of the government."[61] This statement he construed as meaning either that the Russian

[59] Buchanan, op. cit., II, 160.
[60] American Labor Year Book, 1917-1918, 229.
[61] Labour Leader, August 9, 1917.

government was opposed to the conference, or at least less favorably disposed toward it than before. This interpretation was further expounded in a Parliamentary debate—August 15—when the Premier declared that there has been

a most drastic change in the whole policy of the government in Russia. There has been an end put to the fraternization which has destroyed the morale of the Russian army. . . . Naturally under these conditions there would be a different feeling with regard to holding a fraternizing conference with the enemy. . . . Under the old conditions the Russian government was supposed to be not merely in favor of the conference, but to be promoting it . . . now the government had nothing whatever to do with the conference, but they felt that they could not possibly prevent delegates from attending it.[62]

As a result, on August 13, Mr. Bonar Law in answer to a question, announced that

the government has decided that permission to attend the conference will not be granted, and the same decision has been taken by the governments of the United States, of France, and of Italy, with whom His Majesty's government have been in communication on the subject. The four Allied countries have come definitely to the conclusion that if peace terms are to be discussed, they must be discussed by the representatives of a whole nation and not merely a section.[63]

This decision was taken in spite of the fact that the Labour Party Conference of August 10 had decided in favor of going to Stockholm by the overwhelming vote of 1,846,000 to 550,000, after Henderson, the Labour member of the Ministry, had pressed the necessity of going to Stockholm in order to "consolidate the fruits of the Russian Revolution and to safeguard them against a cunning and ruthless foe."[64] As a result of his repudiation by his colleagues, Henderson's position in the Ministry was rapidly becoming intolerable, and on August 13, he resigned, but not before he had taken steps to correct the impression that there had been any change in the attitude of benevolent neutrality which the Provisional Government adopted toward the conference. This view was soon confirmed from official sources.

Kerensky, the Russian Prime Minister, authorized Dr. Soskice, the correspondent of the *Manchester Guardian,* to say

that the Russian government cordially sympathizes with the objects of the conference which is to establish peace and good will among peoples, and in

---

[62] *Parliamentary Debates, Commons,* vol. XCVI, 929.

[63] *Ibid.,* 824.

[64] *Labour Leader,* August 16, 1917.

our conversations with Allied ambassadors and other representatives of Allied countries, we always emphasized our view that no obstacles should be placed to the granting of passports.[65]

Whether this marked a new about face from the position announced by Lloyd George or the reiteration of an old policy which Lloyd George misinterpreted is difficult to say. At any rate, it was clear that the attitude of the Russian government was still favorable to the conference.

Kerensky's statement revived hopes in socialist ranks that a reversal of the policy of the Allied governments on the passport question was still possible. The adjourned Labour Party conference, meeting on August 21, reaffirmed by the close vote of 1,234,000 to 1,231,000 its previous endorsement of the Executive recommendation that the Party send delegates to Stockholm.[66] It was decided to postpone further consideration until after the meeting of the Inter-Allied Socialist Conference.

The Inter-Allied Socialist Conference which met at London, August 28-29, included representatives from eight countries, Great Britain, France, Russia, Italy, Belgium, Portugal, Greece and South Africa.[67] It was agreed that no binding decisions were to be made except by unanimous vote. In the absence of unanimity, the conference was confined to resolutions which revealed the drift of sentiment in its membership. The two important problems before the gathering were (1) the question of going to Stockholm, (2) the attitude toward the refusal of passports by the governments. The conference had before it a letter from the organization Committee of the Stockholm Conference which accepted the September 9 date for the conference, and on the question of passports declared emphatically that "we cannot and you cannot accept that the proletariat be deprived of the primary right to think, to speak, and to exchange its views."[68]

The Inter-Allied Conference approved a resolution in favor of going to Stockholm by a vote of 48 to 13.[69] Representatives of Belgium, South Africa and Greece voted against the resolution. The French majority Socialists and the British Trade Union group abstained from voting. The resolution condemning the refusal of the passports received an overwhelming majority with 50 votes in favor and only 2 dissents.

[65] Ibid., August 23, 1917.
[66] Ibid.
[67] Ibid., September 6, 1917.
[68] Comité Organisateur xxiii-xxv.
[69] Labour Leader, September 6, 1917.

Then came the Blackpool Congress of British Trade Unionists, September 3-4, 1917. It marked the beginning of a retreat on the part of Labor. The report of the Parliamentary committee which was heartily approved by a vote of 2,849,000 to 91,000 declared that

in view of the divergence of opinion, we have come to the conclusion that a conference at Stockholm at the present moment could not be successful, and in the light of all these circumstances we make the following recommendations: (1) we recommend that the Parliamentary committee attempt in every possible way to secure general agreement of aim among the working classes of the Allied nations, as in our opinion, this is a fundamental condition of a successful international conference. (2) We are strongly of the opinion that an international labor and Socialist conference would be of the greatest service, and is a necessary preliminary to the conclusion of a lasting and democratic peace, and we recommend that the Trade Union Congress Parliamentary Committee be empowered to assist to arrange and take part in such a conference. . . .[70]

But the retreat is at least to be an honorable one, and the resolution concludes with a blast of defiance at the government.

We desire to make it clearly understood that the above recommendations arise out of the internal difficulties revealed at the Inter-Allied conference and elsewhere, and are in no way consequent upon the decision of governments to refuse passports to the Stockholm conference. In the opinion of your committee, no government has any right to prevent an expression of feeling by the working class of its country, and we regard the action of the government in this matter as an unwarrantable interference with our rights as citizens. The workers of this country have made enormous sacrifices in life and liberty and we are entitled to a commanding voice in the settlement of peace. We recommend that this conference enters emphatic protest against the action of the government in refusing passports, and demands that, in the event of an international conference taking place on the lines recommended, no obstacle shall be placed in the way of the delegates from any country.[71]

The Bordeaux Congress of the French Socialist Party which assembled in October, 1917, likewise agreed on the principle of an international socialist congress and protested against the refusal of passports, but without any appreciable influence on the policy of the government.[72] The Russian delegation returned from England to Stockholm disheartened, but still refusing to admit complete defeat.

In a manifesto issued soon after their return, the Organizing Commit-

[70] *Ibid.,* September 13, 1917.
[71] *Ibid.*
[72] *Pendant la Guerre,* Resolutions of National Congress of 1917, Oct. 6-9; 182ff.

tee of the Stockholm Conference proclaimed its unwillingness to abandon the proposed meeting.[73]

With the watchword "To Stockholm" still on its lips, the Organizing Committee of the Conference busied itself, during the early days of October, with the preparation of an advance project of a peace program. This document saw the light of day on October 10, and was intended to serve as a basis of discussion for the conference when it assembled.[74] But the conference never met, and the preparatory labors of the conference proved abortive. Feeble efforts continued even after the Bolshevik Revolution of November 7, 1917, to breathe life into the Stockholm conference, but without success.

The responsibility for the failure of the Stockholm conference to materialize rests largely at the door of the Allied governments. The great majority of Allied Socialists expressed their willingness to participate. It was the refusal of passports to delegates by the United States, Great Britain, France and Italy which dealt a death blow to the Stockholm

[73] See *Labour Leader*, September 20, 1917.

"The idea of the Stockholm conference is not abandoned. The enemies of Socialism have employed methods of insinuation and invoked non-existent documents to impress the masses. They have abused the monopoly of the postal and telegraph services to misconstrue and falsify our declarations. This campaign has failed. The Inter-Allied conference in London favored Stockholm.

"If the Blackpool conference is compared with the Manchester resolutions the progress made is obvious. Stockholm is closely connected with the Revolution in Russia. The forces of reaction have tried to render the Revolution responsible for the Anarchy which was due to Tsarism. We hope all our Russian comrades will close their ranks and defend Russian democracy. The working classes of all countries hail with enthusiasm the fall of the Czar, and condemn the efforts at counter-revolution.

". . . we express also our strong hope that the German and Austrian Socialists will do their Socialist duty, and protest energetically against projects and tactics which tend to weaken the Revolution and to make Germany the accomplice of the counter-revolution. The present circumstances prevent us giving a definite reply as to the date of the conference to various requests from France, Austria, Germany, etc., but the committee is resolved to continue its activities and will publish a collection of documents coming from adherents of the conference and a general report.

"Finally the committee has decided to send, if the organizations concerned are willing, delegates to a new inter-Allied conference and to all similar gatherings, and to issue a report on its actions and its views for a future conference.

"The Stockholm conference must inaugurate a new era in the struggle of the proletariat against Imperialism by the reestablishment of an international capable of common action. The working class desires this war to be the last, to democratize the nations, to prevent a new conflict—above all, to create by guarantees of right and of arbitration a pacific disarmed world on land and sea; and democracy and true liberty. The conference is now delayed; but for every organized proletarian the watchword is still 'To Stockholm!'"

[74] *Comité Organisateur* xxviii.

movement. It is true that the governments found support for their policies in the attitude of portions of the labor movement. The hand of the United States government was strengthened by the support of Gompers, the president of the American Federation of Labor, who denounced Stockholm as a piece of "insidious pro-Kaiser propaganda." In England the declaration of Havelock Wilson, the president of the Seamen's Union, that no delegates to Stockholm would be allowed on ships manned by his union, helped to buttress the governmental policy. But in spite of energetic protests against Stockholm by labor and socialist minorities in all the Allied countries, the fact still remains that the majority Socialists were willing and were anxious to go, but were prevented by governmental interference. In the face of governmental opposition, Allied Socialists were compelled to beat a retreat. The only recourse left them was to give the conference a decent burial by a final insistence on their right to attend as a matter of principle, but by actual relinquishing of participation as a matter of fact.

The consequences of the Stockholm fiasco for international socialist organization were highly significant. The Stockholm conference represented an opportunity to bring together within a single international organization majority as well as minority Socialists, government Socialists as well as the more moderate representatives of the Zimmerwald organization. The conference enjoyed the sponsorship of neutral Socialists, of the Executive Committee of the International Socialist Bureau, of Russian Socialists who shared the pacifist views of Zimmerwald. Only the extreme Zimmerwaldians of the Left—the Bolsheviks and their sympathizers—openly renounced the conference, and at the time this group still represented a very small if growing portion of the international socialist movement. The Stockholm conference thus presented a unique opportunity to lay the foundations for a revival of the Second International in all its pre-war strength. It offered a chance to reunite the Right and the Center, to heal the breach which the Left had been so sedulously widening at Zimmerwald and Kienthal. That opportunity was missed by the failure of the Stockholm conference to convene.

The obstacles placed in the way of the Stockholm conference had still another important consequence. Indirectly they helped to make the November Revolution a success, to raise the Bolsheviks to power, and to establish the kernel of the Third International. One of the reasons for the failure of the Provisional Government in Russia was its inability or unwillingness to bring peace to a war-weary people. The Stockholm conference represented a step in this direction, a step which the Provisional Government—in its socialist stage at least—regarded with mild benevolence. The refusal of the Allied Powers to permit this conference to assemble and the supine acquiescence of the Provisional Government in this refusal drove the peace-hungry masses toward the extreme Left, which, whatever its political or economic views, at least promised an immediate end to the bloodshed. The failure of the Stockholm conference to assemble thus combined with other domestic factors to lift the Bolsheviks into a position of supremacy. By establishing the Bolsheviks in power, it helped to create an effective nucleus for the Third International.

CHAPTER VIII

THE ZIMMERWALD ORGANIZATION, STOCKHOLM, AND THE RUSSIAN REVOLUTION

It is now necessary to pick up the threads of the Zimmerwald movement and to trace its activities in the period between the March and November Revolutions in Russia. The International Socialist Commission of the Zimmerwald organization, as might be expected, greeted the outbreak of the Russian Revolution in March with great enthusiasm. It promptly issued a manifesto calling for active support of the Revolution by the world proletariat and heralding the Revolution as a step forward on the road to peace.[1]

The members of the Commission undertook as their first task to facilitate the return of the Russian Socialist exiles who were stranded in Switzerland. On the initiative of the International Socialist Commission, a conference was held of representatives of Russian Socialist parties adhering to the Zimmerwald organization. The conference approved Martov's plan by which the Russian emigrants were to return through Germany and Stockholm "on the basis of exchanging for the emigrants an equal number of Germans and Austrians interned in Russia."[2] Telegrams were dispatched to the Provisional Government in Russia to obtain its consent, but no answer was received.[3]

Meanwhile, Grimm, the secretary of the International Socialist Commission, was instructed to enter into negotiations with the Swiss government. Grimm appealed to Hoffmann, member of the Federal Council in charge of the political department, but the proposal was rejected on the ground that Swiss intervention would be construed by the Entente Powers as a violation of neutrality. Grimm then privately approached representatives of the German government in order to discover whether there was any objection to the plan from that direction. The Russian emigrants now divided into two camps, those supporting Martov who felt it necessary to wait for a reply from Petrograd, and the Bolsheviks who favored an immediate departure if German consent could be obtained. The indiscretion of Lenin and Zinoviev in publishing a circular

---

[1] For text see *Archiv für die Geschichte des Sozialismus* hereafter referred to as *Archiv*) XII, 362.
[2] Lenin, *Works*, XX, Part Two, 382.
[3] *Ibid.* XX, Part One, 81.

147

letter (informing the emigrants of their decision to return) which alluded to the appeal to Hoffmann caused Grimm to withdraw from the negotiations, and Fritz Platten, the secretary of the Swiss Socialist Party, an adherent of the Zimmerwald Left, replaced him. Platten conducted the negotiations through the German embassy in Berne and arranged for the return through Germany in a car which was to be considered extra-territorial. Platten was to accompany the party; no one was to be permitted to enter the car without his permission. In return, the travellers agreed to bring pressure to bear in Russia to secure the return of a corresponding number of Austro-Germans to Germany.[4] Before the departure of Platten's party the representatives of other groups which had decided to stay behind passed a resolution which condemned the decision of the Bolsheviks.[5]

The Bolsheviks, regarding the alternatives before them as either returning to Russia through Germany, or residing abroad till the end of the war, preferred to accept the former, with all its dangers. Their choice was approved and defended in a declaration signed by leading representatives of the Zimmerwald Left.[6]

[4] For documents on the passage through Germany see Lenin, *Works*, XX, Part Two, Appendix, 381-386.

[5] *Ibid*. 384.

"Whereas in view of the obvious impossibility of returning to Russia via England due to resistance offered by the English and French authorities, all parties have found it necessary to ask of the Provisional Government through the Soviet of Workers' Deputies, authorization to exchange a number of political emigrants for an equal number of German citizens;

"and whereas the comrades who represent the Central Committee have decided to go to Russia through Germany without awaiting the outcome of the step undertaken in this direction;

"Therefore we consider the decision of the comrades from the Central Committee to be a political error as it has not been proved that it is impossible to obtain the authorization of the Provisional Government for such an exchange."

[6] *Ibid*., 385-386. Paul Hartstein (Paul Levi) Germany; Henri Guilbeaux, F. Loriot, France; Lindhagen (Mayor of Stockholm), Strom, Deputy, Secretary of the Swedish Socialist Party; Carlson, deputy, Ture Nerman, editor of *Politiken*, Kilbour, editor of *Stormklockan*, Sweden; Hansen, Norway, signed the declaration which declared:

"The undersigned are appraised of the difficulties put by the Entente governments in the way of the Russian internationalists' departure and of the conditions under which the German Government allows them to pass. The undersigned are fully aware of the fact that the German Government allows the passage of the Russian internationalists only in order thus to strengthen the anti-war movement in Russia.

"The Russian internationalists who, during the war, tirelessly and with all their power have been fighting against the imperialism of all nations, particularly that of Germany, now go back to Russia to work for the revolution; by these actions

On April 16, 1917, Lenin and the first party of emigrants arrived in Petrograd. The next day Lenin and Zinoviev appeared before the Executive Committee of the Petrograd Soviet to report on their journey and answer rumors which circulated that they were German agents.[7] After the discussion the Executive Committee decided that the

delegation be instructed to raise the question of the political emigrants before the Government, temporarily to adopt no resolution on the passage through Germany, print all the factual material relevant to this question in the *Izvestia,* and publish a notice in the next number of the *Izvestia* on the report made by comrade Lenin on the day of the arrival concerning circumstances of the journey through Germany.[8]

The threat which Miliukov was alleged to have made to arrest all citizens returning through Germany was not carried out. Lenin and his adherents were permitted full freedom for the time being to carry on their propaganda and organization. In this way the members of the International Socialist Commission who arranged the return of Lenin and other leading Bolsheviks to Russia helped to prepare the ground for the November Revolution. The aid received by Lenin and his followers from the outside helped to cement the unity of the Zimmerwald Left.

The success of the Russian Revolution centered interest in the North, and the International Socialist Commission transferred its headquarters to Stockholm.[9] The *Bulletin* issued by the Commission was transformed and enlarged into a *Nachrichtendienst.* The first number appeared May 5, under the editorship of Fred Strom, the Swedish deputy. In the interval the Dutch-Scandinavian Committee had called for the assembly of a general socialist conference at Stockholm on May 15, later postponed until June 10. The International Socialist Commission was asked to participate in the preparatory work of the conference. Grimm, the

---

they will help the proletariat of all countries and especially the proletariat of Germany to begin their struggle against their governments. The example of the heroic struggle of the Russian proletariat is the best stimulant for such a struggle. For all these reasons the undersigned internationalists of Switzerland, France, Germany, Poland, Sweden, and Norway, consider it not only the right but also the duty of the Russian comrades to take advantage of the possibility offered them to return to Russia. At the same time we wish them the best success in their struggle against the imperialist policy of the Russian bourgeoisie, a struggle that is part of a general struggle of the proletariat for a social revolution."

[7] For text of report see Lenin, *Works,* Part One, XX, 91-93; also *Pravda,* No. 24, April 18, 1917.

[8] Lenin, *Works,* XX, Part One, 361.

[9] *Archiv,* XII, 362.

secretary of the International Socialist Commission, notified all groups affiliated with Zimmerwald, of the impending conference.[10] In accordance with the decision of the Kienthal conference, Grimm called upon these groups to assemble at Stockholm on May 31 in order to decide the attitude to be adopted toward the Stockholm conference called by the Dutch-Scandinavian Committee.[11]

The attitude which the Bolsheviks adopted toward the Stockholm conference as well as the Zimmerwald conference which was to precede it is of considerable importance because of the leading rôle which the Bolsheviks later played in the creation of the Third International. At the all-Russian April conference of the Bolsheviks (May 7-12, Western calendar) Nogin of the Moscow committee who reported on the Stockholm conference, expressed the opinion that a delegation of Bolsheviks ought to participate in the conference if only for purposes of information.[12] This standpoint was vigorously combatted by Lenin. The conference accepted Lenin's point of view and passed a resolution which condemned participation in any gathering sponsored by "patriotic" socialists.[13]

[10] For text, *Ibid.*, 363-364.

[11] *Ibid.* This circular notice was addressed to the Petrograd Soviet of Workers' and Soldiers' Deputies, the Central Committee (Bolshevik) and the Organization Committee (Menshevik) of the Russian Social-Democratic Labor Party, the internationalist wing of the Russian Social-Revolutionary Party, the Jewish Bund, the Independent Social-Democratic Party of Germany, the Zimmerwald group in the minority of the French Socialist Party, the Socialist Party of Italy, the Zimmerwald elements in the Polish, Bulgarian, and Rumanian Socialist parties, the Social-Democratic Party of Switzerland, the Independent Labour Party of Great Britain, and the British Socialist Party, the Left wing of the Swedish Social-Democrats, the Socialist Youth of Sweden, Norway, and Denmark, and the Social-Democratic Party of Norway and Sweden. In addition, all other groups were invited which accepted the Zimmerwaldian slogans of a battle against the civil peace, a renewal of class war, and a peace without annexations and indemnities on the basis of the free self-determination of peoples.

[12] Lenin, *Works*, XX, Part One, 377.

[13] *Resolutions of the All-Russian April (May) Conference of the* R. S. D. L. P. May 7-12, 1917; see Lenin, *Works*, XX, Part Two, Appendix, 401-402.

"In connection with the arrival of the Danish 'Socialist' Borgbjerg and his proposal for participation at a congress of Socialists to support the peace proposed by the German Socialists of Scheidemann's and Plekhanov's orientation on the basis of Germany's renouncing the major part of its annexations the conference decides:

"Borgbjerg appears in the name of three Scandinavian parties, the Swedish, Danish and Norwegian. He received his mandate from that Swedish party which is headed by Branting, a Socialist who has joined the side of his bourgeoisie and betrayed the revolutionary union of the workers of all countries. The Swedish party cannot be recognized as Socialist. We consider as a Socialist party in Sweden only that party of the youth which is headed by Höglund, Lindhagen, Strom, Carlson, and others.

"The Danish party, from which Borgbjerg has a mandate, we also fail to consider

On the question of participation in the Third Zimmerwald Conference there was also disagreement. Zinoviev reported on the situation in the International and sponsored the resolution which was adopted by the conference. Zinoviev declared for participation in the conference planned for May 18, in order to come to an understanding with the Liebknecht group, unify the Zimmerwald Left, and at the conference itself to break with the "Centrist majority on the occasion of big, basic questions, as for example, the question of the Stockholm conference which had been proposed by Borgbjerg, and to organize the Third International in the further course of development."[14]

Lenin took a more extreme position. Despairing of any possibility of attracting the support of the Center, he referred to the breakdown of the Zimmerwald International because of its "vacillation, its indecision, when it came to the most important practical and all-determining question of breaking completely with the social-chauvinists and the old social-chauvinist International headed by Vandervelde and Huysmans."[15] With relentless realism he proclaimed,

we can stand no longer this Zimmerwald mire. We must not, on account of the Zimmerwald Kautskians remain more or less allied with the chauvinist International of Plekhanovs and Scheidemanns. We must break with this International immediately. We ought to remain in Zimmerwald only to gather information.[16]

He called upon his supporters "to organize a third International, bold and honest and proletarian, the kind which Liebknecht would have, an International which will set its face boldly against all traitors, all social-

---

a Socialist party because it is headed by Stauning, a member of the bourgeois cabinet. . . . According to his own admission, Borgbjerg acts in accord with Scheidemann and other German Socialists who have gone over to the side of the German government and the German bourgeoisie. There can be no doubt, therefore, that directly or indirectly, Borgbjerg is in reality an agent of the German imperialist government.

"In view of this the conference considers participation of our party in a conference which includes Borgbjerg and Scheidemann to be inadmissable in principle, since it is our task to unite, not the direct or indirect agents of the various imperialist governments, but the workers of all countries, who already during the war have begun to fight, and are fighting in a revolutionary way against their imperialist governments. . . .

"The party of the Russian proletariat will go to a conference, and will join a brotherly union, only with such workers' parties of the other countries as are fighting in a revolutionary way within their own country for the passing of the entire state power into the hands of the proletariat."

[14] *Ibid.*, XX, Part One, 380.
[15] *Ibid.*, 151.
[16] *Ibid.*, 152.

chauvinists and the vacillating people of the 'centre.' "[17] In spite of a fervent appeal Lenin's amendment to stay in the Zimmerwald union "solely for the purposes of information" was rejected, and the conference adopted the more cautiously worded resolution of Zinoviev.

The Zinoviev resolution, while stressing the weakness of the Zimmerwald movement, still advocated remaining within it to advance the program of the Zimmerwald Left and create the basis for the organization of the Third International.

> The majority in Zimmerwald and Kienthal belonged to the "Centre." This weakened the Zimmerwald bloc from the very start. . . . The Zimmerwald bloc refused to recognize the necessity of a straight split with the social-chauvinists' majority of the old official parties and thus it weakened the Zimmerwald movement. The Kienthal conference in words condemned both bourgeois and Socialist pacifism; in reality, however, the majority of the parties and groups that belong to the Zimmerwald bloc continue a policy of social-chauvinism. The vacillating tactics of the Zimmerwald majority have brought about a situation where in some countries Zimmerwald is already beginning to serve as a brake on the revolutionary movement.
>
> The task of our party . . . is to take the initiative of creating the Third International. . . . The conference warns against organizing international congresses with the participation of the social-chauvinists. . . . Our party remains in the Zimmerwald bloc with the aim of defending the tactics of the Zimmerwald Left wing there, and it authorizes the Central Committee immediately to take steps leading to the establishment of the Third International.[18]

With these considerations in mind the conference decided for participation in the International Conference of the Zimmerwaldians, though it refused to have anything to do with the Stockholm conference.

The Sparticists joined in boycotting the Stockholm conference. Franz Mehring, of the German opposition group, "Internationale," in a letter to Tscheidse, the chairman of the Executive Committee of the Petrograd Soviet of Soldiers' and Workers' Deputies (April 29) renounced participation in any international conference in which the German Social-Democratic majority would be represented and called upon "our Russian comrades to prevent the presence at the Stockholm conference of any representative of the German majority Socialists."[19] The Independent Social-Democrats of Germany agreed to send representatives to Stockholm but only on condition that the Russian Socialists take part.

The decision of the Executive Committee of the Petrograd Soviet on

[17] *Ibid.*, 153.
[18] Lenin, *Works*, XX, Part Two, Appendix, 406-407.
[19] *Archiv*, XII, 370-372.

May 9 to issue an independent call for an international socialist conference injected a new factor into the situation, since Zimmerwaldian groups formed a large part of the membership of the Soviet. The original invitation issued by the Soviet specified that only such parties and organizations could attend as supported the following platform: 1. Peace without annexations or indemnities on the basis of self-determination of nations. 2. Peace to be obtained through mass action of the proletariat carrying out the resolutions of the Stockholm conference. 3. As a precondition, the recognition of the necessity of abandoning the policy of "civil peace" and support of the imperialist governments.[20]

This apparent stiffening of the conditions of admission left the implication that the majority Socialists would have to revise their policies in order to be eligible for participation and seemed to make necessary a reconsideration of the policy of the International Socialist Commission (Zimmerwald) toward the proposed conference. Toward the end of May, Grimm, the secretary of the International Socialist Commission, arrived in Petrograd after encountering considerable obstacles to his entry into Russia.

On May 28-29, the International Socialist Commission engaged in conversations with the representatives of the Russian Socialists affiliated with the Zimmerwald movements.[21] The object of the conversations was to ascertain the sentiment of the participants toward the impending conference.

The discussion revealed two currents of thought.[22] One, represented by Trotsky, Zinoviev, Riazanov and Balabanova, called for a complete boycott of the conference; the other view, supported by Grimm, Rakovsky, Martinov and Bobrov, counselled participation on the ground that the revolutionary Soviet had undertaken the sponsorship of the conference instead of the discredited International Socialist Bureau. No conclusions were reached. In accordance with the Kienthal resolution, decision on the question awaited the assembly of the Third Zimmerwald Conference. In the course of the conference Zinoviev and Lenin called upon the International Socialist Commission to issue a manifesto which would condemn

[20] *Ibid.*, 372.
[21] *Ibid.* 364-365. The participants included R. Grimm, and Angelica Balabanova for the International Socialist Commission, Bobrov for the Social-Revolutionary Internationalists, Zinoviev and Lenin for the Bolsheviks, Abramovitch for the Bund, Lapinski for the Poles and Lithuanians, Riazanov, Trotsky and Urizki for the Interfractional Russian Social-Democrats, Bienstock, Martov, Martinov and Larin for the Menshevik Internationalists, and Rakovsky of the Rumanian Social-Democrats.
[22] *Ibid.*, 365.

the participation of Russian Socialists in the Ministry (Chernov, Sko-
belev and Tseretelli). The majority were, however, of the opinion that
the International Socialist Commission had no power to issue such a
condemnation without a consultation of all groups affiliated with Zimmerwald. As a result of the conversations the International Socialist
Commission issued an invitation on June 10 to affiliated organizations
and called upon them to send delegates to a Third Zimmerwald Conference which was to assemble three days before the opening of the Stockholm conference sponsored by the Soviet.[23] Since the date of the latter
conference was not yet finally determined, the date of the Zimmerwald
conference also remained provisional. The chief business was the attitude to be adopted by the Zimmerwaldians toward the Stockholm proceedings.

Grimm and Balabanova, the representatives of the International Socialist Commission, in the meantime utilized their stay in Russia to develop support for the Socialist minority in the other belligerent countries.
The activity of Grimm led to misunderstanding. Sensational rumors were
circulated in Russia and the Entente countries that Grimm was a German
agent seeking to negotiate a separate peace between Germany and Russia
through the Swiss embassy in Petrograd.[24] As a result of intercepted tele-
graphic correspondence between Grimm and the Swiss minister Hoffman, leading Zimmerwaldians were involved in these charges. Angelica
Balabanova was accused of conducting negotiations for a separate peace
between the Socialist Party of Italy and the German government. Though
the Italian Socialist Party promptly denied these charges and cleared
Balabanova of the insinuations directed against her, the attempt to discredit the Zimmerwald movement met with some success. Grimm was
compelled to leave Russia and later resigned his post in the International
Socialist Commission. A commission consisting of Zimmerwaldians—
Lindhagen and Höglund (Sweden), Krykov (Bulgaria), Otto Lang
(Switzerland), Olausen (Norway), Orlowski (Russia) and Radek (Poland)—was appointed to investigate the charges against Grimm. In a
report issued at Stockholm July 5, the accusation that Grimm was acting
as a German agent was declared to be without foundation.[25] His negotiations with the Swiss minister, Hoffman, it was declared, were intended to

[23] *Ibid.*, 365-366.
[24] *Ibid.*, 366-367.
[25] *Ibid.*, 368-369.

clear away obstacles and facilitate the meeting of a general peace conference in which all governments would be represented. The commission, however, expressed its disapproval of Grimm's action because of his failure to consult with other members of the International Socialist Commission and representatives of Russian Zimmerwaldians and because his independently conceived idea gave enemies of the Zimmerwald movement an opportunity to label the Zimmerwald movement an instrument of German imperialism. For these reasons Zimmerwaldians refused to take any responsibility for Grimm's action and declared his usefulness as a member of the Commission at an end. The Swedish Left Socialists, Höglund, Carlson and Nerman, were constituted a provisional International Socialist Commission, and Angelica Balabanova took over the Secretariat.[26]

The attitude of the Zimmerwald organization toward the proposed Stockholm conference still remained an unsettled problem. The delegates of the Russian Soviet of Workers' and Peasants' Deputies, Rosanoff, Zinoviev and Goldenberg, sought to enlist Zimmerwald support, and on July 3 a conference was held for this purpose at Stockholm.[27]

The willingness of the Soviet delegates to sanction the participation of "patriotic" Socialists in the forthcoming conference aroused the ire of the Left Zimmerwaldians. The original invitation issued by the Soviet which called for a peace without annexations and indemnities and invited the majority Socialists to abandon the policy of civil peace, had been answered by a request from Vandervelde and Thomas for a clarification of the term annexations, and a statement that while the German majority Socialists ought to be compelled to cease to support their government, the French and English Socialists who were fighting a war of defense could not consent to a renunciation of the policy of "civil peace." The Soviet Executive Committee answered that abandonment of "civil peace" would no longer be considered a pre-requisite for admission to the conference.

In the debate of July 3, Karl Radek called for a clarification of the position of the Soviet delegates. Goldenberg answered that the invitation

<hr />

[26] *Ibid.*, 369.

[27] *Ibid.* 372. Among those present were Angelica Balabanova of the International Socialist Commission, Krykov (Bulgaria), Sirola (Finland), Karl Kautsky, Hugo Haase, Louise Zietz and Oscar Cohn (Germany), Lindstrom, Lindhagen and Höglund (Sweden), Olausen (Norway), Lang (Switzerland), Orlowski, Radek and Hanecki (Russia and Poland) and Boris Reinstein for the Socialist-Labor Party of the United States.

of the Soviet permitted the participation of the majority Socialists.[28] A large number of those in attendance then declared against participation in the Stockholm conference. Radek went even further and declared that the Bolsheviks would withdraw from the Zimmerwald movement in the event that the Zimmerwaldians decided in favor of participation in the conference sponsored by the Dutch-Scandinavian Committee and the Soviet. Haase took a contrary position and notified all present of the decision of the Independent Socialist Party of Germany to participate. Thereupon Angelica Balabanova in the name of the International Socialist Commission declared that regardless of the attitude of the Russian Bolsheviks or the German Independents, only a full meeting of the groups affiliated with the Zimmerwald movement could finally determine the attitude of the Zimmerwald organization as a whole. The next day the Bureau of the International Socialist Commission issued a notice that the Zimmerwald conference would assemble five days before the coming together of the Stockholm conference.

Should the Stockholm conference not meet before September 15, and the Bureau be convinced that the conference will not assemble, the International Socialist Commission is empowered to call a conference of affiliated minorities on a date to be agreed upon on consultation with these groups. In the event that such a gathering is rendered impossible through denial of passports or other governmental measures, the International Socialist Commission is instructed to issue a manifesto setting forth the general political situation and calling upon comrades inside and outside of Parliaments to act to obtain a peace without annexations and indemnities on the basis of the self-determination of nations.[29]

On July 9, an official conversation took place between Rosanoff, Rousanoff, and Erlich, representatives of the Russian Soviet, and Carlson, Höglund, and Balabanova for the International Socialistic Commission, to decide whether the latter would join in the call for the Stockholm conference.[30] Again the International Socialist Commission refused; it based its action on the Kienthal resolutions, which provided for a preliminary Zimmerwald conference, and on the unwillingness of sponsors of the Stockholm conference to require renunciation of the policy of "civil peace" from the participants. The delegates of the Soviet, nevertheless, joined with the Dutch-Scandinavian Committee on July 11, in issuing another call for the Stockholm conference; at the same time,

[28] *Ibid.*, 373.
[29] For complete text, *Ibid.*, 373-374.
[30] *Ibid.*, 374.

regret was expressed that the International Socialist Commission did not aid in the preparatory work.

On July 13, the International Socialist Commission held another meeting with representatives of various Zimmerwald organizations in Stockholm.[31] Radek and Kollontai called for a boycott of the Stockholm conference, but the International Socialist Commission again reminded the participants that decision on the question must await a full meeting of the Zimmerwald Union.

The left continued restive. A week later, July 20, representatives of the Zimmerwald Left, including Bolsheviks, Polish and Lithuanian Socialists, "narrow" Bulgarian Social-Democrats, and Swedish Lefts, joined in a manifesto which was made public in the Swedish Left socialist press and was widely reprinted.[32] The manifesto followed the line already made familiar by the April resolution of the Bolsheviks. After pointing out the gathering unrest and disillusion of the masses as revealed by increasingly serious strikes and food riots in the belligerent countries, the authors denounce the Stockholm conference as a desperate effort on the part of the social-patriots to retrieve the situation for their bourgeois masters. The decision of the Lebedour-Haase group in Germany and of the Longuet-Pressemane section of the French party to participate is described as an effort to give the conference a pseudo-socialist character by awakening the confidence of large sections of the socialist masses. In so doing the Centrists were alleged to have played into the hands of the "government" Socialists. It is the task of the revolutionary Social-Democrats, the manifesto continues, to deflate the socialist phraseology in which the call for the Stockholm conference has been embodied, to expose the true objects of the conference, to call for a proletarian revolution as the only means of obtaining a peace free from the yoke of capitalism, to disavow Zimmerwaldians who participate in the conference, and to send delegates to Stockholm to form a real revolutionary union as opposed to the pseudo-socialism of the Right and the Center.

It would be a mistake to suppose that even the Bolsheviks were united in their attitude toward the Stockholm conference. The refusal of the Entente Goverments to grant passports even to "majority" Socialists raised doubts concerning the validity of an analysis which made the

[31] *Ibid.*, 380. Among those who attended this meeting were Radek, Kollontai, Orlowski, Martinov, and Jermanski of Russia, Mohr of Switzerland, Sirola of Finland, Strom and Kilborn of Sweden.

[32] Reprinted, *Ibid.*, 381-388.

majority Socialists the blind tools of their governments. Kamenev, a leading Bolshevik, in a speech before the Central Executive on August 19, called attention to these facts and argued that events had entered a new stage, that the Stockholm conference must now be defended since it raised the banner of the united proletariat against the imperialist governments.[33] Although Kamenev acknowledged that he spoke only in a personal capacity and not on behalf of the party, his speech was the occasion for a sharp rebuke from Lenin who insisted that the official attitude of opposition of the party toward Stockholm had not been altered, and that in spite of the policy of the Entente governments, no compromise was possible between "social-chauvinists" and Bolsheviks.[34]

On July 22, the International Socialist Commission issued an invitation fixing August 10 as the date for the Third Zimmerwald Conference.[35] On August 1, the Commission met with representatives of Zimmerwaldian organizations located in Stockholm.[36] All agreed that it was necessary to summon a Zimmerwald conference, but decided to postpone the date until September 5.

On August 12, the International Socialist Commission issued two manifestoes. The first pointed out that the decision of the Kerensky government to defy the will of the Soviet and carry on the war aggressively had caused the Allies to treat the Stockholm conference with contempt; that the Allied Socialists had shown a weak-kneed resistance to the denial of passports, and called upon the masses to repudiate the policy of tolerating governments which defied their will.[37] The second manifesto dealt with the Russian Revolution. Fearing that the July offensive undertaken by the Kerensky régime and the repression of the Bolsheviks foreshadowed a dictatorship of petty-bourgeois supporters of the counter-revolution, the manifesto appealed to the proletariat of all countries to help save the fruits of the Revolution by undertaking to end the war and combat capitalism. "Will the Revolution kill the War or the War kill the Revolution?" asked the authors. The answer to this question, the manifesto concluded, rested with the proletariat.[38]

---

[33] Lenin, *Sämtliche Werke,* XXI, 639.
[34] *Ibid.,* 97.
[35] *Archiv,* XII, 388ff.
[36] *Ibid.,* 395. Among others, Lindhagen and Lindstrom of Sweden, A. Jermanski of Russia, Sirola of Finland; J. Eads Howe of the United States; Radek and Hanecki of Poland; Strom of Sweden and Ledebour of Germany.
[37] *Ibid.,* 388-390.
[38] *Ibid.,* 390-392.

On September 2, three days before the scheduled Third Zimmerwald Conference, the Commission issued still another manifesto which criticized the Allied Socialist Conference held in London for its failure to agree on a resolution insisting on the meeting of the Stockholm conference and condemning the participants for their abject surrender to the Entente Governments.[39] The whole Stockholm fiasco, in the eyes of the Commission, marked the bankruptcy of the policy of socialist collaboration with bourgeois governments. There was only one way out of the chaos—"a return to the international class struggle, a break with 'civil peace,' a proletarian battle in every land with proletarian tools without regard for the strategic views and wishes of imperialist governments."[40] The impending conference of Zimmerwaldians had as its aim, the manifesto concluded, to unite all those who subscribed to these views.

The third conference of the Zimmerwald Union, which was originally planned for May 18, 1917, did not finally take place until September 5. Its sessions were "rigidly conspiratory."[41] Representatives from the countries of the Entente were prevented from attending because of the denial of passports by the Allied governments. It was decided, nevertheless, that the decisions of the conference were to be binding on all members of the Zimmerwald Union, whether they were represented at the conference or not.

The agenda of the conference included the following points: (1) the reports of the International Socialist Commission; (2) the Grimm affair; (3) the attitude toward the Stockholm conference; (4) the struggle for peace and the attitude of the Zimmerwaldians toward it.[42] The first two

[39] *Ibid.*, 392-395.

[40] *Ibid.*, 394-395.

[41] Lenin, *Works*, XX, Part Two, 380. See also *Archiv*, XII, 396. The participants included Ledebour, Haase, Stadthagen, Kathe Duncker, Adolf Hofer, and Robert Wengels of the Independent Socialist Party of Germany; Orlowski and Alexandrov from the Bolshevik Central Committee; Axelrod and Panin from the Menshevik Organization Committee; Jermanski from the Menshevik Internationalists; Radek and Hanecki from the National Committee of the Polish Social-Democracy; Sirola of Finland; Constantinescu and Prinu from Rumania; Rosa Bloch and Ernst Nobs of Switzerland; Ahsis of the Socialist Propaganda League and J. Eads Howe of the International Brotherhood of the United States; Nissen, Christian and Erwig of Norway; Samuelson, Strom, Lindhagen and Lindstrom of Sweden; Therese Schlesinger and Frau Luzzatto of Austria; and Angelica Balabanova, Carlson, Höglund and Nerman on behalf of the International Socialist Commission. Two Bulgarian delegates—Charlakov and Tinev—arrived too late to participate in the proceedings; two other Bulgarian delegates—Kolarov and Krykov—had to leave before the conference opened. The Bulgarian delegation, however, gave full support to the decisions of the conference.

[42] *Archiv*, XII, 397.

questions aroused no controversy. The report of the investigating committee in the Grimm affair was approved without dissent, and the withdrawal of Grimm from the Commission ended the incident.

The most bitter debate took place over the question of participation in the Stockholm conference.[43] The two Menshevik representatives reported that their instructions were only to participate in the Zimmerwald conference if that gathering decided to take part in the general Stockholm conference. Because of their disagreement with the resolutions of the conference, they found it necessary finally to withdraw. In the discussion of the Stockholm conference, Radek, Duncker, Balabanova, Lebedour, Höglund and Sirola all spoke against participation. Haase and Stadthagen supported participation on the ground that the general conference offered the minorities an excellent opportunity to square accounts with the majority parties. Since the question of participation or non-participation had been rendered largely academic by the refusal of the Allied governments to grant passports to the Stockholm delegates, the Zimmerwald conference found it unnecessary to come to a decision. The discussion, however, revealed a considerable preponderance of sentiment against participation in the event that a general conference should later take place.[44]

The most important question before the conference was the problem of safeguarding the socialist character of the Russian Revolution. The unsuccessful July uprising of the Bolsheviks widened the breach between the Bolsheviks and the alliance of Mensheviks and Social-Revolutionaries which supported Kerensky and took part in his government. This conflict was carried over into the Zimmerwald conference. Orlowski, the Bolshevik representative, protested vigorously against the tactics of the Mensheviks and Social-Revolutionaries in upholding the Kerensky régime on the ground that the latter was dedicated to a more vigorous prosecution of the war, had revived the death penalty in the army to enforce discipline, had arrested prominent Bolshevik leaders and had ordered repressive measures against Bolshevik newspapers and organizations. He therefore called upon the conference to proclaim its solidarity with the Bolsheviks as the best representatives of the Zimmerwald tradition in the Russian Socialist movement.[45] The conference in response to this appeal did issue a declaration of sympathy with Alexandra Kollontai and

[43] *Ibid.*
[44] *Ibid.*, 409.
[45] *Ibid.*, 401-402.

Trotsky who had been imprisoned by the Kerensky government, and also with the Austrian Socialist, Friedrich Adler.

The conference concluded its labors by drafting a manifesto which appealed for international mass action to end the war and to save the Russian Revolution from the forces of reaction.[46] The manifesto called for a concerted international general strike in order to bring about peace and the triumph of Socialism. This manifesto was to be transmitted to the Zimmerwald parties for approval and publication. Pending approval, it was to be kept secret.

On September 28, Louise Zietz, a member of the Central Committee of the Independent Social-Democratic Party, arrived in Stockholm to ask the International Socialist Commission for permission to postpone publication of the manifesto because of the fear that the call for a general strike which it contained would only invite further repressive measures by the German government without securing compensating benefits for the Zimmerwaldians.[47] At this time the Party was in bad repute with the government because of the discovery of revolutionary organizational work carried on in the German fleet by Reichpietsch and Kobis who were alleged to be Party members. Dittman, one of the leaders of the Independent Socialists, denied responsibility for the revolutionary movement in the Reichstag and declared for legality at any price. To issue a call for a general strike at a time when the legal position of the Party was precarious was to face the danger of dissolution. The Party therefore pleaded for delay until circumstances were more opportune. In spite of the insistence of Radek that immediate publication be demanded regardless of the objective situation, the Commission sanctioned delay, though it still insisted on ultimate publication.[48] The incident provided the Bolsheviks with still another text to reinforce their indictment of the Center Socialists as revolutionaries in word but not in deed, who shrank from action when danger threatened.

To Lenin, the spectacle of the Zimmerwald Conference putting off its deliberations from month to month, waiting in vain for the Stockholm gathering to convene, and finally assembling in sheer desperation had been "comedy" in which Bolshevik participation was indefensible.[49] From the first, he had called for the immediate creation of a Third

---

[46] *Ibid.*, 403-406.
[47] *Ibid.*, XII, 232.
[48] *Ibid.*, 233.
[49] Lenin, *Sämtliche Werke*, XXI, 161.

International to be composed of the revolutionary elements adhering to the Zimmerwald Left wing, but he had been overruled by his own party which was still reluctant to cut off all ties with the Centrists in the Zimmerwald movement. The Zimmerwald Union therefore remained. It included within its ranks incongruous elements. In theory at least it commanded the loyalty of individuals as widely apart in their philosophy as Kautsky and Zinoviev. In the clear light of Lenin's pitiless logic, it appeared to be a hollow union of irreconcilable groups, the sooner parted, the better. Yet inspite of logic and inspite of Lenin, both Centrist and Left wingers still clung to Zimmerwald as the sole remaining symbol of international proletarian solidarity in a war-torn world.

The period between the March and November Revolutions thus represents a highly critical stage in the history of the origins of the Third International. At the dawn of the March Revolution the revolutionary vanguard which followed Lenin constituted a small if determined and active band. By the sheer weight of their aggressiveness, they had succeeded in giving an increasingly revolutionary coloring to the resolutions of the Zimmerwald and Kienthal conferences, though numerically these conferences were dominated by Centrist and Pacifist groups which were reluctant to break with the old International. The strategy of the Left was directed toward winning the support of a wavering and irresolute group in the Center, and toward precipitating a break with the old International and creating a new Third International.

The Russian Revolution gave a powerful impetus to the mass desire for peace. Both outside and inside Russia, it stirred Socialists of all descriptions to favor an International meeting which would help prepare the way for peace. The projected Stockholm conference called jointly by the neutral Socialists on the Dutch-Scandinavian Committee and the Soviet, represented the answer to this demand. Enjoying the wholehearted support of the government or majority Socialists and the qualified support of the majority Zimmerwaldians or Centrists, it presented a remarkable opportunity to weld into a single unit all the scattered fragments of the old International, with the exception of the Left Zimmerwaldians. The willingness expressed by Centrist groups to participate in the Stockholm conference revealed that while they had been wooed by the Left, they had not been won. When the crucial test came, they were ready to reunite with the Right.

But the Stockholm conference, due largely to the obstacles placed in the way by the Entente governments, did not assemble. The Zimmerwald Union for all its weakness remained the only active international organization of proletarian elements. The Center was thrown back on the Left for support if it desired to preserve international socialist ties.

The Russian Revolution gave the Bolsheviks the undisputed leadership of the Zimmerwald Left. From the very beginning, Lenin and his co-workers in the Central Committee of the Bolshevik Party constituted the brains and the drive in the Zimmerwald Left wing. As long as they remained in exile in Switzerland and other havens of refuge, their sphere of usefulness was largely limited to literary and organizational contact work. With the triumph of the Russian Revolution the Bolsheviks became a legal party. They could agitate and organize as much as they pleased; they could seek to provide the party with a broad foundation of mass support. The increase in the strength of the Bolsheviks even in the early days of the Russian Revolution enhanced their authority and prestige. Their new-found power prompted the assumption of a kind of arrogance which encouraged Lenin to dispense with Centrist support and to call for the immediate creation of a Third International. The program of Lenin was not, however, followed. The Bolsheviks decided to remain within the Zimmerwald Union and to continue their attempts to impregnate it with a revolutionary character.

The future fate of the Third International became intimately bound up with domestic developments in Russia. The premature July uprising of the Bolsheviks and its unsuccessful end led to a policy of repression by the Kerensky régime and an appeal by the Bolsheviks to the Zimmerwald Union to bring pressure to bear on the Mensheviks and other socialist groups in Russia to withdraw their support from the Kerensky government.

Other events were more favorable to the Bolshevik cause. The failure of the Kerensky government to insist that its Allies grant passports to socialist delegates, doomed the Stockholm conference, and with it, the possibility of an immediate alliance between majority and Centrist Socialists. By closing the way to peace, it only added to the war-weariness of the Russian masses and made them increasingly fertile soil for Bolshevik propaganda. The failure of the Russian offensive against the Central Powers helped to discredit the Kerensky régime. The Kornilov revolt with its threat of counter-revolution compelled Kerensky to invoke Bolshevik aid to repel the attack and thus raised the prestige of the Left wingers. An increasingly critical economic crisis which the Kerensky government seemed powerless to solve only augmented the general air of ineffectuality and aimlessness which surrounded the Provisional Government. All these factors helped to prepare the way for the Bolshevik seizure of power in November, with its slogans of immediate peace, land to the peasants, and workers' control in the industries.

The triumph of the Bolsheviks in Russia had profound consequences on the future history of the Third International. The Bolsheviks had led the Zimmerwald Left even in the Switzerland days; they now dominated the whole Zimmerwald Union. They had demonstrated the success of the revolutionary technique. It is hardly an exaggeration to say that by the November coup d'état they became the most powerful single factor in the international socialist movement. The victory of the Bolsheviks transformed the Third International from the dream of an exile and doctrinaire into a living movement which awaited only the voice of its creator to call it formally into being. The Zimmerwald Union supplied the organizational garment which folded within its sweep those groups most closely akin to the Bolsheviks. But with the success of the November Revolution the real inspiration and driving force toward the creation of a Third International became not the Zimmerwald Union but the Bolshevik Party.

CHAPTER IX

BOLSHEVIK DIPLOMACY AND THE WORLD REVOLUTION

The Bolshevik victory in Russia constituted the greatest single driving force toward the creation of the Third International. Their triumph in the November Revolution meant that the leadership among revolutionary Socialists had passed definitely to the Bolsheviks. Though the Zimmerwald organization still remained in theory the international nucleus around which Left and Centrist Socialists gathered, in practice it consisted chiefly of a secretariat which tended to become an instrument utilized by the Bolsheviks in their appeals for aid to the international proletariat. Since the Bolsheviks were now the dominant unit in the Zimmerwald organization, revolutionaries in all lands looked to them for council, support and inspiration. It is, therefore, to Russia that one must turn in tracing the continuity of leadership which worked to produce the Third International .

The coming of the Bolsheviks to power meant that the destinies of Russia and the Third International became intimately intertwined. As revolutionary Socialists, the Bolsheviks were committed to world revolution. As the responsible administrators of Soviet Russia, their efforts were primarily directed toward preserving the fruits of the revolution in one state. The two tasks were not necessarily incompatible; when by a fortunate juxtaposition of events, both objectives reinforced each other, the Bolsheviks deemed themselves doubly blessed. But as Lenin insisted later in arguing for the acceptance of the Brest-Litovsk peace, "the international policy of the Soviets must be based chiefly on the conditions of the revolution in Russia."[1] In the Leninist philosophy, agitation and propaganda for the world revolution became an instrumentality molded to the diplomatic needs of Soviet Russia in its contacts with the outside world. Bolshevik propaganda for the world revolution must, therefore, be studied in relation to its domestic setting.

When the Bolsheviks seized power they found themselves confronted with a desperate situation. They had been able to win popular support by promising bread to the hungry, freedom to the oppressed, and peace

[1] Louis C. Fraina (editor), *The Proletarian Revolution in Russia,* New York, 1918. N. Lenin, "Why Soviet Russia Made Peace," 256.

165

to the war-weary. With the assumption of the responsibilities of office it became necessary to carry out these promises. Russia was disorganized. The first need was peace—to give the Bolsheviks, in Lenin's phrase, a "breathing space" in order to undertake the tasks of reconstruction and to stamp out the last vestiges of (bourgeois) opposition within Russia.[2]

Soviet diplomacy, therefore, directed all its efforts toward obtaining an immediate peace. Regarding negotiations through the usual diplomatic channels with contempt, the Bolshevik leaders determined to mobilize the popular yearning for peace and bring it to bear on the heads of the belligerent governments. Revolutionary propaganda became the dynamo which Soviet diplomacy utilized to generate a mass will for peace. They even dared to hope that propaganda would light the spark of world revolution and create a union of world socialist states which would relieve Russia of the pressure of both German annexationists and Allied interventionists. Revolutionary propaganda in other lands, therefore, became an important weapon in the Soviet diplomatic arsenal.

Immediately after the seizure of power (November 8, 1917) the All-Russian Convention of Soviets of Workers', Soldiers' and Peasants' Deputies, adopted a decree proposing "to all warring peoples and their governments to begin immediately negotiations for a just and democratic peace."[3] Significantly, the appeal was directed especially "to the class conscious workers of . . . England, France, and Germany."[4] On November 22, Trotsky sent the Allied ambassadors a note which constituted "a formal proposal for an immediate armistice on all fronts and the immediate opening of peace negotiations."[5] The Allies protested vigorously and warned that Russia's defection "might have the most serious consequences," a phrase which was construed by the Russians to contain an implied threat of intervention. When the German High Command agreed to the conduct of peace negotiations, the Bolsheviks still made efforts to avoid a separate peace and postponed the opening of the negotiations five days until December 1, "in order once again to invite the Allied Governments to define their attitude to the question of peaceful negotiations."[6]

On November 28, the Council of People's Commissars directed an

[2] *Ibid.*, 355-360.

[3] Henri Barbusse (introduction), *The Soviet Union and Peace* (collection of documents), London, 1929, 22.

[4] *Ibid.*, 25.

[5] *Ibid.*, 25-26.

[6] *Ibid.*, 26.

appeal to the people of the belligerent countries to join in the negotiations for an armistice.[7] The call of the Soviets for peace was reinforced by similar appeals circulated through the International Socialist Commission of the Zimmerwald Union.[8]

The armistice negotiations with Germany opened December 2. On December 5, negotiations were suspended for a week to give the Allies an opportunity to join, but the hope proved vain. The Council of People's Commissars decided to build a fire under British influence in the East and thus hoped perhaps to spur Great Britain to action. A manifesto addressed to all Mohammedans in Russia and the East, which was issued on December 7, promised them national freedom and called upon them to overthrow "the robbers of European imperialism."[9] The hint was not lost on Sir George Buchanan, the British ambassador in Russia, who wrote that "Mr. Lenin . . . incited our Indian subjects to rebellion."[10]

The Allies did not, however, join in the negotiations, and on December 13, armistice negotiations continued between Russia and the Central Powers. A truce was arranged until January 14, 1918. As one of the conditions of the truce it was provided that "the exchange of views and newspapers is to be permitted." The opportunities which this opened up for Bolshevik anti-war propaganda were not neglected and contributed to the demoralization of the fighting spirit of the German soldiers on the Eastern front.[11]

The Bolsheviks now sought to strengthen their position at Brest-Litovsk by appeals to the people over the heads of the governments. In an "Appeal from the People's Commissariat for Foreign Affairs of the R. S. F. S. R. to the Toiling, Oppressed, and Exhausted Peoples of Europe" (December 19, 1917), Trotsky declared:

[7] *Ibid.*, 27.

"We, the Council of People's Commissars, appeal to the Allied peoples, and, first and foremost, to their toiling masses: Will they consent to drag on with this pointless slaughter, and go blindly to the ruin of the whole of European culture? . . . The government of the victorious revolution does not require recognition from the professional representatives of capitalist diplomacy but we do ask the people: Does reactionary diplomacy express your ideas and aspirations? Do the people agree to allow the diplomats to let the great opportunity for peace offered by the Russian Revolution slip through their fingers? The answer to these questions must be given without delay, and it must be an answer in deeds and not merely in words. The Russian army and the Russian people cannot and will not wait longer."

[8] *Archiv für die Geschichte des Sozialismus*, XIII, 240ff.

[9] *The Soviet Union and Peace*, 30-31.

[10] Louis Fischer, *The Soviets in World Affairs*, New York, 1930, 2 vols., I, 29.

[11] *Ibid.*, 76.

We do not attempt to conceal the fact that we do not consider the existing capitalist governments capable of a democratic peace. Only the revolutionary struggle of the toiling masses against the existing governments can bring Europe nearer to such a peace. Its full realization can only be guaranteed by the victorious proletarian revolution in all capitalist countries.[12]

The purposes of the peace negotiations are two:

first, to achieve the speediest possible cessation of the shameful and criminal slaughter which is laying Europe waste; and second, to assist with all means at our disposal the working class in all lands to overthrow the sway of capital and seize state power for the purpose of a democratic and socialist reconstruction of Europe and the whole of humanity.

The German, Austro-Hungarian, Bulgarian, and Turkish workers are called upon "to oppose to the program of imperialism brought forward by their ruling classes, their own revolutionary program of agreement and cooperation between the toilers and exploited classes in all countries."[13]

The Bolsheviks by no means confined themselves to broadsides and manifestoes. Fearing that a separate peace was inevitable, they also sought to establish direct relations with the German Socialists in order to obtain support for the Russian Revolution and embarrass the German negotiators. As early as November 14, Dr. Helphand, a German Socialist with Russian connections, was asked to come to Stockholm because the Bolshevik representative, Vorovsky, at Stockholm, desired to get in touch with the Socialist Parties of Germany.[14] Dr. Helphand was informed that "big demonstrations and strikes would be most welcome to the Russians."[15] Ebert and Scheidemann, the leaders of the majority Socialists refused to attack the government in the rear by demonstrations, though they were ready with good wishes and resolutions of sympathy. When Vorovsky informed Scheidemann in Stockholm that Russia counted on the possibility of revolution breaking out in all countries in the West, Scheidemann was quick to answer: "Do not be under any illusions on that score, as far as Germany is concerned."[16] The German majority Socialists, however, did use their influence to modify somewhat the harsh conditions which the High Command desired to impose on Russia.

The Brest-Litovsk peace conference opened officially on December 22.

[12] *The Soviet Union and Peace*, 30-31.
[13] *Ibid.*, 31.
[14] Scheidemann, *Memoirs*, II, 101.
[15] *Ibid.*
[16] *Ibid.*, 107.

From the very first session the Russian strategy became evident. In spite of Scheidemann's discouragement, the Bolsheviks still placed their hopes on revolution in Germany and perhaps other countries. Their tactics consisted in delaying the proceedings until the revolutionary leaven would have time to ferment. As Trotsky explained it at the Seventh Party Congress (March, 1918):

> Had we really wanted to obtain the most favorable peace, we would have agreed to it as early as last November. But no one (except Zinoviev) raised his voice to do it. We were all—in favor of agitation, of revolutionizing the working classes of Germany, Austro-Hungary, and all of Europe. . . .[17]

From the first, the Russians insisted on public sessions. They desired to make the peace conference a platform from which the revolutionary tribunes could address the proletariat of all Europe.

On December 28, the conference adjourned for ten days "in order to give the last opportunity to the Allied countries to take part in further negotiations, and by doing this to secure themselves from all consequences of a separate peace between Russia and the enemy countries."[18] Again, the appeal was not heeded, though the Commissariat for Foreign Affairs continued to call upon the working classes to take the power out of the hands of those "who cannot or will not give the people peace."[19] On January 8, the last day of the recess, President Wilson made the famous speech in which he set forth his Fourteen Points as a basis for peace. Thus the Russians on their return to Brest-Litovsk were confronted with a liberal interpretation of Allied War aims, but the Allies themselves did not put in an appearance.

Russia was now face to face with the Central Powers. Without Allied support, the only hope for a favorable peace remained a revolution in Germany and Austria. The strategy of the Russian negotiators, therefore, was directed toward delaying the proceedings in order to allow time for the revolution to mature.

Meanwhile propaganda was not neglected. In the very first week of the Revolution, there was established in the Commissariat of Foreign Affairs a Bureau of the Press under Karl Radek and a Bureau of International Propaganda in charge of Boris Reinstein, a member of the American Socialist-Labor Party. John Reed for a time was in charge

---

[17] Trotsky, *My Life*, 390.
[18] *The Soviet Union and Peace*, 35.
[19] *Ibid.*, 38.

of the English-speaking section of this Bureau.[20] He was later succeeded by Albert Rhys Williams.

The Soviet government subsidized the work by a special appropriation of 2,000,000 rubles.[21] With this financial support an intensive campaign of propaganda was initiated. It was primarily designed to undermine the morale of the German soldiers and gain their support for the Russian Revolution. John Reed who took an important part in the activities, tells the story:

We immediately began publication of a series of daily propaganda newspapers. The first of these was in German, *Die Fackel* (The Torch) issued in editions of half a million a day, and sent by special train to the Central Army Committees in Minsk, Kiev, and other cities, which in turn, by special committees distributed them to different towns along the front where a regularly-organized system of couriers brought them to the front trenches for distribution.

During the daytime at the official fraternization points, bundles of these papers were ostentatiously carried; and they were always confiscated by the German officers. But at night the real work of distribution began. In isolated spots there were continually secret meetings at which the bundles of propaganda literature were put into the hands of German soldiers. At other points Russian soldiers buried bundles of papers in places agreed upon, where they were dug up by the Germans.

After about a dozen numbers the name of *Die Fackel* was changed to *Der Völkerfriede* (The People's Peace). By this time we had daily papers in Hungarian, Bohemian, Rumanian, and Croatian. Williams and I also got out a weekly illustrated paper of four pages, for the simpler, less-educated German

[20] His account of the work of the Bureau may be found in *The Liberator*, January, 1919, "How Soviet Russia Conquered Imperial Germany."

[21] On December 23, the following resolution was passed: "Taking into consideration that the Soviet Union is based on the principle of international proletarian solidarity and the brotherhood of workers of all countries, that the struggle against the war and against imperialism can only lead to victory if it is carried out on an international scale, the Council of People's Commissars deems it necessary to come to the assistance of the Left International wing of the labor movement of all countries, by all possible means, including funds, whether the said countries are at war with Russia, allied to Russia, or occupying a neutral position.

"For this purpose the Council of People's Commissars resolves: That at the disposal of the foreign representative of the Commissariat of Foreign Affairs shall be placed the sum of two million rubles for the needs of the revolutionary internationalist movements." (signed)

Chairman of the Council of People's Commissars
V. Oulianov (Lenin)

People's Commissar for Foreign Affairs
L. Trotsky

See *Ibid.*, 23.

soldiers, called *Die Russische Revolution in Bildern* (The Russian Revolution in Pictures)....[22]

During the armistice and peace negotiations at Brest-Litovsk, the German trenches were flooded with copies of *Der Völkerfriede* which urged the soldiers to upset their government, throw out their Kaiser, and declare a revolutionary peace. Meanwhile the Bolshevik negotiators sought to delay proceedings. They talked and killed time waiting for the revolutionary seeds to sprout. While the German diplomats grew more dictatorial in their annexationist demands, the Russians made speeches, carried on an intensive propaganda, and placed their hopes in the revolutionary potentialities of the German proletariat.

Toward the middle of January their reward seemed to come. A great strike movement broke loose in Austria. To Trotsky these strikes "signified the first recognition of our method of conducting the peace negotiations, the first recognition we received from the proletariat of the Central Powers anent the annexationist demands of German militarism."[23] Spontaneous labor risings spread through Germany and Austria where the desperate food shortage and war-weariness had prepared the soil. For a while, the strikes seemed to presage revolution, but the more conservative labor leaders and Social-Democrats assumed control and succeeded in appeasing the demands of the strikers.[24]

The Spartacists and their sympathisers in Germany sought to exploit the prevailing unrest to foment revolution. Broadsides and pamphlets in the thousands were circulated illegally among the masses.[25] The International Socialist Commission helped to circulate similar appeals.[26] In spite of persistent and vigorous agitation the workers of Germany were not yet ready to follow the call for revolution. A revolutionary ferment was at work, but the revolution itself proved abortive. The

---

[22] *Ibid.*, 19-23.

[23] Leon Trotsky, "At Brest-Litovsk": See Fraina (editor), *op. cit.*, 350.

[24] *Ibid.*, 321.

[25] *Ibid.*, 322. Also Drahn and Leonhard, *op. cit.*, 91ff for other examples. Their general import may be gathered from the following sample: "There is only one means of putting an end to the present butchery and misery of the workers— the overthrow of the government and the bourgeois class, in the way that this was done in Russia. It is solely by mass effort, by the revolt of the masses, by a mass strike, paralyzing all economic activity and all war industries; it is solely by a revolution and the setting up of a people's republic in Germany by and for the working class that an end may be put to the murder of the toilers of all lands that a general peace can be achieved."

[26] *Archiv für die Geschichte des Sozialismus*, . . . XIII, 43ff.

January strikes raised false hopes in Russia. As the editors of *Izvestia* put it: "We were deceived by the Austro-German strike, which made us —to use Herzen's expression—mistake the second month of pregnancy for the ninth." The response of the German proletariat had proved disappointing.

Meanwhile the Bolsheviks also sought to secure support for their peace policy among the masses of the Entente countries. In France they received a rude rebuff. The Socialist group in the Chamber of Deputies, numbering among its members representatives of such various shades of opinion as Albert Thomas, Jean Longuet, and Marcel Cachin, appealed to their Russian comrades not to conclude a separate peace. "Such a consummation," they held, "would not only permit the Central Empires to prepare for, or to actually achieve a military victory and finally to dictate their conditions in the name of force, it would even serve—it already serves—the machinations of all the enemies of democracy and Socialism in the world by permitting them to invoke the Russian Revolution as an example of disintegration and of demoralization."[27] Trotsky answered with a bitter attack on the war record of the French Socialists and again called upon the French proletariat "to demand from its government participation in the peace negotiations."[28] The French Socialists, however, adhered to their original decision "to do nothing to weaken the resistance of the army and people of France."

Maxim Litvinov, the accredited Soviet representative in Great Britain, sought to enlist the support of British labor in the effort to turn the Brest-Litovsk pour-parlers into a general peace conference. In an appeal "To the Workers of Great Britain" he declared:

The further prolongation of the war must lead to the defeat of the Russian revolution and to the triumph of militarism and reaction everywhere. An immediate, just, and democratic peace on the principle of no annexations, no indemnities will spell the downfall of militarism in all countries. This peace can be achieved if only labor will speak in full voice and act with all its might. Workers of Britain! peace is in the balance. The Russian workers appeal to you to join them in their efforts to turn the scale. Labor—speak![29]

While British labor was slow to speak, there were some indications of rising revolutionary ardor. At the Seventeenth Annual Conference of the Labour Party held at Nottingham in January, 1918, there was spontaneous singing of the *Red Flag*, cheers when Trotsky's name was men-

---

[27] *Labour Leader*, January 3, 1918.
[28] Fraina (ed.), *op. cit.*, 23-24.
[29] *Labour Leader*, January 10, 1918.

tioned, and a mild ovation for Litvinov who was invited to address the gathering. Again he appealed for aid:

The Russian workers are fighting an unequal fight against the imperialists of all the world for democratic principles honestly applied. They have begun the proceedings for a general peace, but it is obvious they cannot finish it alone. I would say to the representatives of British labor, "Speed up your peace."[30]

An editorial in the *Labour Leader* took up the cry and declared that "the time is now ripe for the democracies to unitedly rise and sweep their stupid and incompetent governors aside and take the settlement of the war into their own hands."[31] This sentiment became the battle cry of the more revolutionary elements in the British Socialist movement. It did not, however, eventuate in any action.

The Italian Socialists went to the greatest extreme in promising support to the Bolsheviks. The deputy, Morgari, declared in the Chamber of Deputies that the Italian Socialists "favored an immediate peace not only on the Bolshevist terms, but by Bolshevist methods."[32] Still his colleagues took no steps to precipitate an open revolt.

As a result, the Bolsheviks were isolated at Brest-Litovsk. Abandoned by the Entente governments, disappointed in their expectations of support from the proletariat of the belligerent countries, they were virtually at the mercy of the Central Powers. The Austro-German diplomats were quick to press their advantage. Fischer sums up the situation at this point in the negotiations as follows:

the Germans had dropped their mask and were appearing as frank annexationists and militarists. They had agreed to the principle of non-annexation and they insisted on the indefinite occupation of the Russian border states. They had accepted self-determination as one of the bases of the pour parlers and then submitted that self-determination had already taken place, though the expression of "popular will" was in reality the voice of Baltic-German land barons and of German agents. They had consented to the formula of no indemnities and at Brest they presented a bill which would amount to between four and eight billion rubles.[33]

On February 9, representatives of the bourgeois Rada, speaking on behalf of an independent Ukraine, signed a separate peace with Germany though Red troops occupied the larger part of the area which the

[30] *Ibid.*, January 24, 1918.
[31] *Ibid.*, February 7, 1918.
[32] Fraina, (ed.) *op. cit.*, 322.
[33] Fischer, *op. cit.*, I, 50.

Ukrainian representatives claimed to represent.[34] The next day Trotsky brought the conference to a close with his famous "no peace—no war" speech. Refusing to sanction the territorial aspirations of the Germans by a peace treaty, Trotsky declared: "We are withdrawing from the war, but we are forced to refuse to sign a peace treaty."[35]

Trotsky believed that "the position we have taken in this question has made attack more difficult for German militarism."[36] He was soon undeceived. The German attack came quickly; the Russian troops melted away in panic. On February 17, the Bolshevik Central Committee met to decide whether to sue for peace or to fight. Lenin's relentless logic carried the day. Realistically he argued that Russia was not ready for a revolutionary war, that peace was the only salvation for the revolution. As he put it even earlier, "Here in Russia a perfectly healthy child—the Socialist republic—has already been born. We may kill it if we start a war."[37] On February 23, the German terms arrived, accompanied by an ultimatum that they must be accepted within 48 hours. Though the terms were far beyond the territorial demands which Trotsky had deemed extreme at Brest, they were accepted over the bitter opposition of Bukharin and his adherents who still called for a revolutionary war against Germany. On March 3, the peace terms were signed; "at the point of a sword," the Soviet delegates put it.[38]

The treaty still remained to be ratified by the Party Congress and the All-Union Soviet Congress. At the Seventh Party Congress (March 6-8, 1918), Lenin was again the victor. His hard practical point of view punctured the revolutionary soap bubbles of the Bukharinites. The army was in no condition to fight. The international proletariat could not be depended upon to come to the aid of Russia. The Russian Revolution was in jeopardy. It had to be safeguarded at all costs. To the argument that peace with Germany meant abandoning the world revolution, Lenin answered:

The German revolution will absolutely not be made more difficult by the conclusion of a separate peace. It will probably be weakened for a time by chauvinism, but the conditions in Germany will remain very critical. . . . The example of the Russian Revolution will continue to inspire the peoples of the world, and its influence will be enormous. . . . By a separate peace we free ourselves . . . from the two imperialist coalitions. . . . We shall utilize the time

[34] Fraina (ed.), *op. cit.*, 352.
[35] *Ibid.*, 353, for Trotsky's explanation; also Barbusse, *op. cit.*, 39-41.
[36] Fraina (ed.), *op. cit.*, 353-354.
[37] Fischer, *op. cit.*, 49.
[38] For text see *Texts of the "Russian" Peace*, Government Printing Office, Washington, 1918, 12ff.

so gained in order to strengthen the Socialist Republic in Russia . . . the reorganization of Russia, based on the dictatorship of the proletariat, the nationalization of banks and of big industry, the exchange of the products of the cities with the cooperatives of small peasants in the country, is economically quite feasible, provided we have a few months to devote energetically to the job. Such an organization will make Socialism unconquerable in Russia, and will provide a permanent basis for the formation of a powerful red army of peasants and workers.[39]

The All-Union Soviet Congress met on March 12. Even at that late date, Lenin still flirted with the idea of bringing in Allied aid to fight the Germans, but when no aid was forthcoming from that direction, Lenin made the final speech for ratification and was upheld by a large majority of the Congress. Lenin referred to Brest-Litovsk as a Peace of Tilsit. "History," he declared, "moves in zig-zags and in round-about paths." From the ashes of Brest-Litovsk, he predicted, a rich and powerful Russia would yet rise up.[40]

The period that followed the signing of the Brest-Litovsk peace did not afford the expected "breathing space" upon which Soviet Russia relied to build up domestic economy and consolidate internal strength. Again questions of foreign policy pushed themselves to the fore. The danger of foreign intervention absorbed the vital energies of the state. The threat came from two directions: (1) the German policy of encroachment, infiltration, and extension of control in the Ukraine, Finland, the border states, and the Caucasus; (2) the beginning of Allied intervention marked by the landing of Japanese troops in Vladivostok, Allied support of the counter-revolutionary insurrection of the Czecho-Slovaks, and the landing of Allied troops at Murmansk and Archangel.

This is not the place for an extended discussion of the tortuous diplomacy of the intervention period. That subject has been dealt with elsewhere.[41] To the student whose attention is centered on tracing the origins of the Communist International, the aspect of the subject which is of greatest interest, is the renewed emphasis on world revolution as a method of relieving pressure from the armed attacks of foreign interventionists. Chicherin in his report on Foreign Policy to the Fifth Soviet Congress July, 1918, reveals the value which was being placed on outside proletarian assistance:

In the last four months (March to June, 1918), we were compelled to make it our object to avoid all the dangers which menaced us from all sides and to gain

[39] N. Lenin, "Why Soviet Russia Made Peace." Fraina (ed.) *op. cit.*, 355-360.
[40] N. Lenin, "Peace and Our Task," *Ibid.*, 361-364.
[41] See Fischer, *op. cit.;* also F. L. Schuman, *American Policy Toward Russia Since 1917,* New York, 1928; also Chicherin, *Two Years of Foreign Policy,* London, 1920.

as much time as possible, to assist the growth of the proletarian movements in other countries, and in the second place, to establish more firmly the political and social ideals of the Soviet government amongst the broad masses of the people of Russia and to bring about their united support for the program of the Soviets.[42]

Assistance to outside proletarian movements became a recognized mode of conducting revolutionary diplomacy. The Bolsheviks still placed great hope on the revolutionary potentialities of the German masses, particularly the Spartacist section which was led by Karl Liebknecht. It became their objective therefore to develop these potentialities by assiduous propaganda. A Soviet Germany would mark a great step forward toward the world revolution. To attain this objective became one of the goals of Soviet diplomacy. Failing that Soviet diplomats hoped that pressure from the German proletariat might contribute toward forcing the German armies to withdraw from Russian soil.[43]

After the signing of the Treaty of Brest-Litovsk, conditions in Germany did not favor a revolutionary outbreak. The triumph on the Eastern Front aroused high hopes of victory, even in the ranks of German labor; the temporarily successful offensive of April and May, 1918, on the Western Front lifted these hopes still higher. With the checking of the German offensive on the Western Front and the successful counter-attack of the Allies, the tide of sentiment in Germany began to shift. As American troops poured into France in ever-increasing numbers and the balance of power turned strongly in favor of the Allies, a spirit of defeatism spread among the masses. Hunger and suffering intensified the unrest. The medium with which revolutionary propagandists had to work in the second half of 1918 was, therefore, much less refractory than in the earlier years of the war. To say this is not to deprecate the important rôle which revolutionary propaganda played in bringing on the German Revolution.

After the conclusion of the Treaty of Brest-Litovsk, diplomatic relations between Germany and Russia were resumed.

According to the provisions of the treaty, the Bureau of Revolutionary Propaganda was abolished. But the first act of the new Council of People's Commissars was secretly to reorganize this work, appointing an unofficial committee to take charge of it and appropriating for this purpose twenty million rubles.[44]

[42] For text of report see Fraina (ed.), *op. cit.*, 409-427.
[43] *Ibid.*
[44] *The Liberator*, January 1919, 24.

At the same time Adolph Joffe was appointed the Soviet diplomatic representative in Berlin. He arrived in Berlin toward the end of April with ten expert propagandists, who spoke German, in his entourage. "His first act in the German capital was to hoist over the Russian embassy the Red Flag, lettered with the device of the Soviet Republic, Russian Socialist Federative Soviet Republic, Workmen of all countries, unite! He refused to present his credentials to the Kaiser and invited to his first state banquet, Haase, Ledebour, Dittman, Franz Mehring, Rosa Luxemburg, Clara Zetkin, and Karl Liebknecht (then in prison)," all leading representatives of the Left and Left Center of the German Socialist movement.[45] It was soon evident that Joffe had come as an emissary of revolution as well as the diplomatic representative of his country.

Well supplied with funds, Joffe used them to good revolutionary advantage. The Russian embassy became a center from which anti-government and anti-war propaganda was distributed. Ten Left Social-Democratic newspapers were supported by the embassy. Members of the Independent Social-Democratic Party advised freely with Joffe.[46]

The German government made repeated protests, charging the Soviet government with violation of paragraph two of the Brest treaty, which prohibited either government from carrying on agitation against the institutions of the other government. On September 2, the German Foreign Office protested against the "inflammatory articles" of the Russian press. On September 13, an even more caustic note was dispatched concerning the agitation which the Russians were carrying on in Germany.[47]

The military collapse of the Central Powers raised hopes in Russia that the long-awaited revolution was imminent. Toward the end of September, Bulgaria withdrew from the coalition. On October 2, Prince Max of Baden formed a coalition government in which majority Socialists in Germany—Scheidemann and Bauer—participated. Democratic concessions were promised to placate the masses. The next day—October 3—the All-Russian Central Executive Committee promised to assist a German revolutionary workers' state if it were threatened by the aggression of Anglo-French imperialism. On October 5, the German government sent a request for an armistice to President Wilson. While the government sought to come to terms with the Entente governments, "broad sheets

[45] Ibid.
[46] Fischer, op. cit., I, 75.
[47] Chicherin, op. cit., 23.

were being constantly circulated, especially in Berlin and other big towns, with the object of inciting the workers to Bolshevism."[48] On October 21, Karl Liebknecht was released from prison. Escorted by thousands of workers in a flower-filled carriage, he went straight to the Russian embassy from the balcony of which he made a speech which urged that the time had come for the German people to follow Russia's example."[49]

The next day (October 22, 1918) Lenin addressed the All-Russian Executive Committee. He was in a highly optimistic mood.

Comrades—now in the fifth year of the World War the general collapse of imperialism is an evident fact; now it is clear that the revolution in all the belligerent countries is unavoidable . . . the revolution has broken out in Bulgaria . . . the Bulgarian soldiers are organizing councils, or Soviets, after the Russian model. . . . In Austria too, the revolution of the workers and peasants is knocking at the door everywhere.

In Germany the press already talks openly of the abdication of the Kaiser and the Independent Social-Democratic Party now dares to speak of the German republic. This certainly means something! The German revolution is already a fact.[50]

With the rising revolutionary wave in Germany, the propaganda activities of the Soviet embassy became increasingly obnoxious to the authorities. According to Scheidemann, "the number of Russian carriers with a vast amount of luggage, boxes and bags travelling between Moscow and Berlin was enormous."[51] To put an end to this traffic which enjoyed diplomatic immunities, the Cabinet determined upon the expulsion of the Soviet mission. At the suggestion of Scheidemann, one of the boxes destined for the Soviet embassy was conveniently dropped by a porter in such a way as to break open and spill its contents.[52] It was found to contain inflammatory tracts. On November 5, the Soviet representatives were ordered out of Germany on the ground that they had violated the second article of the Treaty of Brest-Litovsk.[53]

The full contribution of the Soviet embassy to the support of the Left wing Socialists in Germany did not become widely known until some time later. After the successful establishment of the German Soviets, Joffe revealed that the Embassy had made substantial contributions in the way of arms and finances. In a radio message dated December 15,

[48] Scheidemann, *Memoirs*, II, 210.
[49] *The Liberator*, January, 1919.
[50] Fraina (ed.), *op. cit.*, 449.
[51] Scheidemann, *Memoirs*, II, 212.
[52] *Ibid.*
[53] *Ibid.*, 213.

1918, which was broadcast by Joffe to the German revolutionary Soviets, he not only admitted that he had paid 100,000 marks for the purchase of arms for revolutionaries, but announced that he had established a 10,000,000 ruble fund in Germany for the support of the revolution.[54] This fund was entrusted to Oscar Cohn, an Independent Social-Democratic Deputy, who had served as counsellor of the Soviet legation. As a result Joffe felt justified in wiring to Haase: "I congratulate myself and I rejoice on having personally in accord with the Independent ministers contributed to the victory of the German revolution."[55]

The German revolution, however, did not take the form which Joffe and Lenin had anticipated. On November 9 came the uprising of the Berlin proletariat, Prince Max turned over the reins of government to Ebert, the majority Socialist leader who immediately organized a coalition cabinet composed of three majority and three Independent Socialists. The Bolsheviks looked to see the revolution turn more to the Left as in Russia. "The Scheidemann gang will not remain at the helm very long," said Lenin, "it does not represent the broad masses of the people."[56] The Russians fully expected to see Liebknecht and his Spartacist friends seize power and join in an entente with Soviet Russia. The expectation was doomed to disappointment. The trial of strength came in the first weeks of January, 1919. The majority Socialists retained control of a considerable section of the armed forces, and under the leadership of Noske, the Spartacist uprising was ruthlessly suppressed. Karl Liebknecht and Rosa Luxemburg, the Spartacist leaders, were killed. Though the Spartacists continued restive, it became clear in the early months of 1919 that the government had the situation well in hand, and there would be no working agreement between the majority Socialists in control in Germany and the Bolsheviks.[57]

The majority Socialists recognized that the Bolsheviks were the driving force behind the Spartacist movement.[58] Karl Radek, the emissary sent

[54] Fischer, *op. cit.*, I, 76.

[55] *Frankfurter Zeitung*, Dec. 10, 1918.

[56] Fraina (ed.), *op. cit.*, 449.

[57] For a more detailed description of the part of the Spartacists in the German Revolution, see:

Scheidemann, *Memoirs*, II, a majority Socialist's view.

Heinrich Ströbel, *The German Revolution and After*, London, 1923. The author was an Independent Socialist.

M. Philips Price, *Germany in Transition*, London, 1923. Sympathetic to the Spartacist movement.

[58] Scheidemann, *Memoirs*, II, 280-281.

by the Bolsheviks to aid the Spartacist leaders, in his pamphlets of November, 1918, denounced the Scheidemann government as "lackeys of capitalism," and advised the Spartacists to seize power by a coup d'état and ally themselves with Soviet Russia.[59] Radek appeared at the First Congress of the Communist Party of Germany (the Spartakusbund) December 30, 1918, to January 1, 1919, and appealed for a Communist revolution.[60] Together with Liebknecht he played a leading rôle in directing the Spartacist uprising of the next weeks and was later arrested by the German government.

The German government, therefore, was in no mood to treat with Revolutionary Russia. While the Berlin Soviet demanded the re-establishment of diplomatic relations, the German government marked time. As early as November 17 the German government decided to refuse bread sent from Russia to feed the hungry populace of Germany. The German government was unwilling to help Bolshevism ingratiate itself with the German masses. On January 20, 1919, the German government, taking into account "the support given by Russian Bolsheviks to the Spartakus mutiny," sent a wireless "lodging the strongest protest against this inadmissable and criminal interference in the internal affairs of Germany" and warned "that the sharpest measures will be taken against all those Russians who have been guilty of supporting the revolutionary movement."[61] The unsuccessful Spartacist uprising only increased the tension between Germany and Soviet Russia. Not even yet did the Bolsheviks despair of a successful Communist revolt in Germany. For the moment they were forced to admit that their plans had received a checkmate.

Meanwhile danger threatened the Bolsheviks from other quarters. Allied military intervention in Russia began in April, 1918. Ostensibly the object of this intervention was to re-establish the Eastern Front against Germany. Though some British, American and French representatives advised working with the Bolsheviks instead of against them, it soon became evident that the method by which the Allies proposed to attain their objective was to join with counter-revolutionary forces in Russia to overthrow the Bolsheviks and establish a government willing

[59] Karl Radek, *Die Deutsche Revolution,* Moskau, 1918, 20. "Die erste Pflicht der deutschen Sozialistischen Republik wäre es, sich aufs engste an die Sozialistische Schwester Republik anzuschliessen."

[60] *Berichte über den Gründungsparteitag der Kommunistischen Partei Deutschlands (Spartakusbund) vom Dezember 30, 1918, bis 1 Januar, 1919.*

[61] Paul Miliukov, *Bolshevism: An International Danger,* London 1920, 138.

to continue the struggle against the Central Powers.[62] Again the Bolsheviks relied heavily on propaganda to ward off this new menace.

The Bolsheviks appealed to the masses of the Entente countries to compel the Allied governments to withdraw their troops. In Great Britain, Maxim Litvinov formed the focal point of revolutionary propaganda. His activities caused considerable concern to the British government.[63]

When Kerensky addressed the Labour Party Conference of June, 1918, favoring intervention, Litvinov promptly addressed a letter to the delegates of the Labour Conference in which he said:

> When Mr. Kerensky promises you in exchange for this intervention in Russian internal affairs to re-create a Russian army for the resumption of the war on a large scale . . . he promises what he knows full well that neither he nor any anti-Soviet party can perform. . . . No! the re-creation of the Russian front is not the purpose of the much-talked-of Japanese or Allied intervention. The real object is, of course, the crushing of the worker's government and of the Revolution, the spread of whose influence to other countries is a standing menace to international capitalism. . . . Is British labour going to be a party to these dark schemes? Is the British proletariat prepared to take upon itself the responsibility before history for the crushing of the great Russian Proletariat Revolution?[64]

While the Labour Party took no action on this appeal, the National Council of the Independent Labour Party issued a manifesto which urged British organized labor "to express the strongest condemnation of the participation of the British government in an act which constitutes a crime against national independence and against the Russian Revolution."[65]

In French labor and socialist circles opposition to the Allied intervention was more outspoken. The General Conference of the Confédération Général du Travail, meeting on July 15, 1918, condemned armed intervention in Russia by the Entente nations against the will of the Russian

[62] See Jacques Sadoul, *Notes Sur la Révolution Bolchévique,* Paris, 1920. Sadoul, Raymond Robins and Bruce Lockhart were among those who counselled collaboration with the Bolsheviks. See also, R. H. Bruce Lockhart, *British Agent,* New York, 1933, 195-198.

[63] *Foreign Relations of the United States, 1918, Russia,* Washington 1931, 722-723. "The Bolshevik authorities in Russia have . . . the opportunity of sending sealed mail bags to London and have used these bags for the transmission of the party's literature, which thus escapes censorship. Some of the British papers have already published very violent speeches from Russian sources, and if no means of checking the importation of the literature through the Bolshevik representative is adopted, there seems little doubt that an active anti-war and revolutionary propaganda will be started in all parts of the country through the efforts of Russian agents."

[64] *Labour Leader,* July 4, 1918.

[65] *Ibid.,* August 1, 1918.

people.[66] The National Council of the French Socialist Party, meeting on October 11, 1918, also adopted a resolution denouncing Allied intervention.[67]

The appeals of the Bolsheviks to the proletariat for aid continued. On August 1, Lenin, Trotsky and Chicherin joined in a warning to the proletariat of the Entente nations that "in the interests of Capital, you are to be the hangmen of the Russian Revolution."[68] The plight of the Bolsheviks was serious. Lenin, in a "Letter to American Workingmen" (August 20, 1918), declared: "We are in a beleaguered fortress, so long as no other international Socialist revolution comes to our assistance with its armies . . . we are counting upon the inevitability of the international revolution."[69]

The appeals to the Allied proletariat awakened little response. In the autumn of 1918 the war was still on; the Russian intervention was still conceived as a method of fighting the Germans. The Allies were flushed with impending success, and a very considerable portion of the Allied labor world was more interested in pushing the war to a victorious conclusion than in listening to the fancied grievances of the Bolsheviks.

The armistice worked a profound transformation in the attitude toward Allied intervention in Russia. The argument that the object of Allied intervention was the restoration of the Eastern Front was no longer applicable. The Allied statesmen who now defended intervention and support of the counter-revolution in Russia justified their course of action on the ground that Bolshevism was a world menace which had to be exterminated.

Shortly after the Armistice, the Allies took steps to isolate the Bolsheviks in order to prevent the virus of Bolshevism from infecting the proletariat of the Allied countries. A steady stream of Bolshevik propaganda was flowing at this time through the Soviet embassies of Switzerland and the Scandinavian countries for distribution in France, England and the United States. The Allied governments became alarmed, and Great Britain initiated concerted action by the Allied and Associated Powers to "invite neutral governments to break off diplomatic relations with Bolsheviks, and to control spread of propaganda, among other ways, by bringing pressure to bear on banks to cut off Bolshevik financial

---

[66] *Ibid.*, July 25, 1918.
[67] *Ibid.*, Oct., 17, 1918.
[68] *The Soviet Union and Peace*, 41-46.
[69] See the *Class Struggle*, December, 1918.

transactions."[70] Toward the end of 1918 the results of this policy began to be manifest. The Soviet representatives were ordered out of Switzerland. Chicherin continues the story:

> Comrade Rosin whom we appointed to Holland, notwithstanding the official consent of the latter to his mission, could not get further than Berlin, and immediately thereafter the Dutch government recalled all its representatives from Russia. Similar action was taken by Spain. In December Comrade Vorovsky was requested to leave Stockholm. His final departure took place about the end of January. After Norway and Denmark had broken off diplomatic relations with us, the sole foreign representative in Russia was the Danish Red Cross, which left Russia in the summer of 1919.[71]

By enforcing the diplomatic isolation of Russia, the Allies proposed to cut off all channels for the introduction of Bolshevik propaganda into Allied countries.

The quarantine was not altogether effective. The Allied Socialist parties refused to accept the view that Bolshevism was an international menace which had to be stamped out by force. On November 12, the day after the armistice, the Executive of the French Socialist Party declared:

> In the belief that some of the armistice conditions justify the suspicions that the Allied governments intend to extend their criminal military intervention against Revolutionary Russia on a wider scale, the party declares that it will appeal to all the forces of the French proletariat to prevent the Socialism that is springing up in Russia from being crushed by a coalition of foreign capitalists.[72]

On December 5, the Independent Labour Party, the British Socialist Party, and the Socialist-Labour Party joined in a call to British labor to "demand the immediate withdrawal from Russia of the Allied armies now waging war against the Russian Revolution."[73]

The revolutionary temper of the masses in the Allied countries was rising. In Great Britain labor and socialist organizations in all parts of the country drew up resolutions demanding that Great Britain cease to interfere with the internal affairs of the Russian people. There was talk of a general strike in order to secure the withdrawal of the British forces. "Hands off Russia" meetings were heavily attended.[74]

[70] *Foreign Relations of the United States, 1918, Russia,* 726.
[71] Chicherin, *op. cit.,* 28-29.
[72] *Labour Leader,* Nov. 21, 1918.
[73] *Ibid.,* Dec. 5, 1918.
[74] *Ibid.,* Jan. 16, 1919.

Meanwhile the Bolsheviks were plying the Allied soldiers in Russia with leaflets and pamphlets which sought to undermine the patriotism of the soldiers by appealing to their class loyalties.[75]

The ugly mood of the British and French workers and the feeling of the Allied soldiers in Russia that the war was over and that it was time to go home gave British statesmen, in particular, serious concern. Lloyd George with his finger on Labor's pulse declared: "If a military enterprise were started against the Bolsheviks,—that would make England Bolshevist and there would be a Soviet in London."[76] Sir Henry Wilson noted in his diary on January 17, 1919, "We are sitting on the top of a mine which may go up at any minute."[77]

The net result of this unrest was to make Allied statesmen more receptive to the peace overtures of the Bolsheviks. Litvinov's appeal of December 24, 1918, to President Wilson, "impartially to weigh and investigate the one-sided accusation against Russia" struck a responsive chord.[78] On January 16, 1919, the situation in Russia was discussed by the Allied diplomats.[79] Lloyd George pointed out that there seemed to be three possible policies: (1) military intervention; (2) a cordon; (3) a meeting with the Bolsheviks and other Russian parties in order to arrange a settlement. Military intervention was impossible. "If he now proposed to send a thousand British troops to Russia for that purpose, the armies would mutiny. The same applies to United States troops in Siberia; also to Canadians and French as well." The cordon was rejected as inhuman since it meant death for the "people that the Allies desired to protect." The third alternative was negotiation, and this was decided upon. On January 22, President Wilson issued the proposal for a conference at Prinkipo of all *de facto* governments in Russia, to meet with representatives of the Allies to draw up a program upon which agreement might be reached.[80] The note of the Soviet government of February 4,

---

[75] *Ibid.*, Jan. 16, 1919. See also pamphlet published by English speaking Communists in Russia, *Capitalist England—Socialist Russia*. "Comrades," the manifestoes ran, "You will be fighting not against enemies, but against working people like yourselves. We ask you, are you going to crush us. . . . Be loyal to your class and refuse to do the dirty work of your masters. . . . Go home and establish the industrial republics in your own countries, and together we shall form a world-wide co-operative commonwealth."

[76] C. K. Cumming, and Walter W. Pettit (ed.), *Russian-American Relations* (Documents and Papers), New York, 1920, 287. (Hereafter referred to as R. A. R.)

[77] Quoted in Fischer, *op. cit.*, I, 163.

[78] For text see *R. A. R.*, 270ff.

[79] *Ibid.*, 284ff.

[80] *Ibid.*, 297.

accepted the Prinkipo invitation, but the conference failed to take place because of the refusal of some of the non-Bolshevik Russian governments to attend.[81]

The Allies still attempted to bring about peace by negotiation. A detailed statement of proposed peace terms was drawn up by the Soviet government on March 14, and submitted to Mr. Bullitt who had been sent to Russia by President Wilson with the knowledge of Lloyd George. Nothing came of these proposals.[82]

The successes of Kolchak again raised Allied hopes that the Bolshevik government would be overthrown, and negotiations were therefore abandoned. It became the policy of the Allies to refrain from sending large additional reinforcements to Russia while at the same time they supported Kolchak and other counter-revolutionary leaders with money, ammunition, and supplies. The èconomic blockade of Russia continued. The answer of the Bolsheviks was two-fold: (1) a willingness to call a truce if suitable terms could be arranged; (2) failing that, continued military resistance and revolutionary propaganda among the Entente masses to force withdrawal.

Propaganda for world revolution thus played an important rôle in Soviet diplomacy between November, 1917, and January, 1919. Immediately after the November Revolution, the Bolsheviks appealed to the masses to bring about a general peace. The appeal was not heeded. The Bolsheviks then sought to conclude a separate peace with Germany. They placed their reliance for favorable terms on the revolutionary potentialities of the German masses which they sought to develop by intensive propaganda. Again their efforts failed to bear immediate fruit, and they were forced to conclude the Peace of Brest-Litovsk on dictated terms. They continued, nevertheless, to carry on revolutionary propaganda in the fertile German soil and by undermining the morale of the German troops on the Eastern Front, they contributed to the breakdown of the German military machine. When the German revolution broke out on November 9, 1918, they sought to turn it into revolutionary channels by supporting the Spartacists but were rebuffed again when the Spartacist uprising was put down in January, 1919.

When the Allies embarked on their schemes of military intervention in April, 1918, the Bolsheviks again utilized revolutionary propaganda as a means of forcing the withdrawal of the troops. Although their efforts

[81] *Ibid.*, 291ff.
[82] Chicherin, *op. cit.*, 30.

were rewarded by sympathetic declarations on the part of Allied Socialists who denounced intervention, the Allied occupations continued.

With the signing of the armistice, the appeals of the Bolsheviks met with more success. Allied Socialist and labor organizations redoubled their protests against intervention and contributed to the more conciliatory attitude which the Allied diplomats adopted at Versailles. Prinkipo and the Bullitt mission were a direct tribute to the ominous temper of the masses in the Allied countries in the first months of 1919.

The spectre of a Communist revolution sat at the table with the diplomats at Versailles. Clemenceau, who was no dreamer, said on January 21:

> Bolshevism was spreading. It had invaded the Baltic provinces and Poland, and that very morning they received very bad news regarding its spread to Budapest and Vienna. Italy was also in danger. If Bolshevism after spreading in Germany were to traverse Austria and Hungary and also reach Italy, Europe would be faced with a very great danger. Something must be done against Bolshevism.[83]

In the last analysis, it was not the statesmen who were going to repulse the rising revolutionary wave, but the masses themselves. The world of labor and Socialism was by no means convinced that revolution after the Russian fashion offered the only salvation for their misfortunes. After Stockholm efforts were continued to rally the more moderate Socialists around the banner of the old International. The result was the Berne Conference of January, 1919. It is to the history of these efforts, of the Berne meeting, and the resulting split in the ranks of Socialist internationalism that attention is now turned.

[83] *R. A. R.*, 292.

CHAPTER X

TOWARD THE REBUILDING OF THE SECOND INTERNATIONAL

The Bolshevik appeal for revolutionary mass action in 1918 failed to command the support of the world proletariat. The explanation lies chiefly in the lack of unity in socialist ranks. A large part of the labor and socialist world still followed the Right wing and Centrist leaders who were committed to a moderate, evolutionary program and had little sympathy for the methods of Bolshevism. Throughout the year 1918 there was going on in the socialist movement a gradual consolidation of Right wing and Centrist strength which aimed at the rehabilitation of the Second International rather than its overthrow. This movement was given a strong impetus by the Armistice and resulted in the Berne Conference of January-February, 1919. It is this process of reuniting the Right and Right-center against the Left which will now be traced.

The failure of the Stockholm Conference to assemble in the autumn of 1917 was a blow to the Right and Center Socialists who sponsored the project. Yet the main onus for the Stockholm fiasco fell upon the Allied governments who refused to grant passports rather than upon the Socialists who, however reluctantly, had expressed their willingness to attend. In spite of the obstacles which the Allied governments placed in the way, the organizers of the Stockholm Conference refused to give up the idea. The Committee prepared an advance project of a peace program[1] which was issued under neutral sponsorship on October 10, but without important results. The organizing committee was still powerless to bring about an international conference.

With the organizing committee paralyzed, the initiative passed to the British Labour Party which conceived of another line of procedure for securing peace and the successful restoration of the International. The scheme was first, to produce unity of view on war aims within the British labor movement, then to create the same unity of view among Inter-Allied labor, and finally to appeal for unity to the workers of the world. The process threatened to be time-consuming, but in the eyes of its sponsors it was justified because it ensured adequate preliminary preparation. In accordance with this program the Executive Committee of the

[1]*Comité Organisateur de la Conférence Socialiste internationale de Stockholm.* xxvii.

British Labour Party met at Blackpool immediately after the Trade Union Congress on September 24, 1917, and decided upon joint action with the Parliamentary Committee of the Trade Union Congress to secure "first national, secondly inter-Allied, and ultimately international agreement."[2] The two committees met and appointed a joint international sub-committee to draft a Memorandum on War Aims. The Memorandum was intended to represent the agreed policy of the British Labor movement and was to be presented subsequently to an Inter-Allied Conference. The Memorandum was drawn up and approved by a joint conference of the societies affiliated with the Trade Union Congress and Labour Party on December 28, 1917.

The British Labour Party in its annual conference at Nottingham on January 23, 1918, approved arrangements for an Inter-Allied Conference to be held in London, on February 20, 1918, as a preliminary to a more inclusive international conference of Socialists to be held in Switzerland at a later date.[3] The Third Inter-Allied Labor and Socialist Conference opened in London on the date scheduled.[4] Among the groups represented were the British Labour Party and Trade Union Congress, the French Socialist Party and Confédération Général du Travail; the Belgian Labor Party, the Italian Socialist Party and the Italian Socialist Union. The Bolsheviks boycotted the conference and prevented representatives of the Mensheviks and Social-Revolutionaries from leaving Russia to attend the gathering. The American Federation of Labor was not represented. In a subsequent letter, Gompers indicated that the notice given did not allow sufficient time for the appointment of delegates to be arranged.

The conference adopted a resolution declaring in favor of an international conference of Labor and Socialist organizations to be arranged "by a committee whose impartiality cannot be questioned." The conference was to be "fully representative of all the Labour and Socialist movements in all the belligerent countries accepting the conditions under which the Conference is invoked," and was to "be held in a neutral country under such conditions as would inspire confidence." The resolution called for precise statements of peace terms by all participating organizations, including Socialists of the Central Powers, in order to "ar-

[2] *Report of the 17th Annual Conference of the Labour Party*, Nottingham, 1918, 12.
[3] *Ibid.*, 105.
[4] *Inter-Allied Labour and Socialist Conference, Report*, London, 1918.

range a programme of action for a speedy and democratic peace."[5]

Albert Thomas of France, Vandervelde of Belgium and Henderson of Great Britain were appointed members of a Commission "to secure from the governments a promise that at least one representative of Labour and Socialism will be included in the official representation at any governmental conference and to organize Labour and Socialist representatives to sit concurrently with the official conference." A committee was appointed to go to the United States to "confer with representatives of the American democracy" since American representatives had not participated in the Inter-Allied Conference and their approval of the decisions reached was desired.[6]

The Conference also worked out a War Aims Memorandum on the basis of the British proposals. This document was to be submitted to the Socialists of the Central Powers in order to secure unanimity on the proposed principles of a people's peace. This did not prove an easy matter. The German and Austrian censors prevented transmission. The answer of the Germans was delayed.

On July 16, 1918, the *Vorwärts* published the following letter from Hermann Mueller, dated June 26, and addressed to Huysmans:

Dear Comrade Huysmans:—Your letter of March 10th, which Comrade Branting sent us on April 29th, did not reach us until June 3d. . . . As regards the summoning of an international Socialist conference to a neutral country we are ready to take part in such a conference, just as we have been ready at all times during the war, to support the efforts which aimed at a meeting of the representatives of the Socialist parties.

We regard it as obvious that admission to this conference must be open to the representatives of all Socialist parties. . . . We agree that the conference can be held only under the leadership of Socialists of neutral countries, because that is the only way by which all appearance of partiality can be avoided.

Now your letter further expresses the wish that the Social-Democratic Party of Germany shall make in public a declaration about its peace conditions. The Germany party has already made such declarations on many occasions. . . .[7]

Mueller enclosed the memorandum submitted by the German Socialist parties to the Organizing Committee of the Stockholm Conference. The German Socialists of Austria, and the Hungarian and Bulgarian Social-

[5] *A Clean Peace—The War Aims-of British Labour,* Complete text of the official War Aims Memorandum of the Inter-Allied Labour and Socialist Conference held in London, Feb. 23, 1918, by Chas. A. McCurdy, New York, 1918, 25ff.

[6] *Ibid.*

[7] *Inter-Allied Labour and Socialist Conference—The Replies of the Socialist Parties of the Central Powers to the "Memorandum on War Aims"*—London, 1918, 8.

Democrats answered in a similar vein with statements of their war aims.[8]

It was now the turn of the Allied Socialists to make the next move. But again there was governmental interference. The refusal of the British government to allow P. J. Troelstra, the leader of the Dutch Labor Party, to attend the British Labour Party Conference in June, 1918, in order to submit a statement on behalf of the German Social Democracy in reply to the war aims memorandum of the Allied Labor Parties, and the subsequent refusal of both the British and French governments to permit a British labor deputation to visit Switzerland to confer with Troelstra and other representatives of International Labor, hindered an agreement between the belligerent Socialists. The protests of the Executive Committee of the Labour Party and the Parliamentary Committee of the Trade Union Congress against the restrictive policy of the government brought no relief.[9]

While negotiations with Socialists of the Central Powers were made difficult even through intermediaries, it was still possible to take action on the replies at hand. Arrangements were now made for a Fourth Inter-Allied Socialist and Labor Conference which was held at London from September 17 to 20.[10] The American Federation of Labor, which was not a socialist organization, sent representatives for the first time. The American delegation under the leadership of Samuel Gompers took a prominent part in the proceedings. One of the objects of the conference was to "see how far the Americans were prepared to fall in with the Inter-Allied Memorandum on War Aims."[11] The Conference also dealt with the Austrian Peace Note of September, 1918, the problem of Allied intervention in Russia, and the reconstitution of the International.

Among the notable absentees were the Bolsheviks, the American Socialist Party, and the Italian Socialist Party. Their absence clearly emphasized the breach in socialist ranks. The conference was under predominantly Right sponsorship.

The presence of the American delegation and the influence of the recent military successes of the Allies on the Western Front stiffened the ranks of the "war to victory" faction, with the result that little progress was made toward the rebuilding of the International. By a vote of 57 to 10 the conference adopted a resolution which, while expressing satisfaction with the replies of the Bulgarian and Hungarian Socialists, held the

[8] *Ibid.*, 10ff.
[9] *Labour Leader*, August 22, 1918.
[10] *The Labour Year Book, 1919*, 40-41.
[11] *Ibid.*, 40.

response of the German majority Socialists unsatisfactory because the party "does not accept the London proposals and fails officially to accept even the neutral's proposals as a basis of discussion." But an effort was to be made "to get the German attitude changed," and the proposal of the American Federation of Labor, that "we will meet in conference with those only of the Central Powers who are in open revolt against their autocratic governors" was overwhelmingly rejected.[12]

The resolution on the "Russian Situation" revealed how far the labor and socialist organizations represented at the Inter-Allied Conference were from making a common front with Bolshevism. In taking note of the military intervention of the Allied governments in Russia, the conference contented itself with a mild warning that "the present effort of the Allied Governments to assist the Russian people must be influenced only by a genuine desire to preserve liberty and democracy in an ordered and durable world peace in which the beneficent fruits of the Revolution shall be made permanently secure."[13]

The action of the Inter-Allied Conference did not mean the complete abandonment of efforts to rebuild the International. At the French Socialist Congress of September, 1918, the Longuet resolution which authorized the Executive to work for an immediate meeting of the International, denounced the government's attitude toward Soviet Russia, and protested against intervention in Russia, was carried by a large majority and became the official policy of the party.[14] The French Socialist Executive meeting on October 22, expressed a desire that the committee appointed by the Inter-Allied Conference meet at the earliest possible moment to discuss the summoning of an international conference.[15]

Arrangements were made for a meeting of the committee, composed of Albert Thomas, Vandervelde, Gompers and Henderson, in Paris on October 26. Henderson in company with Huysmans was prevented from boarding the vessel by members of the Seamen's and Firemen's Union, who acted on instructions from Havelock Wilson, the head of the Union, whose opposition to an inter-belligerent conference had been expressed before by similar action.[16] These obstacles and delays dragged on the negotiations until the war was over.

The signing of the armistice and the cessation of hostilities cleared

[12] *Report of the 19th Annual Conference of the Labour Party—Southport*, 1919, 9.
[13] *Ibid.*, 10.
[14] *Labour Leader*, Oct. 17, 1918.
[15] *Ibid.*, Oct. 31, 1918.
[16] *Report of the 19th Annual Conference of the Labour Party*, 10-11.

the way at last for an International Labour and Socialist Conference. The governments withdrew their objections, and the Socialist parties were assured that passport facilities would be available. Preparations began immediately to convoke an international conference. The Executive of the Confédération Général du Travail issued a manifesto on November 14, three days after the signing of the armistice, announcing its decision to bring about an immediate meeting of the International.[17]

The machinery of organization now began to swing into action. Huysmans, the secretary of the International Bureau, worked in close collaboration with the committee appointed by the Fourth Inter-Allied Labor and Socialist Conference to prepare for the proposed gathering. It is important to note that the actual authorization for the conference came not from the International Socialist Bureau, which under the constitution of the Second International alone had power to convoke periodic congresses, but from the committee appointed by the Inter-Allied Conference of September, 1918, which worked in conjunction with Huysmans.[18]

The method of representation also departed from the practice of the old International.[19] Invitations were extended to groups not affiliated with the Second International such as the American Federation of Labor, which, however, refused the invitation. Industrial as well as political labor bodies were represented. In the case of the British section, the separate representation of the Socialist parties was abolished, and they received their representation only indirectly through their affiliation with the Labour Party. The conference was therefore not a regular Congress of the Second International. It was an extraordinary gathering of Socialists and labor parties meeting under highly irregular conditions which had as its object to prepare the way for a revival of the Second International.

The Conference was scheduled to open in Berne on January 27, 1919. The original intention had been to hold the Conference at Paris concurrently with the Peace Conference, but Clemenceau's opposition to the presence of German delegates in Paris compelled the transfer of the Conference to neutral soil.[20]

[17] *Labour Leader*, Nov. 28, 1918.
[18] *Report of the 19th Annual Conference of the Labour Party*, 12.
[19] Pierre Renaudel, *L'Internationale à Berne*, Paris, 1919 (contains documents), 23-30.
[20] *Labour Leaders*, Dec. 26, 1918.

The tasks which faced the Berne Conference may be summarized as follows: (1) the re-establishment of international connections within the labor and Socialist movement; (2) agreement on the terms of peace and reconstruction so that the presence of united labor and Socialist sentiment might be brought to bear on the official representatives who were negotiating peace; (3) agreement on a charter of labor legislation to protect and improve the position of international labor; (4) the determination of a policy toward the revolutionary movements in Eastern and Central Europe.

The first task did not promise to be easy. The organizers of the Conference had to bring together not only Socialists of the Central Powers and Allied Socialists who still nursed war grudges, but also majority and opposition Socialists of the same country who were bitter in their criticisms of each other. The prospect of such an all-embracing conciliation was not very radiant.

Rebuffs came from both directions—Right and Left. Of the two, the opposition of the Right was less serious. The Belgian Labor Party with war memories still fresh refused to go to Berne to sit at the same table with enemy Socialists who, they argued, were responsible for the devastation of their country. Prior to the conference an informal meeting of Allied Socialists (Belgium, France, Russia, and Great Britain) was held in Paris at the invitation of the French in order to overcome the Belgian objections.[21] The Belgian delegations were impressed by the arguments of their colleagues and agreed to ask the General Council of the Belgian Labor Party to reconsider its decision at a special meeting. The Council remained unmoved and decided against participation. Representatives of Belgium therefore were not present at Berne. The American Federation of Labor took a similar stand.[22]

Much more serious were the defections on the Left and Center. Among the important groups which were not represented at Berne because they considered the conference too reactionary were the Russian Bolsheviks, the German Spartacists, the "narrow" Bulgarian Social-Democrats, and the official Socialist parties of Italy, Switzerland, Serbia and Rumania.[23] Even among those who came to Berne there was by no means unanimity.

[21] *Report of the 19th Annual Conference of the Labour Party*, 12.
[22] *Ibid.*, 13.
[23] *Ibid.*, 13. Prior to the Conference the Swiss Social-Democratic Party voted by a majority of 238 against 147 to decline to take part in the conference. The majority declared in favor of an international conference based on Zimmerwaldian principles.

A Centrist group led by Jean Longuet of France and Friedrich Adler of Austria took an independent stand on the question of Bolshevism. With representatives of the extreme Left absent, Berne became a more or less unstable union of Right and Center Socialists with the Right in the majority and in substantial control of the proceedings.

The official opening of the Conference was delayed by the difficulties of travel until February 3.[24] Meanwhile the delegates who had come earlier held private conferences and made a preliminary survey of the agenda and procedure of the conference. At the opening session, 80 delegates were present from 21 countries; before the close 102 delegates had arrived from 26 countries. Branting of Sweden was unanimously elected President of the Conference.[25]

At the very outset the Conference was faced with the danger of dissolution when a resolution offered by Albert Thomas of France precipitated a debate on war guilt. The Thomas resolution proposed that the question of the war responsibility of the Socialist Parties have first place on the agenda, and that in view of the dangers threatening Socialism from Bolshevism, the second point on the agenda should be the part of Democracy in the establishment of the Socialist order.[26]

The debate on war responsibilities was bitter, but was not allowed to precipitate an open split.[27] The French Right Socialists led by Thomas and Renaudel demanded that Socialists who had made themselves accomplices of the guilty governments of the Central Powers should be denounced and repudiated by the International. Finally this proposal, together with a statement made by the German majority Socialists, was referred to a special commission consisting of Branting(Sweden), Wibaut (Holland), Buchinger (Hungary), Renaudel and Longuet (France), Eisner and Wels (Germany), and Henderson and Stuart-Bunning (Great Britain). The report of the commission which contained a declaration made by the German majority party disposed of the question with the following conciliatory resolution:

> The Berne Conference acknowledges that, so far as it is concerned, the question of the immediate responsibility of the war has been made clear, both by the discussions and by the declaration of the German majority, affirming the revolutionary spirit of New Germany and its complete separation from the old system which was responsible for the war.

[24] *Report of the 19th Annual Conference of the Labour Party,* 12.
[25] *Ibid.*
[26] *Ibid.,* 13.
[27] Renaudel, *op. cit.,* 35ff.

In welcoming the German Revolution and the development of democratic and Socialistic institutions which it involves, the Conference sees the way clear for the common work of the International.

The further declaration made by the German delegates in the course of the debate on the League of Nations, has convinced the Conference that, from now onward, the united working classes of the whole world will prove the most powerful guarantee for the suppression of all militarism and of every attempt to destroy international democracy.

The Conference sees fruitful preliminary work in the debates which have taken place and leaves to a future international Congress, convened under normal conditions, the task of formulating the judgment of the International on the world historic question of the responsibility for the war.[28]

The report which was adopted with only one dissenting vote in effect disposed of the issue by postponing it. In this way an open break was avoided.

The resolutions on the League of Nations, territorial questions, international labor legislation, and prisoners of war caused little trouble, and were all approved unanimously.[29] While their contents have considerable intrinsic interest for the student who is tracing the influence of the Berne Conference on the decisions of the Peace Conference, they do not illuminate the conflicts within the international socialist movement and may be passed over.

The critical question before the Conference from the point of view of the relations of the Second and the Third International was the policy to be adopted by the Conference toward the revolutionary movements in Eastern and Central Europe. What attitude was the Conference to take toward Bolshevism? The masses were restive. Their allegiance was divided between the leaders of the Left who sought to capture power by violence and revolution and the more moderate Socialists who were willing to rely on democratic institutions for the realization of their aims. The issue as the Conference saw it was—Democracy versus Dictatorship. It is hardly an exaggeration to say that in the stand which the Conference adopted toward the problem was implicit the success or failure of the Bolshevik call for a revolution in Europe. The revolutionary movement could not be successful without the support of the masses who followed the lead of the Socialists gathered at Berne. And if these leaders decided to fight Bolshevism and were able to hold their supporters in line, the revolutionary uprisings were doomed in advance to futility. For these

[28] *Report of the 19th Annual Conference of the Labour Party*, Appendix, 196.
[29] For texts, *Ibid.*, 196-204.

reasons the decisions of the Berne Conference were pregnant with momentous consequences.

The committee which was charged with framing a resolution on Democracy and Dictatorship consisted of nine members sharply divided in their views.[30] Branting, Wels, Eisner, Soukhomlin, and Renaudel supported the majority, or Branting, resolution which vigorously condemned dictatorship. Adler and Longuet who embodied their views in a minority resolution took a more conciliatory position and desired to leave the way open for a reunion of Revolutionary Socialists and other branches of the Socialist movement. Axelrod and MacDonald abstained from voting in the committee.

The resolutions deserve to be considered in more detail. They contain the nearest equivalent to an official statement of the attitude of the Second International toward the Third at this time.

The Branting resolution began by hailing "the great political revolutions which in Russia, Austria, Hungary and Germany have destroyed the old régimes of imperialism and militarism." It continued:

The Conference urges the workers and Socialists of these countries to develop democratic and republican institutions which will enable them to bring about the great Socialist transformation. In these momentous times, when the problem of the Socialist reconstruction of the world is more than ever before a burning question, the working class should make up their minds, unanimously and unmistakeably, about the method of their emancipation.

In full agreement with all previous Congresses of the International, the Berne Conference firmly adheres to the principle of democracy. A reorganized society more and more permeated with Socialism, cannot be realized, much less permanently established, unless it rests upon triumphs of Democracy and is rooted in the principles of liberty.

Those institutions which constitute Democracy—freedom of speech and of the press, the right of assembly, universal suffrage, a government responsible to Parliament, with arrangements guaranteeing popular cooperation and respect for the wishes of the people—the right of association etc. . . . these also provide the working classes with the means of carrying on the class struggle. . . .

Since in the opinion of the Conference, effective Socialist development is only possible under democratic law, it is essential to eliminate at once any method of socialization which has no prospect of gaining the support of the majority of the people.

A dictatorship of this character would be all the more dangerous if it were based upon the support of only one.section of the working class. The inevitable consequence of such a régime would be the paralysis of working class strength through fratricidal war. The inevitable end would be the dictatorship of reaction.

[30] Renaudel, *op. cit.,* 133ff.

The Russian delegates have proposed that a Commission composed of representatives of all Socialist tendencies should be appointed by the Conference to visit Russia for the purpose of making an impartial report to the International on the political and economic situation there. The Conference fully realizes the difficulties involved in such a task; nevertheless, considering the general interest Socialists of all countries have in exact knowledge of the facts bearing on these popular upheavals, the conference authorizes the Permanent Commission to arrange for a delegation to be sent to Russia on this mission.

The Conference decided to put the question of Bolshevism on the agenda of the next Conference, and recommends the Permanent Commission to carry out the necessary preparatory work.[31]

Thus the majority resolution, while refraining from condemning Bolshevism by name and suspending judgment pending the report of the investigating commission, nevertheless sharply criticizes the category of revolutionary Socialism in which Bolshevism falls. Against this criticism by indirection the minority resolution protests.

The Adler-Longuet resolution deserves to be reprinted at length as a statement of the Centrist position:

The leading idea of the policy which we have resolutely and tirelessly pursued throughout the whole course of the War, was the reconstitution of the international front of the conscious revolutionary proletariat. This same fundamental principle also determined our attitude towards the Berne Conference.

We maintain that this conference runs the risk of provoking grave criticism, not because of what is contained in its resolutions, but because certain commonplace truths have been expressed too late, not during the war, but after the war is over.

On the other hand, the resolution on Democracy and Dictatorship gives cause for most serious objections. The same men who have passively or actively hindered international action for four and a half years, who have thought it their duty to abstain from any international meeting, now eagerly utilize the Conference for a course of action which will inevitably increase the difficulties of the International.

We warn the working classes against any kind of stigma which may be applied to the Russian Soviet Republic. We have not sufficient material for a judgment. One thing only we do know with certainty, that the shameful campaign of lying in which the press and agencies of the Central Empires and the Entente have continued with each other during the war continues unchanged today.

We do not wish by passing premature judgment on political methods to be the victims of the manoeuvres and interested calumnies of bourgeois governments. To our great regret, we are unable to rely solely on the information received from those Russian delegates present at the conference, who represent only a minority of the Russian working class. We do not cast the slightest doubt on their good faith, but we must demand that the International remain

[21] For text see *Report of the 19th Annual Conference of the Labour Party,* 198-199.

true to its old principle of hearing both sides before coming to a decision. The Berne Conference is but a first feeble attempt at an international assembly. Whole parties, such as the Italian, Serbian, Roumanian and Swiss are standing aside! Others are taking part reluctantly.

We have warned you against any decision which would make the meeting of the working classes of all countries more difficult in the future. We desire to reserve free entry into the International for the Socialist and Revolutionary parties of all countries conscious of their class interests.

The majority of the Commission have not listened to our warnings. We do not wish to be parties to any action against the International and we cannot be bound by the resolution as a whole since certain paragraphs can be exploited by the bourgeoisie.[32]

Thus the Adler-Longuet resolution adopted the point of view that there was not sufficient information to pass judgment on the Bolsheviks. Its framers apparently were motivated by a sincere desire to reconstitute the international Socialist front by leaving the way open for the re-entry into the International of the Zimmerwaldians who boycotted the Berne Conference.

The debate on the resolutions revealed a widespread hostility to the methods of Bolshevism.[33] The German delegates were particularly virulent. As the governors of Germany they had already come face to face with the Spartacists' threat and had been compelled to use force to put down the Spartacist uprisings. For them Bolshevism represented a menace which had to be exterminated. Bernstein expressed the view of this group when he said:

The question of Bolshevism is for the German Revolution a question of life or death. The Bolshevists are the true counter-revolutionaries in Europe; they will kill the revolution. Their interpretation of Marxian theories on the dictatorship of the proletariat is absolutely false. They have known only how to create an army commanded by the officers of the Czar and intended to combat the will of the people. Their rule is the rule of corruption. . . . Germany has had experience with it. Bolshevism leads directly to the decadence of humanity.[34]

As the debate proceeded, three currents of opinion emerged. The great majority favored the Branting resolution. A very considerable minority supported the Adler-Longuet resolution. Further to the Left were a small group of Zimmerwaldians led by Loriot who advocated the principle of the dictatorship of the proletariat and urged that it merely rep-

[32] For text, *Ibid.*, 199-200.
[33] Renaudel, *op. cit.*, 125ff.
[34] *Ibid.*, 141.

resented a revival of the principles proclaimed by the old International.[35]

Only the Branting and Adler-Longuet resolutions were put to a vote. The division was as follows:[36]

Branting		Adler-Longuet
Germany	Bulgaria	France (new majority)
Sweden	Armenia	Norway
Russia	Hungary	Spain
Esthonia	Finland	Greece
Lettland	Great Britain	Holland
Georgia	Canada	Half of German-Austrian delegation.
Alsace	French minority	
Argentine	Italy (Social Reformists)	
Denmark	Ukraine	
Palestine	Half of German-Austrian	
Poland	delegation	

The vote revealed the Right wing still dominating the proceedings, but it also disclosed an important Centrist group somewhat vacillating and uncertain in its attitude toward Bolshevism but sincerely desirous of promoting a reconciliation of every shade of opinion if such a reconciliation were humanly possible.

The Berne Conference thus represented the first step toward the revival of the Second International. It was dominated by the Right wing of the international Socialist movement, which stood committed to the policy of attaining Socialism by peaceful and democratic means. It attracted the qualified support of such Centrist leaders as Jean Longuet and Friedrich Adler, Ramsay MacDonald and Hugo Haase. It expressed a very considerable body of sentiment within labor and socialist ranks which was opposed to the revolutionary tactics fostered by the Bolsheviks. It helped to erect a bulwark among the Socialist masses to check the rising revolutionary wave which swept Central and Eastern Europe in the early months of 1919.

If the Berne Conference helped to cement the alliance of the Right and Right-center Socialists, it also served to demarcate more clearly the revolutionary Socialists from the evolutionary Socialists. The Berne Conference failed to attract the attendance of important parties in the old International which stood on the principles of Zimmerwald and sympathized with the Bolsheviks. The Italian, Swiss, Rumanian, Serbian and American Socialists did not take part in the Berne Conference.

[35] John de Kay, *L'Esprit de L'Internationale à Berne*, Lucerne, 1919, 80.
[36] Renaudel, *op. cit.*, 133.

The split in the International which had been developing through the war was now a reality. A call for a new revolutionary International had issued from the north. "The dulcet jingling of the bells of the Second International," ran a flamboyant Communist announcement, "may soon be drowned by the tocsin of the Communist International. The north wind of Russia will soon sweep the political horizon of Western Europe clear of the spiritual fog-banks of the social patriots."[37]

[37] *The Communist International,* May 1, 1919, 66.

CHAPTER XI

THE FOUNDING OF THE COMMUNIST
INTERNATIONAL

On January 24, 1919, three days before the scheduled opening of the Berne Conference, a wireless message went out from Moscow summoning revolutionary class parties of all lands to organize a new International. The invitation was extended to thirty-eight party groups which were identified with the Left revolutionary movement or showed a tendency toward the Left in their development.[1]

[1] The following groups were invited to take part:
1. Spartacist Union (Germany);
2. Communist Party (Bolshevik Party, Russia);
3. Communist Party of German Austria;
4. Communist Party of Hungary;
5. Communist Party of Poland;
6. Communist Party of Finland;
7. Communist Party of Esthonia;
8. Communist Party of Lettland;
9. Communist Party of Lithuania;
10. Communist Party of White Russia;
11. Communist Party of Ukraine
12. The revolutionary elements in the Czech Social Democracy;
13. The Bulgarian Social Democratic Party "Narrows;"
14. The Rumanian Social Democratic Party;
15. The Serbian Social Democratic Party;
16. The Left Swedish Social Democratic Party;
17. The Norwegian Social Democratic Party;
18. The "Class Struggle" Group of Denmark;
19. The Communist Party of Holland;
20. The Revolutionary elements in the Belgian Labor Party;
21. and 22. The groups and organizations of the Socialist and Trade Union movement in France which agree on fundamental questions with Loriot.
23. The Left Social Democrats of Switzerland;
24. The Italian Socialist Party;
25. Left elements in the Spanish Socialist Party;
26. Left elements in the Portuguese Socialist Party;
27. The British Socialist Party (especially the tendency represented by Mac-Lean);
28. The Socialist Labour Party (England);
29. I. W. W. (England);
30. I. W. of Great Britain;
31. The revolutionary elements of the Shop Stewards movement in England;
32. The revolutionary elements of the Irish Labour Organizations;
33. The Socialist Labor Party (America);
34. The Left elements of the American Socialist Party (in particular the tendency

The call was issued in the name of eight parties and was signed by various persons who purported to represent these organizations.[2] Not all of the signers had authority to speak for their parties. The call was issued with the object of giving it as broadly representative a character as possible. The real drive for the conference came from the Russian Communists.

What considerations impelled the Bolsheviks to take the initiative in convoking the new Revolutionary International? The invitation discloses at least three motives: (1) "the rapid and enormous progress of the World Revolution;" (2) "the danger which this [Russian] Revolution runs of being strangled by the alliance of capitalist states organized against the Revolution under the hypocritical banner of the League of Nations;" (3) "the attempts of the traitorous Socialist parties to come to an understanding amongst themselves and after mutual pardons to assist their governments and their bourgeoisie to deceive the working class once more."[3] These considerations need to be enlarged upon.

First, "the rapid and enormous progress of the World Revolution." The breakdown of the German military machine and the signing of the armistice opened the flood gates of revolution. Republican and Socialist governments were formed in Austria, Hungary, and Germany. In Germany the revolutionary Spartacists struggled with the more moderate

---

represented by Debs, as well as the tendency represented by the Socialist Propaganda League);

35. I. W. W. of America;
36. I. W. W. of Australia;
37. Workers' International Industrial Union (America);
38. The Socialist groups of Tokio and Yokohama represented by Comrade Katayama.

The Young Socialist International was represented by Comrade Muntzenberg. See *The Communist International*, #1, May 1, 1919.

[2] *Ibid.*

1. Lenin and Trotsky for the Central Committee of the Russian Communist Party.
2. Karsky for the Foreign Bureau of the Polish Comunist Labor Party.
3. Roudniansky for the Foreign Bureau of the Hungarian Communist Party.
4. Douda for the Foreign Bureau of the German Austrian Communist Party.
5. Rozine for the Russian Bureau of the Central Committee of the Lettish Comunist Party.
6. Sirola for the Central Committee of the Finnish Communist Party.
7. Rakovsky for the Executive Committee of the Revolutionary Social-Democratic Federation of the Balkans.
8. Reinstein for the Socialist Labor Party of America.

[3] The text of the invitation to the Moscow Congress is reprinted in R. Palme Dutt, *The Two Internationals*, London, 1920. Appendix B, 63ff.

Socialists for mastery of the state. Even the masses of the Allied countries were restive. Conditions seemed peculiarly ripe for the organization of world revolution under the impetus of a successful Bolshevik uprising in Russia.

The second object which inspired the organization of the Third International was the necessity of getting outside aid from the world proletariat to assist Soviet Russia to resist the interventionists. The Bolshevik Revolution was in great danger in the early months of 1919. Russia was surrounded by a "cordon sanitaire" which cut off all trade with the outside world. Allied troops were at Vladivostok, Archangel and Murmansk. Counter-revolutionary armies, subsidized by the Allies, formed a ring around Bolshevik Russia and were closing in on the Bolsheviks. In the districts under Bolshevik rule there was much hunger and suffering. Under such circumstances, the idea of a world revolution spreading through Europe seemed like the promise of salvation. Even if the dream of a world revolution proved futile, the organization of Revolutionary Socialists in all lands in close alliance with the Russian Communists still had its value. If workmen abroad could be induced to cease producing arms and supplies to support the counter-revolution or could be made to demand the withdrawal of Allied troops from Russia, the Revolution in Russia might be saved. Thus the Third International became from the very outset an instrument upon which Soviet diplomacy relied to safeguard the integrity of the Soviet state.

The third and more immediate inspiration for the organization of the Third International was the attempt to revive the Second International. The Berne Conference, dominated as it was by Right Socialists who had supported their governments through the World War and who were opposed to revolution as a means of deliverance for the proletariat, represented a challenge to the Bolsheviks that could not be ignored. The world revolution upon which the Bolsheviks placed their hopes could not be successful without the support of the masses. If the masses followed the lead of the Right Socialists and abjured the violent tactics of the Bolsheviks, the revolutionary movement was condemned in advance to failure. It therefore became necessary for revolutionary Socialists to organize on an international scale to prevent the masses from falling under the spell of the Berne Conference. The proposed Third International represented the counter-appeal from the Left for mass support. The Moscow Conference was an answer to the Berne gathering, which the Communists regarded as an assembly dominated by Socialist "traitors" who in assisting their governments and their bourgeoisie would once more deceive the working class.

The efforts of the Center at Berne led by Longuet and Adler to leave the way open for a reconciliation of Right and Left wing Socialists were contemptuously rejected. When the Berne Conference appointed a Commission of Inquiry to visit Russia, Chicherin replied that:

> though they did not consider the Berne Conference either Socialist or in any degree representative of the working class they nevertheless would permit the Commission's journey into Russia, and would give it every opportunity of becoming acquainted from all sides with the state of affairs, just as they would any bourgeois commission directly or indirectly connected with any of the bourgeois governments, even with those then attacking Russia.[4]

Such a reply was not calculated to mollify the feelings of the recipients. It can only be explained by the widespread conviction which Bolsheviks held that the Berne Socialists were tools which the Allied governments wished to utilize to mobilize Socialist sentiment in favor of intervention in Russia to overthrow the Bolsheviks.[5] The decision of the French and British governments to refuse passports to the members of the Commission challenged the validity of this hypothesis. Yet the convictions of the Bolsheviks that the Berne International had to be combatted remained unshaken. The Third International was summoned into being to divert the masses from the "bankrupt" leadership of the old International to the uncompromising revolutionary road upon which the Bolsheviks had already set foot.

The invitation laid down a tentative platform for the proposed Third International. The platform, the invitation stated, had been "drawn up in agreement with the programme of the Spartacist Union in Germany and of the Communist Party in Russia."[6] It set forth fifteen propositions which embody the objects and tactics of the proposed International. The first seven deal with general objectives and methods. The call points out that this is "the epoch of the decomposition and breakup of the world capitalist system." Consequently the task of the working class is (1) the immediate seizure of state power and the suppression of the "bourgeois" governmental machinery; (2) the abandonment of "false

---

[4] Arthur Ransome, *Russia in 1919*, New York, 1919, 156-157.

[5] The view of Litvinov was typical. Of the proposed Berne Commission he said: "In this case a group of men already committed to condemn the revolution are coming to pass judgment on it. If they were not to condemn the revolution, they would be condemning themselves." See Ransome, *op. cit.*, 158.

[6] For text see Dutt, *op. cit.*, 64-68.

bourgeois democracy" for the dictatorship of the working class dedicated to the "systematic suppression and expropriation of the exploiting classes;" (3) the use of the dictatorship of the proletariat to suppress private property in the means of production, and to secure the centralization of economic function in the hands of the proletarian dictatorship; (4) the arming of the proletariat and disarming of the bourgeoisie and their agents; (5) the maintenance of contact between various parts of the revolutionary proletariat and the consolidation of countries where the Socialist revolution is already victorious. The method of the struggle is to consist of "the action of the proletarian masses even to open armed conflict with the power of the capitalist state."

The next six points deal with the relations to other Socialist parties. The old International is divided into three groups: first, the avowed Social-Chauvinists who "are fighting against the proletarian revolution with arms in their hands; against them only a fight without mercy is acceptable;" second, the Center led by Kautsky which is "an association of changeable elements incapable of any settled policy;" the policy of the Communists toward the Center ought to be to "criticize it relentlessly, unmask its leaders, and separate out the more revolutionary elements;" third, and finally, there is the revolutionary Left wing. The task of the Third International is to form a bloc of all organizations and tendencies identified with the revolutionary labor movement.

The last two points in the program outline the plan of the proposed International. The Congress of the Third International is to be transformed into a common organ of combat with a view to permanent struggle and the systematic direction of the movement. "The interests of the movement in each country are to be subordinated to the general interests of the revolution from an international point of view." The elaboration of organizational detail is left to the Congress.

With this clarion call to action summoning the cohorts of revolution together, the first Congress of the Communist International assembled at Moscow from March 2 to 6, 1919. Under the prevailing conditions, a thoroughly representative gathering of revolutionary Socialists was not possible. The tremendous haste with which the Conference was called and the difficulties of gaining entrance into Russia were partly responsible for the small number of delegates. Representatives with full voting rights came from nineteen groups, chiefly from Eastern and Central Europe. Advisory delegates were present from France, Great Britain, Czecho-Slovakia, the United States, Switzerland, Jugo-Slavia, Holland, Bulgaria,

Turkey and some parts of Asia.[7] Represented at the gathering were many of the participants in the Zimmerwald movement, including Angelica Balabanova, the secretary of the International Socialist Commission. Thus the way was prepared for the merging of the Zimmerwald organization and the Communist International. Some of the delegates lacked official credentials from the parties which they purported to represent. Some of them were merely party members who happened to be in Russia and sympathized with the aims of the proposed International. Ransome, the only non-Communist journalist present, pointed out this aspect of the gathering. "There was a make-believe side to the whole affair in which English Left Socialists were represented by Finberg and the Americans by Reinstein neither of whom had or was likely to have any means of communicating with his constituents."[8]

The opening of the conference was attended with some mystery. Ransome has an interesting description of the gathering.[9] The meeting was in a small room in the Kremlin, decorated in red and draped with banners with "Long live the Third International" inscribed upon them in many languages. "The præsidium was on the raised dais at the end of the room, Lenin sitting in the middle behind a long red covered table

[7] A complete list of the delegates may be found in *First Congress of the Communist International* (stenographic report of the proceedings in Russian), Petrograd, 1921, 5-6. The following were represented:

Delegates with Full Voting Rights	Votes
Armenia (Communist Party)	1
Austria (Communist Party)	3
Esthonia (Communist Party)	3
Finland (Communist Party)	1
Germany (Communist Party)	3
Hungary (Communist Party)	5
Lettland (Communist Party)	3
Lithuania (Communist Party)	1
Norway (Social Democratic Labor Party)	3
Poland (Communist Party)	3
Russia	5
Sweden (Left Socialist Party)	3
Switzerland (Social Democratic Party)	3
Ukraine (Communist Party)	3
United States (Socialist Labor Party)	5
Balkan Revolutionary Socialist Federation	3
Communist Party of German Colonies in Russia	1
Group of Oriental Nationalities in Russia	1
Left Zimmerwaldians.	5

(This list does not include advisory delegates)

[8] Ransome, *op. cit.*, 217-218.

[9] *Ibid.*, 213-220.

with Albrecht, a young German Spartacist on the right and Platten, the Swiss, on the left. . . ."[10] Business was conducted and speeches were made in all languages though German was used most commonly. "It was really an extraordinary affair," wrote Ransome, "and in spite of some childishness I could not help realizing that I was present at something that will go down in the histories of Socialism . . ."[11]

The agenda of the conference included the following items of business: 1. Presentation of reports by the delegates on the situation in the different countries; 2. programme of the Communist International; 3. bourgeois democracy and the dictatorship of the proletariat; 4. Attitude toward the socialist parties and the Berne conference; 5. international situation and the policy of the Allies; 6. election of committees and organization.[12] The chief work of the conference consisted first in the establishment of the provisional organization of the Third International and second in the preparation of a manifesto and programme which set forth the policies of the International.

The Congress established its continuity with the Zimmerwald-Kienthal movement by dissolving the Zimmerwald organization and absorbing the International Socialist Commission into the Communist International. Rakovsky, Lenin, Zinoviev, Trotsky and Platten, all representatives of the Zimmerwald Left, issued the following "Declaration of participators in the Zimmerwald Conference":

The Zimmerwald and Kienthal Conferences were significant at the time when it was important to unite all the elements of the proletariat, who were ready to protest in one way or another against imperialistic murder. But, together with decided communistic elements, the Zimmerwald agreement or coalition embraced elements of the Centre, pacifists and wavering elements. These elements of the Centre, as the Berne Conference shows, now join the Social patriots in fighting against the revolutionary proletariat, and in this way Zimmerwald is used in the interest of reaction.

At the same time the Communist stream is gathering force in many countries, and a conflict with the Centre elements, who check the development of the Socialist revolution, has become one of the most urgent tasks of the revolutionary proletariat.

The Zimmerwald Union or Coalition has outlived its purpose. All that was really revolutionary in it goes over to the Communist International.

The subjoined signatories and participators in the Zimmerwald arrangement declare that they consider the Zimmerwald organization as liquidated, and they

[10] *Ibid.*, 215.
[11] *Ibid.*, 217.
[12] *First Congress of the Communist International*, 3.

beg the Bureau of the Zimmerwald Conference to hand over all its documents to the Executive Committee of the Third International.

In the response to this declaration the Congress passed the following resolution.

After receiving the explanation of the secretary of the Zimmerwald International Socialist Conference, Comrade Balabanova, and the declaration of the participators in the Zimmerwald Conference, Comrades Rakovsky, Platten, Lenin, Trotsky and Zinoviev, the first Congress of the Communist International resolves that the Zimmerwald agreement be considered as liquidated.[13]

With Zimmerwald out of the way, the Congress went on to make provisional arrangements for the constitution of the Third International. Albrecht, the young German, opposed the immediate founding of the Third International on the ground that "not all nations were properly represented and that it might make difficulties for the political parties concerned in their own countries." [14] He was overruled. The gathering was officially proclaimed the First Congress of the Third International. Although the final draft of the constitution was left for the next full congress, provision was made for an Executive Committee to carry on activities. The Congress passed a resolution which provided the necessary organs of administration:

In order to be able to begin work without delay, the Congress at once proceeds to elect the necessary organs of administration, in the belief that a constitution in conformity with its aims should be given to the Communist International on the proposal of the Bureau at the next Congress.

The guidance or management of the Communist International will be confided to an Executive Committee to consist of one representative each of the Communist Parties in the most important countries.

The parties in Russia, Germany, German-Austria, Hungary, the Balkan Federation, Switzerland and Scandinavia shall forthwith send their representatives to the first Executive Committee.

Comrades of the country in which the Executive Committee is located shall assume the burden of work until the arrival of representatives from abroad.

The Executive Committee shall elect a Bureau of five persons.[15]

Zinoviev was selected as chairman of the Committee and Angelica Balabanova was made its secretary. The Executive Committee chose Zinoviev, Lenin, Trotsky, Rakovsky and Platten to make up the first Bureau.

The chief work of the convention was the formulation of a new Com-

---

[13] *Ibid.*, 138-139.
[14] Ransome, *op. cit.*, 119.
[15] *First Congress of the Communist International*, 124-125.

munist Manifesto which was issued March 10, under the signature of the Bureau. The document deserves to be considered in some detail for it contains the first authoritative exposition of the principles of the Third International.[16] The founders of the new International begin by announcing themselves as the spiritual descendants of "the two greatest teachers of the proletarian revolution, Karl Marx and Friedrich Engels."

The manifesto itself is divided into six parts. Part One deals with the war. "Now that Europe is covered with smoking ruins, the most ruthless of the incendiaries are searching for some one to blame for the War. . . ." The majority Socialists have fastened upon the German Kaiser as a convenient scapegoat "to erase the memory of their own guilt. . . ." The manifesto continues:

the real blame for the war lodges with finance-capital in all capitalist countries generally which subordinated the power of the state for its own nefarious ends. The War revealed the inescapable contradictions of the capitalist system. Its fruits were mass slaughter on a monumental scale and the intensification and the misery of the working class. Its heritage is a disorganized and shattered world economy. The capitalists have demonstrated their incompetence.

Only by means of a proletarian dictatorship can the present crisis be solved because it "will bear in mind the necessity of saving starving multitudes; it will introduce a general obligation to work and a régime of discipline in work, and will, in this manner in a few years, not only heal the gaping wounds caused by the war, but succeed in raising mankind to heights hitherto undreamed of."

Part Two deals with National states. The multiplication of small national states is declared to be inconsistent with the most fruitful development of their productive forces. The right of self-determination is illusory as long as small states remain pawns of the large imperialist nations. "Only a proletarian revolution can secure the best interests of small nations since it offers them an opportunity to develop their national cultures independently at the same time that it units all people in the closest economic cooperation on the basis of a universal economic plan."

Part Three treats of colonies. The last war which was a war to gain colonies was also a war fought with the aid of colonies. "Indians, Arabs, Madagascans, all fought on the European continent . . . and for what? For the right to remain in the future the slaves of England and France." At the same time the war witnessed a series of colonial insurrections which

---

[16] For text see *Communist International* #1, May 1, 1919. Russian text may be found in *First Congress of the Communist International*, 162ff.

the imperialist powers ruthlessly suppressed. Under capitalist rule the inhabitants of the colonies can expect no better treatment. "Liberation of the colonies can only come through liberation of the working class of the oppressed nations." This section of the manifesto concludes with a final appeal for revolt in the colonies. "Colonial slaves of Africa and Asia! The hour of proletariat dictatorship will be the hour of your release!"

The Fourth Part is devoted to answering the accusation that Communists destroy liberty and democracy. Since in the Communist analysis, the state is an instrument of class rule, in a bourgeois state liberty and democracy do not exist for the proletariat. The capitalist class dominates the machinery of political democracy; it controls all the wellsprings of political life and thought. "To demand of the proletariat in the final life and death struggle with capitalism that it should follow lamb-like the demands of bourgeois democracy would be the same as to ask a man who is defending his life against robbers to follow the artificial rules of a French duel that have been set by his enemy but not followed by him." The proletariat must therefore create its own forms of democracy. It can secure real freedom by the creation of workers' Soviets.

The Fifth Part discusses the Workers', Soldiers' and Peasants' Soviets which are to be the basic reliance of the proletariat in its struggle for the world revolution. By means of the Soviets the class-conscious working class will be able to achieve and hold power. But they must first overthrow the machinery of the capitalist state. The imperialist war which pitted nations against nations is passing into a civil war which lines up class against class. This makes necessary the disarming of the bourgeoisie, and the arming of the proletariat to safeguard the victories of the working class. "The Soviet army is inseparable from the Soviet state."

The last Part deals with the problem of international union and with the relations of revolutionary Socialists to other branches of the Socialist movement. The Second International is declared to be bankrupt. "Just as the War of 1870 dealt a death blow to the First International by revealing that there was not in fact behind the Social-revolutionary programme any compact power of the masses, so the War of 1914 killed the Second International by showing that above the consolidated labor masses there stood labor parties which converted themselves into servile organs of the bourgeois state." Again, Communists are called upon to fight the Social-patriots who act as the "hangmen" of the working class and "the hazy, fickle and irresolute Center" which gives verbal recognition to the programme of Social revolution while denying it in substance.

The members of the Third International regard themselves as the "direct successors of the heroic efforts and martyrdom of a long series of revolutionary generations from Baboeuf to Karl Liebknecht and Rosa Luxemburg. As the First International foresaw the future developments and pointed the way; as the Second International gathered together and organized millions of the proletarians, so the Third International is the International of open mass action, the INTERNATIONAL OF DEEDS." The manifesto concludes with a final plea:

We appeal to laboring men and women in all countries to join us under the Communist banner under which the first great victory already has been won. Proletarians in all lands! Unite to fight against imperialist barbarity, against monarchy, against the privileged classes, against the bourgeois state, and bourgeois property, against all kinds and forms of Social and National oppression. Join us—proletarians in every country—flock to the banner of the workmen's councils, and fight the revolutionary fight for the power and dictatorship of the proletariat.

With this call to action the Third International was launched on its career, a career that was to be marked by many vicissitudes of fortune. In the international labor movement the cleavage which had been precipitated by the war was complete.

CHAPTER XII

SUMMARY AND INTERPRETATIONS

A study in the origins of the Third International is necessarily a study in the disintegration of the Second International. In the preceding pages that process of disintegration has been traced through three stages: (1) the attitude of Socialists at the outbreak of the World War; (2) the attitude of Socialists toward the war once it become a reality; (3) the attitude toward the Bolshevik revolution. The contrast in the tactics of Right, Center and Left Socialists in each of these stages may be recapitulated in general terms.

At the outbreak of the war, the Right supported the war credits; the Center vacillated in its attitude; the Left opposed the credits. During the war the Right desired to push the war to a victorious conclusion and opposed dealings with enemy Socialists. The Center offered pacific resistance to the war and called for a revival of international solidarity among Socialists. The Left attempted to transform the war between nations into a revolutionary war between classes. With the triumph of the Bolsheviks in Russia, the problem of the relations of the various wings of the socialist movement was presented in acute form because the Bolshevik victory had been won at the expense of other branches of the Russian socialist movement. The Right Socialists condemned the methods of Bolshevism and in Germany virtually conducted a civil war with the Spartacists. The Center pleaded for a "Hands off Russia" policy and suspended judgment on the Russian experiment pending more information. The Left sought to follow the Russian example by fomenting revolution on a world-wide scale even if it entailed open conflict with Right Socialists for the control of the state machinery, as in Germany.

The policies of the Right, Center and Left will be discussed separately in order to illuminate the process of disintegration in the Second International from which the Third International emerged.

First, the attitude of the Right. Before the outbreak of the World War, the Right Socialists joined with other wings of the Socialist movement in protesting against the impending war and in bringing pressure to bear on the governments to maintain peace. These efforts failed because of: (1) the constitutional infirmity of the Second International as an effective instrument of international collaboration among Socialists; (2) the

212

failure to agree on effective tactics to be universally applied by Socialists to paralyze the war-making power of national states; (3) the general agreement among Right Socialists that in the event of a defensive war the proletariat was bound to support the Fatherland; (4) the absence of reliable information to determine whether the belligerents were fighting a defensive war; (5) the difficulties of communication in the period of crisis which hindered agreement among Socialists on a common course of action; (6) the identification of the interests of their socialist masses with the political and economic organizations of the national states.

When war became a fact that could not be ignored, Right Socialists supported the belligerent governments on both sides of the trenches. They gave their votes for the war credits in Germany and France; supported recruiting campaigns in Great Britain, and mobilized all their power to carry the war to a victorious conclusion for their own states. For the duration of the war they declared for a policy of civil peace which meant suspension of the class struggle and collaboration between socialist and bourgeois parties for the common welfare of the state. For the greater part of the war they opposed the revival of the International and vied with each other in the bitterness with which they reproached enemy Socialists for their abandonment of socialist ideals.

The Right Socialists organized conferences of Inter-Allied Socialists and conferences of Socialists of the Central Powers, in order primarily to strengthen the bond of union among Socialists against the enemy. They argued that the International was essentially an instrument of peace which was suspended for the duration of the war. They opposed the Zimmerwald and Kienthal gatherings in 1915 and 1916. The Right Socialists of the Allied countries accepted the Stockholm conference reluctantly as a result of pressure from the Center and because they were afraid that a separate peace between Germany and Russia might result from a meeting of German and Russian Socialists without the presence of representatives of Allied Socialists.

At the same time they proclaimed their adherence to a peace which would embody such Socialist and democratic principles as the self-determination of nations, limitations of armaments, compulsory arbitration of all disputes between states, and parliamentary control of foreign policy. But the realization of these aims was to be left to negotiation after the war. Socialists were expected only to exert pressure on the governments to compel them to base the war settlement on these principles of a lasting peace.

The position of the Right was made more difficult by the November Revolution. In Germany the Right Socialists had to decide whether to help the German government fight the Bolsheviks or whether to answer the call of the Bolsheviks to upset the German government by force. The Right Socialists of the Allied Powers had to decide whether to force their governments to heed the Bolshevik call for a general peace or whether to ignore the Bolshevik appeal for aid. With the beginning of Allied Intervention in Russia, the Right was forced to determine whether to support a movement of capitalist nations which sought to overthrow a Left Socialist government or whether to oppose that movement. In each case the Right Socialists identified their interests with the states to which they owed allegiance. The German Right sought to moderate the demands which Imperial Germany made on the Bolsheviks, but in the end they supported the Treaty of Brest-Litovsk, refused to organize a revolutionary mass uprising in Germany, and when the German revolution arrived took over its direction and forcibly suppressed the attempt of the Left Socialists to seize control.

The Right Socialists of the Allied countries used their influence to keep the Bolsheviks in the war, and when that effort failed supported intervention in Russia as a method of restoring the Eastern Front. They denounced the violent methods of the Bolsheviks and their summary treatment of the more moderate Russian Socialists. Only after the armistice, under the influence of mass unrest and war weariness, did they begin to call upon the Allied armies to withdraw from Russia.

After the armistice the Right sought to restore the Second International at the Berne Conference, but even there some of the more intransigent among the Socialists of the victorious powers, with war hatreds still fresh, attempted to brand the defeated Socialists with the responsibility for the catastrophe. Only by avoiding the whole question and indulging in a mutual white-wash were the Right Socialists able to unite on a socialist program for the peace settlement. The Rights could not agree on war responsibility; they found a common ground in their animosity to the Bolsheviks, and while avoiding any indictment by name, they condemned the methods and tactics for which the Bolsheviks stood.

The Rights suffered a steady diminution of strength during the war. At the beginning of the war, they dominated the socialist movement in France and Germany, the two countries in which Socialists were in the best position to prevent the war, or put a stop to it once it had begun. In Germany the opposition gained in strength from month to month and in April, 1917, organized itself into a separate political party, the Independent Social-Democratic Party. In France the party split did not come so soon, but the majority strength dwindled so much that the rôles were reversed and in 1917, the "minoritaires" led by Longuet, became the majority while the Right sank into a subordinate position. The prolongation of the war revealed that the policy of the Right Socialists was becoming increasingly unpopular among the rank and file of Socialists.

The Rights were subjected to a running fire of criticism from two directions. The Centrists felt that the efforts of Socialists should be directed toward obtaining an immediate peace, while the Left insisted that since the workers had no Fatherland, the duty of true Socialists was to wage a revolutionary class war to dispossess the master class in all nations.

It is the Left indictment of the Right which need to be considered here, for it is the fundamental antagonism between these two positions which produced the split in the Second International. The Left accused the Right of treason to Socialism on the ground that the latter had transformed Socialist parties into servile organs of the bourgeois state. The revised programme of the Communist International sums up the indictment:

The war crisis of 1914-1918 was accompanied by the disgraceful collapse of the Social-democratic Second International. Acting in complete violation of the thesis of the "Communist Manifesto" written by Marx and Engels, that the proletariat has no Fatherland under capitalism and in complete violation of the anti-war resolutions passed by the Stuttgart and Basel Congresses, the leaders of the Social-democratic parties in the various countries, with a few exceptions, voted for the war credits, came out definitely in defense of the imperialist Fatherland (i.e., the state organizations of the imperialist bourgeoisie) and instead of combating the imperialist war, became its loyal soldiers, bards and propagandists. In the subsequent period Social-democracy supported the predatory treaties (Brest-Litovsk, Versailles); it actively aligned itself with the militarists in the bloody suppression of proletarian uprisings (Noske), and conducted armed warfare against the first proletarian republic (Soviet Russia).[1]

Is this indictment and bill of particulars which condemned the Right as "traitors" to Socialism justified? Did the Right betray the Second International during the World War? There is a grave danger of becoming involved in fruitless polemics in attempting to frame an answer to such a question. The existence of the danger makes caution necessary, but it does not excuse an evasion. It is in this spirit that the following considerations are advanced.

[1] *Programme of the Communist International*, New York, 1929, 20.

The Communist case is based on the assumption that there is only one proper kind of Socialist tactics, that which is based on the proposition that the proletariat has no Fatherland and that the class struggle must be ceaselessly waged. That the action of the Right Socialists during the war did not conform to such an internationalist class struggle ideology is undeniable. But on the other hand, it is too often forgotten that Right Socialists never accepted such an ideology, even before the war.

To accuse the Right of forsaking the revolutionary doctrines of Marx is to accuse most of its adherents of something which they never claimed to profess. To accuse the Right of abandoning the class struggle and the international solidarity of the proletariat is also to accuse them of abandoning theories to which most of them never subscribed. For the position of the Right even before the war was based on the proposition that the capitalist state grows by a process of peaceful development into the Socialist people's state; that the instruments for working this transformation are trade unions, the cooperative movement, social reform, and democracy. As this transformation takes place, the interests of the proletariat and the state tend to become identical. The workers therefore do not renounce love of country; they become attached to their country more intimately as the state makes additional provision for their welfare. In such a state, workers deplore war and do what they can to avoid it, but if war comes, the working class is not disposed to bend its neck to foreign rule.

That is essentially the theoretical position of the Right, proclaimed by Bernstein before the war and by Scheidemann and a host of Right leaders during and after the war. With that position the attitude of Right Socialists during the World War was not fundamentally contradictory. It is possible to challenge the wisdom of the theoretical position of the Rights or even the effectiveness of the tactics adopted to reach the socialist goal. It is a less satisfactory kind of argument to impeach the sincerity of the Right leaders and theorists or to test the action of the Right during the war by standards to which they did not subscribe; but to which the critics contend they should have subscribed.

The intention of the writer has not been to pass on the respective merits of the position and tactics adopted by the Right and Left Socialists in reaching the desired end. The object has been rather to emphasize the fact that Right Socialists started with a different premise from Left Socialists. They therefore behaved differently. Whether they behaved better or worse is a question which can only be effectively answered by the judgment of posterity.

The attitude of the Center Socialists during the war will be considered next. Was their conduct also foreshadowed by the ideals and tactics proclaimed by their intellectual leaders? Kautsky's position as a typical exponent of the Centrist view had already been reviewed earlier. There is a great danger, however, in settling upon any Centrist theory as typical. For the Centrist position was not sharply defined. It ran the gamut of a vast number of possible variations and combinations between the Right and the Left. It varied from time to time as the result of the interplay of idea and circumstance. Generalizations must therefore be framed with caution and qualified by numerous exceptions in applying them to specific cases.

With these considerations in mind, the following principles are set down as forming the more fundamental characteristics of the Center position: (1) an acceptance of the Marxian laws of the decay of capitalist society, but an interpretation of those laws in terms of peaceful development rather than violence and struggle. The theorist of the Center envisaged a long period of preparation for Socialism as fore-ordained. Because the process cannot be hurried, premature uprisings against the capitalist state are doomed to defeat and ought to be discouraged. (2) The process of preparation may be used by the proletariat to develop its powers. Within the framework of the capitalist state the proletariat may gain the political experience which will enable it to manage the machinery of a socialist state. Utilizing the tools of democracy in a capitalist state, the working class can make clear its strength and obtain the concessions which are indispensable to avoid violence. The Centrist philosophy is permeated with a horror of useless bloodshed. It is therefore easy to understand how such a philosophy would justify an attitude of pacifism during the World War. (3) It is on the question as to whether the first loyalty of the Socialist is to his class or to the state that the Centrist position is least clear. The quandary of the Center is revealed by two quotations from Kautsky's articles in the *Neue Zeit*. On October 2, 1914, he takes an avowedly national-defensist position.

One thing is clear: every people, and the proletariat of every people, has a pressing interest in this: to prevent the enemy of the country from coming over the frontier, as it is this way that the terror and devastation of war reach their most frightful form; that of a hostile invasion. And in every national state the proletariat, too, must use all its energy to see that the independence and integrity of the national territory is maintained. That is an essential part of democracy, and democracy is a necessary basis for the struggle and the victory of the proletariat.

On November 27, 1914, in the *Neue Zeit,* he suggests a different standard which may be called "the theory of proletarian interests." If "one takes sides, not according to the interests of one's country, but according to that of the whole proletariat, and if one asks oneself whose victory gives better prospect for the progress of our cause, not only in the home country but in the whole world" then the fundamental unity of the world proletariat is not violated. True, this criterion may not produce the same action in every country. It may even produce the same practical results as fighting in defense of the Fatherland, since each Socialist Party makes its own practical applications. Socialists may still fight against Socialists, but at least, Kautsky argues, the criterion is an international one, and the fundamental principles of the International are not violated.

Thus the theory of Kautsky as expressed in the first quotation does not differ in any important essentials from the views of moderate Rights. In the second quotation a view is taken which is internationalist in theory, but nationalist in its applications. It is this view which the Revolutionary Left wing had in mind when it condemned the Center for being Socialist in thought, but chauvinist in deed. It was this view which represented the most considered effort of Center Socialists to rationalize their conduct in war time.

The position of the Center was a difficult one. Believing that the time was not ripe for the armed class warfare which the Left desired to wage, they could not throw their support to the Left. On the other hand, retaining a belief in the fundamental solidarity of the international proletariat, they had to find an internationalist formula which would justify the conduct of Right Socialists. Their theoretical rôle was one of mediation and conciliation. They sought to reconcile the diversity of views among Socialists with unity of organization. The impact of events revealed that the task was an impossible one. As the hostility between the Right and Left grew more intense and a split in organization seemed inevitable, the position of the Centrists grew constantly more embarrassing. Alliance with either the Right or the Left represented for the Centrists a choice between two evils rather than that affirmation of the unity of the proletariat which they held most sacred. Consequently the rôle of the Center during the World War became one of vacillation and uncertainty as between Right and Left, while they strove by all means to preserve the unity of the proletariat.

The tactics of the Center during the war illustrate this dilemma. At the outbreak of the war, the "theory of proletarian interests" led Center Socialists to vote the war credits in France, to take similar action in Germany as a matter of party discipline while opposing the credits in the meeting of the party group, and to deny the war credits in Russia. At the same time all Center Socialists were quick to disclaim responsibility for the conduct of the war. They condemned the chauvinistic utterances of their Right colleagues and directed all their efforts to bring a speedy end to the conflict.

During the war they sought to convoke a full meeting of the International Socialist Bureau. When the Right Socialists of France and Germany prevented this meeting, the more radical Centrists were thrown into the arms of the Left. At Zimmerwald and Kienthal they joined with the Left in protesting against the war and criticizing the conduct of the Right Socialists. They grew rapidly in strength as the discontent with the war mounted. Under pressure from the Left their opposition to the war drove some of them to adopt more vigorous tactics. They refused to vote war credits or support recruiting campaigns and carried on an active peace propaganda. In Germany the opposition Centrists split off from the party and formed an independent organization. In France the Center led by Longuet and Pressemane finally captured the party organization. Most of the neutral Socialist parties threw their support to the Centrist side.

In spite of the increasing alienation of the Right and Center, the Center still refused to support the revolutionary class war tactics of the Left. It clung to the conviction that it was still possible to revive the old International. The Russian Revolution of March, 1917, provided the opportunity. Under the joint inspiration of neutral Socialists and Russian Socialists of the Center, the Stockholm project was hatched, and preparations were made to resurrect the International. The Right joined with Center Socialists in plans for the Conference; the extreme Left decided to boycott the gathering. Governmental opposition prevented the Conference from meeting, but Stockholm remained as a symbol of unity to which both the Right and the Center subscribed.

The Bolshevik revolution called for a definition of attitude by the Center. The result was division and disintegration. Some Centrists went over to the Left. Others were drawn back to the Right. Still others tried to maintain an attitude of neutrality by suspending judgment. The Berne Conference of 1919 offered the first organizational test of Centrist loyalties.

The more moderate Centrists led by Kautsky abjured the violent road of dictatorship and turned for support to the Right which took its stand upon the platform of peaceful democratic progress toward Socialism. Kautsky disagreed fundamentally with the Bolsheviks on the question of tactics. As he saw it, the issue was "democracy versus dictatorship." He refused to throw his support to a party "which gained power in fighting against other Socialist parties and exercises its power while excluding other Socialist parties from the executive."[2] Socialism without democracy Kautsky regards as "unthinkable." Therefore he turned his back on the Left and joined with the Right at Berne in efforts to revive the Second International.

Even at Berne, however, there was represented a group of Centrists led by Adler and Longuet who still resolutely argued the necessity of reconstituting the international proletarian front by bringing together representatives of all currents of thought in the Socialist movement. They therefore asked the conference not to condemn Soviet Russia for fear that such a decision would make a meeting of representatives of the working classes of all countries more difficult in the future. Their efforts to avoid the split were doomed to futility. The call which they sounded could not be heard amid the recriminations engendered by four and a half years of mounting bitterness.

The third and most radical of the Centrist groups represented by the Italian and Swiss Socialist parties refused to send representatives to the Berne Conference and declared their agreement with the programme of the Communist International. The end of the period therefore found the Center divided. An influential group led by Kautsky identified itself with the Right at Berne. Another group led by Longuet and Adler still hoped for the reunion of all branches of the Socialist movement; the third group threw in its lot with the Revolutionary Left.

The attitude of the Left toward these groups varied with the nature of the groups. The tactics of the Communist International toward the Center were directed toward separating out and absorbing its more revolutionary elements, while criticizing and unmasking the so-called "opportunist" leaders. Toward Kautsky, the Left was particularly vindictive.

[2] Karl Kautsky, *The Dictatorship of the Proletariat*, London, 1919.

Lenin's *State and Revolution* had as one of its chief purposes to combat and expose the so-called "Kautskian perversions" of Marx.[3]

The theoretical position of the Left has already been referred to. It will be briefly summarized here. Its sources are the revolutionary aspects of Marx's thought. The state in the Left analysis is an instrument of class rule. The capitalist state exists to ensure the domination of capitalists. To it the worker owes no loyalty. It is not his state. "Democracy, so-called, that is 'bourgeois democracy' is nothing more nor less than veiled dictatorship by the bourgeoisie."

As the process of capitalist disintegration bears with increasing heaviness on the proletariat the capitalist régime becomes unbearable for the worker. The exploited masses then rise up in rebellion against the whole régime, throw off their oppressors, and assume power. For the capitalist state they substitute a proletarian state, which is also an organ of suppression but one directed by the vanguard of workers to secure rights for workers and to break the opposition of the bourgeoisie. The difference between the dictatorship of the proletariat and the dictatorship of the bourgeoisie consists in this, that while the latter is designed to maintain the class structure of society, the former represents a transition stage toward a classless society when the state as such will wither away.

Such in broad outline was the theoretical position of the Left at the outbreak of the war. Its conduct and strategy during the war was based on these theoretical premises. The war was condemned as an imperialist slaughter caused by the ruling class in all countries.

"The war is the beginning of the disintegration of the Capitalist system," said a Bolshevik manifesto on the imperialist war. "It calls forth the growth of the forces which make for an economic and political crisis; it intensifies and accentuates the discontent of the toiling masses; it

---

[3] Into the merits of this controversy the writer refuses to be drawn, except to indicate the difficulties involved in passing judgment. Insofar as Lenin and Kautsky both seek to reinforce their position by quotations from Marx, the problem becomes one of Marxian exegesis, of interpreting passages, weighing their significance, and reconciling their deviations. Both Kautsky and Lenin are able to select passages which serve their purposes. By emphasizing different aspects of Marx's thought, they bend eclecticism to the purposes of controversy. For the scope of this study, it is less important to determine which interpretation distorts Marx the least, than it is to be aware of the conflict between these diverse interpretations. For it is this conflict in theory which helps to illuminate the differences in the behavior of Left and Center Socialists during the World War. It helps explain why that very considerable section of Socialist opinion which took its lead from Kautsky threw in its lot with the Right rather than the Left when the crisis came and the choice had to be made.

leads them to civil war. The task of the Socialists does not consist in being afraid of civil war, but in getting ready for such a civil war and for a proletarian revolution."[4]

From the beginning of the war the efforts of the Left were therefore directed toward transforming the war between nations into a war between classes. Lenin and his collaborators endeavored to weld together those forces in the international labor movement which were united on the necessity of revolutionary mass action. Weak in numbers but strong in leadership, compact in organization, realistic in capitalizing the mistakes of opponents, and possessed of a driving power and vitality that brushed aside obstacles, the Revolutionary Left accumulated strength, seized power in Russia, made a bid for leadership in other countries, and organized the Third International to challenge the hegemony of the Second International in the labor and socialist world.

Even in the earliest days of the war, the Left allowed no opportunity to escape to expose the "chauvinistic" weaknesses of its opponents and to popularize its own uncompromising program. Left delegates advanced their theses at the International Women's Congress at Berne in the spring of 1915 and at the International Youth Conference at Berne in April of the same year. They participated in the work of the Zimmerwald Conference in September of 1915 together with Center Socialists. Though they failed to give the Conference a revolutionary orientation, they deepened the gulf between Right and Center Socialists and laid the basis for the Third International by organizing the Zimmerwald Left.

During the next year they gained fresh recruits; at Kienthal the strength of the Left was greatly increased. The pressure from the Left was so strong that the Center became impregnated with Left ideas. The scission which occurred in the British Socialist Party, and the rapidly approaching split in the German Party evidenced the tension resulting from the increasing animosity between the Right and Center as a result of the Left pressure.

After Kienthal the Left consolidated its strength while not abandoning all cooperation with the Center. The Left leaders—particularly Lenin —became convinced that no real compromise with the Center was possible, and that the Third International would emerge only from the fighting group of revolutionaries who constituted the Zimmerwald Left.

The outbreak of the Russian Revolution in March, 1917, enabled the Bolsheviks, the leaders of the Zimmerwald Left, to return to Russia

[4] *Sotzial Demokrat* #33.

where they played an increasingly active rôle in the political life of that country. Within Russia they sought to deepen the Revolution by seizing power. In the labor and socialist world they formed the rallying point around which revolutionary Socialists gathered. They opposed participation in the Stockholm Conference because they professed to see in the Stockholm gathering a meeting of pseudo-Socialist agents of the imperialist governments. The failure of the Stockholm Conference to convene reacted to their benefit.

The Stockholm Conference presented a unique opportunity to reunite the Right and Center and lay the foundations for the revival of the Second International in all its pre-war strength. The refusal of the Allied governments to allow the conference to gather prevented this consummation and thus indirectly strengthened the case for the Left and its tactics. The Stockholm fiasco worked even more directly to lift the Left to power. For the inability of Socialists to come together at Stockholm to bring peace to war-weary Russia condemned the tactics of the Socialist ministers of the Provisional Government who participated in the project, and drove the peace hungry masses to the extreme Left. Thus the failure of the Stockholm Conference helped to prepare the way for the Bolshevik seizure of power.

The triumph of the Bolsheviks in Russia raised the prestige of the revolutionary Left wing immeasurably. The Bolsheviks were now faced with the double task of carrying on the government of Russia and waging a world-wide revolutionary offensive. Propaganda played a highly important rôle in Soviet diplomacy between the November Revolution and the founding of the Communist International. While not potent enough to prevent Germany from imposing the Peace of Brest-Litovsk, Left wing propaganda helped to prepare the way for the German Revolution. Bolshevik aid was also given to the Spartacist uprising which was suppressed by a Right Socialist government. Revolutionary propaganda among the masses met some success in limiting the scope of Allied aid to the counter-revolution in Russia.

In the early months of 1919 a revolutionary offensive was well under way in Central and Eastern Europe. Bolshevism was spreading among the masses. The Socialists of the Right and moderate Center found themselves placed on the defensive. They were in danger of losing the right to speak for the masses. In February, 1919, they gathered together at Berne to consolidate their strength. The conference was only partially successful. Influential Socialist parties representing such important countries as Italy, Switzerland, and the United States, refused to answer the call. A restive Centrist minority at Berne led by Longuet and Adler was not altogether happy at such a reunion.

The reason was the impending organization of the Communist International. From the north had come the call for a new International of the revolutionary proletariat. The basic appeal of the call was the success of the Revolution in Russia. It came at a time when a revolutionary wave was rising, when Communism threatened to engulf all of Central and Eastern Europe. With the meeting of the Communist International at Moscow in March, 1919, as a counter-blast of defiance to the Berne Conference, the disintegration of the Second International was complete.

The World War marked the end of an era in the history of labor and socialist internationalism.[5] The schism which had been dimly foreshadowed by the internal disagreements in the pre-war International had at last matured. The World War was not responsible for the cleft, except in a very proximate sense. The war merely accelerated a process of dissolution which was implicit in the incompatible positions of Right, Center and Left Wing Socialists. If there is to be community, there must first be consensus. Proletarian solidarity yielded to the surge of rival nationalisms during the World War because the builders of the international labor community had failed to agree upon the theoretical foundations which could make it possible.

[5] The author expects to deal with the post-war vicissitudes of the international labor movement in a forthcoming volume on the Third International.

BIBLIOGRAPHY

NOTE: In gathering the material for this study it was necessary to draw upon a large variety of documents, periodicals, reports, books, and pamphlets. The list which is here presented does not exhaust the subject. It represents material consulted which proved immediately helpful. It has seemed desirable to classify the bibliography under the four following heads: (1) Primary sources (2) Semi-official sources (3) Periodicals (4) Secondary material.

I. PRIMARY SOURCES—These are classified as far as possible according to subject matter. Some overlapping is unavoidable when the same source contains material bearing on several aspects of the subject.

1. The Second International Before the War.
   Proceedings of the Congresses of the Second International (1889-1910) especially:
   VII° Congrès Socialiste International (Stuttgart), compte rendu analytique publié par le Secretariat du Bureau Socialiste International, Bruxelles, 1908.
   VIII° Congrès Socialiste Internationale (Copenhagen), 1911.

2. Socialism at the Outbreak of the War.
   Grünberg, Carl, *Die Internationale und der Weltkrieg*, Leipzig, 1916. A valuable collection of documents on the action of socialist parties in all parts of the world at the beginning of the World War; also contains the resolutions of the Second International on the War in convenient form.
   Walling, William E., *The Socialists and the War*, New York, 1915. A similar collection in English, rich in reprints from the European socialist press, with incidental comments by the editor.

3. Reports of Party Conferences and Party Resolutions During the World War.

   A. *Germany*
   Protokoll über die Verhandlungen des Parteitages S. D. P. (Deutschland) 1918-1919. Berlin.
   Bericht über den Gründungsparteitag der Kommunistischen Partei Deutschlands (Spartakusbund) vom 30 Dezember 1918 bis 1 Jan. 1919. Berlin, 1919.
   Drahn, Ernst and Leonhard, S., *Unterirdische Literatur im Revolutionären Deutschland während des Weltkrieges*, Berlin, 1920. Extracts from the voluminous pamphlet literature circulated secretly by the Left German opposition during the War.
   Meyer, Ernst, (editor), *Spartakus im Kriege*, Berlin, 1927. A valuable collection of Spartacist letters and broadsheets.

   B. *Austria*
   Die Verhandlungen der Sozial-demokratischen Arbeiterpartei Deutschösterreichs, Vienna, 1916.
   Brügel, Ludwig, *Geschichte der Oesterreichischen Sozial-Demokratie*. 5 vols. Vienna, 1925. Contains extensive reprints of important documents of the war period.

   C. *France*
   Pendant la Guerre—Le Parti Socialiste, la Guerre, et la Paix—toutes les

Résolutions et tous les Documents du Parti Socialiste de Juillet 1915 à fin 1917. Paris, 1918.

Confédération Général du Travail, *Reports of Conferences,* especially *Report, Congrès de Lyon* (1919).

D. Belgium

The Belgian Labor Party, *Memorandum on Peace Terms,* New York, 1918.

E. *Italy*

Le Parti Socialiste Italien et L'Internationale Communiste, Paris, 1921.

F. *Russia*

Vsesoiuznaya Kommunisticheskaya Partiya, Resolutsiach (Resolutions of the All-Union Communist Party at its Congresses and Conferences), Moscow, 1927. The resolutions quoted in the foregoing pages may be found in more accessible form in the Appendices to Lenin's *Collected Works,* vols. XX-XXI.

G. *Great Britain*

Reports of the Annual Conferences of the Labour Party, especially:

15th Annual Conference—Bristol, 1916.
16th Annual Conference—Manchester, 1917.
17th Annual Conference—Nottingham, 1918.
18th Annual Conference—Southport, 1919.

McCurdy, Charles A., (editor), *A Clean Peace, The War Aims of British Labour,* New York, 1918.

H. *Miscellaneous*

The American Labor Year Book, Rand School of Social Science, New York.
The Labour Year Book, London.

4. The Zimmerwald Movement

Balabanova, Angelica, "Die Zimmerwalder Bewegung," *Archiv für die Geschichte des Sozialismus und der Arobeiterbewegung,* vols. 12-13. An invaluable collection of documents on the Zimmerwald movement.

Bulletin of the International Socialist Commission. The official voice of the Zimmerwald Bureau.

Lenin, V. I. *Collected Works,* especially

Vol. XVIII. *The Imperialist War*
Vol. XIX. *Imperialismus und Revolution*
Vol. XX. Part I and Part II. *The Revolution of 1917.*
Vol. XXI. *Die Revolution von 1917, Die Vorbereitung des Oktober.*

(Edition in English, International Publishers, New York, in German, Verlag für Literatur und Politik, Vienna, Berlin.) Rich in appendices which contain documentary material on the growth of the Left during the War which is not readily accessible elsewhere.

5. The Stockholm Conference

Comité Organisateur de la Conférence Socialiste Internationale de Stockholm, 1918. A comprehensive collection of documents dealing with the Stockholm Conference.

Balch, Emily, *Approaches to the Great Settlement,* New York, 1918. Contains documents dealing with the attitude of socialist parties toward the Stockholm Conference.

Parliamentary Debates—Official Report—Fifth Series—Commons, 1917. See especially debates on the Stockholm Conference.

6. The Revival of the Second International

Inter-Allied Labour and Socialist Conference—the Replies of the Socialist Parties of the Central Powers to the "Memorandum of War Aims." London, 1918.

Renaudel, Pierre, *L'Internationale à Berne—Biens et faits,* Paris, 1919. Contains the resolutions of the Berne Conference.

7. The Communist International.

Perveui Kongress Kommunisticheskovo Internatsionala (First Congress of the Communist International), Petrograd, 1921. (Stenographic report of the proceedings.)

Manifesto and Governing Rules of the Communist International, Chicago, 1919.

Die Komintern und der Krieg (Dokumente über den Kampf der Komintern gegen den imperialistischen Krieg und für die Verteidigung der Sowjet Union), Hamburg, 1928.

Programme of the Communist International, New York, 1929.

8. Miscellaneous

Barbusse, Henri (introduction), *The Soviet Union and Peace,* London, 1929. Convenient collection of documents, especially valuable for the diplomacy of the period 1917-1919.

Cumming, C. K. and Pettit, Walter W., *Russian-American Relations* (Documents and Papers), New York, 1920.

Texts of the "Russian" Peace, Government Printing Office, Washington, 1918. A translation of the Treaty of Brest-Litovsk and supplementary agreements between Russia and Germany.

Foreign Relations of the United States—Russia—1918, Washington, 1931. Throws light on the cordon sanitaire against Russia and Russian propaganda reprisals.

II. SEMI-OFFICIAL SOURCES—Memoirs; statements of policy by party leaders; expositions of socialist theory, etc., arranged alphabetically.

Balabanova, Angelica, *Memoirs of a Zimmerwaldian,* Leningrad, 1925.

Bernstein, Eduard, *Evolutionary Socialism,* New York, 1909. A standard statement of the Right position before the War.

Bolshevism in Russia or Revolutionary Socialism in Practice. Extracts from reports to British Foreign Office on Bolshevism in Russia. London, Department of Social Economics, 1918.

Briefe und Auszüge aus Briefen von Becker, Dietzen, Engels, Marx an Sorge. Stuttgart, 1921.

Buchanan, George, *My Mission to Russia and Other Diplomatic Memories,* Boston, 1923.

Bukharin, N. I. and Prebrazhenski, E., *The A. B. C. of Communism,* London, 1921.

Chicherin, George, *Two Years of Foreign Policy,* New York, 1920. Written from the Communist point of view; the writer's former position as Commissar for Foreign Affairs gives it authority.

Chicherin, George (Tschitscherin), *Die Internationale Politik Zweier Internationale,* Hamburg, 1920.

DeMan, Henri, *The Remaking of a Mind,* New York, 1919. The author accompanied Mueller on the mission to Paris before the outbreak of the War and also journeyed to Russia with Vandervelde.

Ebert, Friedrich, *Schriften, Aufzeichnungen, Reden,* Dresden, 1926.

Haase, Ernst (editor), *Hugo Haase, Sein Leben und Werken,* Berlin, 1930.

Huysmans, Camille, *The Policy of the International,* London, 1916. A defense of the course pursued by the Executive Committee of the Bureau of the Second International, by its secretary.

Hyndman, R. T., *Last Years of H. M. Hyndman,* London, 1923.

Kautsky, Karl, *Road to Power,* Chicago, 1909. A standard exposition of the Center position before the War.

Kautsky, Karl, *The Dictatorship of the Proletariat,* London, 1919. A criticism of the tactics and ideology of the Bolsheviks by a Center Socialist who takes his stand on Democracy as the road to socialism.

Kautsky, Karl, *Die Internationale,* Vienna, 1920.

Kautsky, Karl, *The Labour Revolution,* London, 1925.

de Kay, John, *L'Esprit de l'Internationale à Berne,* Lucerne, 1919. The author was an observer at the Berne Conference; valuable for its summary of the debates at Berne.

Kommunistische Partie Deutschlands (Spartakusbund), *Was Will der Spartakusbund,* Berlin, 1919. A statement of the program of the Spartacists.

Krupskaya, N. K., *Vospominaniya o Lenine (Memories of Lenin),* 2 vols., Moscow, 1931.

Lenin, N., *The War and the Second International* (Little Lenin Library), New York, 1930. The Left indictment of the "chauvinist" International.

Lenin, N., *Imperialism—The State and Revolution* (Vanguard Press), New York, 1929. Marxian exigesis from the point of view of a Revolutionary Socialist.

Lenin, N., and Trotsky, Leon (Louis Fraina, editor), *The Proletarian Revolution in Russia,* New York, 1918. A valuable collection of the writings of Lenin Trotsky in the months immediately following the Revolution.

Liebknecht, Karl (Julian Gumperz, editor), *Reden und Aufsätze,* Hamburg, 1921. A collection which sets forth the views of the leader of the German Left.

Liebknecht, Karl, *Das Zuchthausurteil,* Berlin, 1919.

Lockhart, R. H. Bruce, *British Agent,* New York, 1933.

Luxemburg, Rosa, *The Crisis in the German Social-Democracy,* New York, 1919.

MacDonald, J. R., *Parliament and Revolution,* London, 1919. Valuable for its criticism of the tactics of Revolutionary Socialism.

MacDonald, J. R., *Socialism after the War,* Manchester, 1918.

Marx, Karl, *Collected Works,* Available in various editions.

Paléologue, Maurice, *An Ambassador's Memoirs,* London, 1925.

Plekhanoff, G. V. *Le Social-Democratie et la Guerre,* Paris, 1916. The views of a Menshevik who favored the Allied cause.

Memoirs of Raymond Poincaré (1915) (Sir George Arthur—translator and adapter), New York, 1931.

Radek, Karl, *L'Evolution du Socialisme de la Science à l'Action.* 1918. The author is one of the most talented of Bolshevik pamphleteers. He played an important rôle in the Spartacist uprising.

Radek, Karl, *Die Deutsche Revolution,* Moscow, 1918.

Radek, Karl, *Die Entwicklung der Weltrevolution—und die Taktik der Kommunistischen Parteien im Kampfe um die Diktatur des Proletariats,* K. P. D. (Spartakusbund), 1919.

Ransome, Arthur, *Russia in 1919,* New York, 1919. The author was the only non-Communist journalist present at the First Congress of the Communist International.

Ribot, Alexandre, *Lettres à un Ami—Souvenirs de ma Vie Politique,* Paris, 1924. Throws light on the reasons for the opposition of the French Government to the Stockholm Conference.

Rosenberg, Arthur, *History of Bolshevism,* London, 1934.

Scheidemann, Philipp, *Der Zusammenbruch,* Berlin, 1921.

Scheidemann, Philipp, *Memoirs,* 2 vols., New York, 1929. A valuable record of events in Germany during the War years, from the point of view of a Right Socialist.

Schmid, Jacq, *Die Kommunistische Internationale (Dritte Internationale) und wie stellen wir uns zu ihr,* Olten, Switzerland, 1919.

Stalin, J. V., *Leninism,* London, 1928.

Troelstra, P. J., *De Stockholmsche Conferentie,* Amsterdam, 1917.

Trotsky, L., *Terrorismus und Kommunismus,* Hamburg, 1920. An answer to Kautsky.

Trotsky, L., *War and Revolution,* Moscow, 1924.

Trotsky, L., *My Life,* New York, 1930.

Vandervelde, Emile, *Three Aspects of the Russian Revolution,* London, 1918. An account of the Vandervelde mission to Russia in 1917.

Zinoviev, G., *La Révolution Russe et le Proletariat International,* 1920.

Zinoviev, G., *War and the Crisis of Socialism,* Petrograd, 1920.

Zinoviev, G., and Lenine, N., *Contre le Courant* (2 vols.), Paris, 1927. A valuable collection of the writings of the authors during the war years of 1914-15-16; record of the rise of the Left.

III. PERIODICALS AND NEWSPAPERS—The list here given is not intended to be an exhaustive catalogue of socialist periodicals and newspapers published during the War years. Only publications which were immediately useful for this study are listed.

Arbeiter-Zeitung—Organ of the Austrian Social Democracy.

Archiv für die Geschichte des Sozialismus und der Arbeiterbewegung—contains valuable source material for the history of Socialism.

Avanti—organ of the Italian Socialist Party.

Berner Tagwacht—edited by Robert Grimm, the Swiss Center Socialist; contains full reports of the Zimmerwald and Kienthal Conferences and the activities of the Opposition during the War.

La Bataille Syndicaliste—organ of the Confederation General du Travail.

Bremer Bürger-Zeitung—Left Social-Democratic newspaper.

Bulletin Communiste—contains valuable historical articles and memoirs of the War period.

The Class Struggle.

Communist International—contains official reports of the Third International.

Die Glocke—organ of the extreme German Right.

L'Humanité—daily paper published by the French Socialist Party; in the hands of the Right majority for the greater part of the War; later Pierre Renaudel was replaced as editor by Marcel Cachin, who became a Communist and carried the paper with him.

Die Internationale—the organ of the Mehring, Luxemburg, Liebknecht group.

International Press Correspondence—from time to time reprints material of historical interest.

Justice—The official organ of the British Socialist Party until the Party split, when it was replaced by the *Call.*

Labour Leader—the weekly journal of the Independent Labour Party of Great Britain; contains valuable notes on developments in the international labor and socialist world.

Labour Monthly—theoretical organ of the British Communist Party.

The Liberator—edited by Max Eastman and sympathetic to the Third International; valuable for the year 1918.

Le Militant Rouge—French Communist publication; occasional articles of historical interest.

Neue Zeit—a fortnightly journal edited by Kautsky and expressive of the views of the German Center.

Pravda—organ of the Central Committee and the Moscow Committee of the Communist Party; translations in the Appendices to Lenin's Works and in Fraina's *The Proletarian Revolution in Russia.*

La Revue Communiste—French Communist publication.

Die Rote Fahne—November 1918-January 1919, a Spartacist newspaper, later the organ of the German Communist Party.

Sozialistische Monatsheft—theoretical organ of the German Right.

Sotzial Demokrat—organ of the Foreign Committee of the Bolsheviks, published in Switzerland during the War; reprints in Lenin's *Collected Works.*

Vorwärts—the daily journal of the German Social Democracy, dominated by the Opposition in the early years of the War.

IV. SECONDARY MATERIAL—Arranged alphabetically.

Adler, Friedrich, *Die Erneuerung der Internationale,* Vienna, 1918.

Alazard, Jean, *Les Socialistes Italiens et La Guerre,* Paris, 1916.

The American Socialists and the War, New York, 1917. Rand School.

Andler, Charles, *La Décomposition politique du Socialisme Allemand* (1914-1919), Paris, 1919.

Axelrod, Paul, *Die Krise und die Aufgaben der Internationalen Sozialdemokratie,* Zurich, 1915.

Baumann, Wilhelm, *Krieg und Proletariat,* Vienna, 1924.

Beer, Max, *History of British Socialism,* 2 vols., London, 1921.

Berger, Richard, *Die Deutsche Sozial-Demokratie im dritten Kriegsjahr,* 1917.

Bernstein, Eduard, *Die Internationale der Arbeiterklasse und der Europäische Krieg.* See *Archiv für Sozialwissenschaft und Sozialpolitik,* vol. 40, p. 267.

Bernstein, Eduard, "Der Riss in der Sozialdemokratie," *Die Zukunft,* April 21, 1917.

Bevan, Edwyn, *German Social Democracy during the War,* London, 1918.

Bloch, Camille, "Les Socialistes Allemands pendant la Crise de Juillet, 1914," *Revue d'Histoire de la Guerre Mondiale,* #4, Oct. 1933.

Boudin, L. B., *Socialism and War,* New York, 1916.

Bridgman, Daisy, "Les Socialistes Anglais et la Guerre," *Revue Politique Internationale,* Lausanne, 1915, Vol. 4, 55-71.

Ciccotti, Ettore, "Le Parti Socialiste Officiel Italien et la Guerre," *Revue des Nations Latines,* Paris, 1916, Annee 1, pp. 201-228.

Cole, G. D. H., *Labour in Wartime,* London, 1915.

David, Eduard, *Die Sozialdemokratie im Weltkrieg,* Berlin, 1915.

Destrée, Jules, *Les Socialistes et la Guerre Européenne,* Paris, 1916.

Dutt, R. Palme, *The Two Internationals,* London, 1920.

Eckstein, Gustav, "Der Krieg und der Sozialismus," *Neue Zeit.,* Stuttgart, 1915, vol. 34, Bd. 1, pp. 229-236, 334-346.

Fay, Sidney B., *The Origins of the World War*, New York, 1930. (Second edition, revised.)

Fendrich, Anton, *Die Kluft—Ergebnisse, Briefe, Dokumente aus dem Kriegsjahren (1914-1917)*, Stuttgart, 1919.

Fester, Richard, *Die Internationale*, Halle, 1919.

Fischer, Louis, *The Soviets in World Affairs*, 2 vols., New York, 1930.

Gorter, Hermann, *Der Imperialismus, der Weltkrieg und die Sozialdemokratie*, Amsterdam, 1915.

Group of English Speaking Communists in Russia, *Capitalist England—Socialist Russia*, 1919.

Grumbach, Salomon, *Der Irrtum von Zimmerwald Kienthal*, 1916, Berne.

Gurevitch, A., *Zarozhdene i Razvitie Kommunisticheskovo Internationale (Origins and Development of the Communist International)*, Kharkov, 1926.

Haenisch, Konrad, *Die Deutsche Sozialdemokratie in und nach dem Weltkriege*, Berlin, 1916.

Hamon, A. F. A., *Der Sozialismus im Frankreich von 1914-1920*, Vienna, 1920.

Humphrey, A. W., *International Socialism and the War*, London, 1915.

Jaroslawski, E., *Aus der Geschichte der Kommunistischen Partei der Sowjet Union (Bolschewiki)*, 2 vols., Hamburg, 1929-31.

Kabaktschieff, Christo, *Die Entstehung und Entwicklung der Komintern*, Berlin, 1929.

Kabaktschieff, Christo, *Die Gründung der K. P. Italiens*, Hamburg, 1921.

Kautsky, Karl, "Die Sozialdemokratie im Weltkrieg," *Die Neue Zeit*, June 11, 1915.

Kautsky, Karl, *Rosa Luxembourg et la Bolschévisme*, Brussels, 1922.

Kautsky, Karl, *Die Internationale und Sowjet-Russland*, Berlin, 1925.

Kellogg, Paul U., and Gleason, Arthur, *British Labor and the War*, New York, 1919.

Komar, I., *Ten Years of the Communist International* (pamphlet), London, 1929.

Kurella, Alfred, *Geschichte der Kommunistischen Jugend-Internationale* (Vol. II. *Gründung und Aufbau der K. J. I.*), Berlin, 1931.

Laidler, Harry W., *Socialism in Thought and Action*, New York, 1921.

Laidler, Harry W., *A History of Socialist Thought*, New York, 1927.

LaChesnais, P. G., *La Paix de Stockholm*, Extrait de la Grande Revue, Paris, 1918.

Laski, H. J., *Communism*, New York, 1927.

Lefas, Alexandre, *Le Parlement et L'Equivoque de Stockholm*, Paris, 1917.

Lenz, J., *Die II Internationale und Ihr Erbe (1889-1929)*, Berlin, 1930. Available in English, *The Rise and Fall of the Second International*, New York, 1932.

Lorwin, Lewis L., *Labor and Internationalism*, New York, 1929.

Louis, Paul, *La Crise du Socialisme Mondial de la II° et III° Internationale*, Paris, 1921.

Maurras, Charles, *Les Chefs Socialistes Pendant la Guerre*, Paris, 1918.

Maxe, Jean, *De Zimmerwald au Bolchévisme (1914-1920)*, Paris, 1910.

Miliukov, Paul, *Bolshevism: An International Danger*, London, 1920.

Monatte, Pierre, and others, *Left Wing Trade Unionism in France*, London, 1921.

Postgate, R. W., *The International During the War*, London, 1918.

Postgate, R. W., *The Workers' International*, London, 1920.

Price, M. Philips, *Germany in Transition*, London, 1923.

Rappoport, Charles, *Le Socialisme et la Guerre*, Paris, 1915.

Renner, Karl, *Marxismus, Krieg, und Internationale*, Stuttgart, 1917.

Sadoul, Jacques, *Notes Sur la Révolution Bolchévique*, Paris, 1921.

Saposs, David, *The Labor Movement in Post-War France*, New York, 1931.

Sassenbach, J., *Twenty-Five Years of International Trade Unionism*, Amsterdam, 1926.

Schön, Curt, *Der Vorwärts und die Kriegserklärung*, Berlin, 1919.

Schuller, Richard, *Geschichte des Kommunistischen Jugend-Internationale* (Vol. I, *Von den Anfangen der Proletarischen Jugendbewegung bis zur Gründung der K. J. I.*), Berlin, 1931.

Schuman, F. L., *American Policy toward Russia Since 1917*, New York, 1928.

Snowden, Mrs. Philip, *A Political Pilgrim in Europe*, New York, 1921.

Sombart, Werner, *Der Proletarische Sozialismus* (2 vols.), Berlin, 1924.

Souvarine, B., *La Troisième Internationale*, Paris, 1919.

Steklov, G. M., *History of the First International*, New York, 1929.

Ströbel, Heinrich, *The German Revolution and After*, London, 1923.

Varga, Eugen, *Die Sozial-Demokratischen Parteien*, Hamburg, 1926.

INDEX

233